Anna Theresa Sadlier

Names That Live in Catholic Hearts

Memoirs of Cardinal Ximenes, Michael Angelo, Samuel de Champlain, Archbishop Plunkett, Charles Carroll, Henri de Larochejacquelein, Simon de Montfort

Anna Theresa Sadlier

Names That Live in Catholic Hearts
Memoirs of Cardinal Ximenes, Michael Angelo, Samuel de Champlain, Archbishop Plunkett, Charles Carroll, Henri de Larochejacquelein, Simon de Montfort

ISBN/EAN: 9783337092665

Printed in Europe, USA, Canada, Australia, Japan

Cover: Foto ©Lupo / pixelio.de

More available books at **www.hansebooks.com**

MICHAEL ANGELO AND HIS DYING SERVANT.

IN

CATHOLIC HEARTS:

MEMOIRS OF

CARDINAL XIMENES, MICHAEL ANGELO, SAMUEL DE CHAMPLAIN, ARCHBISHOP PLUNKETT, CHARLES CARROLL, HENRI DE LAROCHEJACQUELEIN, SIMON DE MONTFORT.

BY

ANNA T. SADLIER.

"Lives of great men all remind us
We may make our lives sublime,
And departing, leave behind us
Footprints on the sands of time."
—*Longfellow.*

NEW YORK, CINCINNATI, AND ST. LOUIS

BENZIGER BROT

PRINTERS TO THE HOLY APOSTOLIC SEE

Copyright, 1882, by BENZIGER BROTHERS.

INTRODUCTION.

It was with no ordinary pleasure that I watched the progress of this work, which has been truly a labor of love for my daughter. Some four or five years have already passed since she began the present series of biographical sketches of illustrious Catholics, not canonized Saints, yet worthy of everlasting remembrance.

How few, of our young people especially, know more than the names—if even so much—of Michael Angelo—of Francisco Ximenes—of Oliver Plunkett—of Samuel de Champlain—of Simon de Montfort—of Henri Larochejaquelein—of Charles Carroll of Carrollton! And yet each one of these names is an heirloom of the Catholic family. Each one held a foremost place among the men of his time, whether as the prince of painters, of sculptors, of architects, like Michael Angelo Buonarotti; as Christian statesman and wise counsellor of kings, like the great Spanish Cardinal; as Martyr-prelate and faithful sentinel on the watch-towers of Israel in a dark and troublous time, like Oliver Plunkett, the last martyr of Ireland; as captains and leaders of Christian armies, valiant champions of the holiest of causes, like Simon de Montfort and Henri Larochejaquelein; as one of the founders of a new and eminently Christian nation amongst the yet unexplored forests of Northern America, like the Sieur de Champlain; as the high-souled, upright, and enlightened patriot, worthy of the proud distinction of being one of the sponsors of the Great Republic of the West, like Charles Carroll of Carrollton!

What stern devotion to principle, what noble disregard of selfish interests, what lofty chivalry in its truest sense, is manifested throughout the whole career of these truly great men! What a singleness and unity of purpose in all, though their lots were cast in times so far apart, amid scenes so varied! Some, like the heroic leader of La Vendée, were called early to their reward; others when mid-way up life's steep acclivity; while still others passed away in the ripeness of venerable age, crowned with years and with honors. All, however, faithfully accomplished the work appointed for them by the Great Master of the vineyard, and went down to the grave in the glory of renown.

Of these great names that truly " live in Catholic Hearts," the young author of these memoirs has taken from various lands the few that could be compressed into a small volume, for the reason that it gives a greater variety to the series in thus changing from one country to another the scene on which her illustrious actors played their heroic part. This, with the difference in manners, ways, and customs of the several nations embraced in the vast fold of the Church, and the ever-changing circumstances wherein the Christian people were placed at different periods of the world's history, contributes to give a more dramatic and attractive character to the work.

It has been the author's design from the first to make her memoirs as little dry as possible, and to bring out, as far as strict historical truth permitted, whatever there is of high moral beauty and poetry in these truly noble lives, each presenting in itself a grand and most complete epic.

If we would really combat the immoral and anti-Christian literature so alarmingly prevalent at this day, we must make our Catholic books and serials " readable." Even Catholic writers, going to work with the highest and purest motives, cannot afford to ignore the lighter elements of fancy and imagination, or dispense with the graces of style.

This volume of " Names that Live in Catholic Hearts" will most likely be followed by one or two more of uniform size, as the author has still a wide range before her, in order to represent even a few of the other countries of Europe and America. Her female characters will form a separate volume.

Commending this first volume, then, of the series to the reading public, and bespeaking for it a kindly welcome, I leave it to its own merits.

MARY A. SADLIER.

MONTREAL, CANADA, March 23, 1882.

CONTENTS.

	PAGE
CARDINAL XIMENES, Grand Chancellor of Spain	9
MICHAEL ANGELO, Painter, Poet, Architect and Sculptor	49
SAMUEL DE CHAMPLAIN, Explorer and Founder of Quebec	81
OLIVER PLUNKETT, Archbishop of Armagh and Primate of Ireland	125
CHARLES CARROLL, of Carrollton, Signer of the Declaration of Independence	175
HENRI DE LAROCHEJAQUELEIN, the Hero of La Vendée	217
SIMON DE MONTFORT, Champion of the Cross and Defender of the Faith	251

Cardinal Ximines

Grand Chancellor of Spain.

O thou divinely gifted man,
Who made through strength thy merit known,
And lived to grasp the golden keys
To mould a mighty state's decrees,
And shape the whisper of the throne;
And moving up from high to higher,
Became on Fortune's crowning slope
The pillar of a people's hope,
The centre of a world's desire.
                        TENNYSON.

Cardinal Ximenes.

GRAND CHANCELLOR OF SPAIN.

WE are far back in the past; we thread our way within the ancient walls, along the picturesque streets, of the former capital of Spain—the famed Toledo. We enter through the Puerta del Sol, observe its massive arches, arabesque ornaments, Moorish inscriptions, and its vivid orange color. We pass on in the shadow of the tall projecting houses, which somewhat obscure the light and modify the heat of a southern sun. We are struck by the coolness of the *patio*, a sort of interior courtyard, paved with many-tinted marbles, which add to its oriental character. This *patio* is attached to each dwelling, and has a temporary cover for the day, which is always withdrawn at night, in order that the balmy freshness of the Castilian night air may penetrate the apartment. We are lost in thought. Our minds are full of the old legends that cluster like dim shades in every nook and corner of these quaint streets; the pale, yet splendid *manes* of departed kings and warriors throng the ambient air; but our purpose is not with them: their glory and their splendor and their power fade from before us. One giant form alone towers above them all, nor needs the heralds cry, "Room for the Cardinal!" Transported in spirit to that city of his fame, we will endeavor to bring into these pages, as clearly and concisely as possible, the chief events in the life of Spain's illustrious citizen, Francisco de Cisneros Ximenes, Archbishop of Toledo, and Prince of the Church. Most biographers agree that he was born in or about the year 1437, of a noble but impoverished family, in the town of Torrelaguna. He pursued his studies principally at the University of Salamanca, for it was the ardent and cherished wish of both his parents that he should become a priest. For some six years, we are told, he defrayed the expenses of his education by giving lessons in civil and canon law. Later on, we find him setting out for Rome to seek his fortune. Twice upon the journey thither he was attacked by robbers, so that it was through the generosity of an old schoolfellow, whom he chanced to meet upon the road, that he was enabled to reach the Eternal City. Called into Spain by some domestic trouble, he obtained from the Holy Father a Bull empowering him to fill the first vacancy in the city of Toledo. This was a curious episode in Ximenes' eventful life. The celebrated Alphonso Carillo, then Archbishop of Toledo, however, refused to grant him the benefice. Ximenes stoutly maintained the higher authority of Rome, at which the archbishop became so incensed that he cast the young ecclesiastic into prison, where he remained six years. During this period of confinement a priest prophesied to him that he should one day be Archbishop of Toledo.

"Father," replied Ximenes, "such a commencement certainly does not promise so happy an end."

These six years of imprisonment in the strong tower of Uzeda seem to us fraught with interest, when we consider that the life of solitude and retirement then led by him may have had its influence in preparing him for that wonderful hereafter. It is a fine picture: that grave though youthful figure, with its background of captivity patiently endured, thrown into strong relief by the light of its future greatness.

Once released from prison, he exchanged his benefice for the chaplaincy of Siguenza, a neighboring diocese, but as the salary was larger than that of his own benefice, he arranged that the difference might be returned to the former chaplain of Siguenza. In a short time after, he so gained the esteem and good-will of his bishop, that he was made Grand Vicar and administrator of the diocese by Cardinal de Mendoza. But the Grand Vicar heard within him the divine call, and the whisper, "Come up higher." He renounced the world, and took the habit of a gray or Franciscan friar, in a convent of the Observantines, so called from their strict adherence to their primitive rules. The fame of his penitential life and great holiness crowded his confessional, and brought him visitors from far and near. This so disturbed him, that he retired to an obscure convent, that of Our Lady of Castañar, remote from all the thoroughfares of men, where he led a life of wonderful austerity. He himself, according to his chroniclers, gives us a delightful though austere picture of his life in this retreat. He speaks of it as a charming oasis. There he devoted himself to that which had always been a joy forever to his mind—that is, his biblical studies. Clad in a hair shirt, holding, as he expresses it, the Bible in one hand and the scourge in the other, he pondered upon eternal truths. While there, his elevation to the archiepiscopal See was again foretold. Once he was on a journey to Toledo with a companion, Pedro Sanchez. Night came on, and the belated travellers were obliged to sleep on the grass. Suddenly, Sanchez awoke, crying out:

"I dreamt only a moment ago, Father Francis, that

you were Archbishop of Toledo, and that I saw a Cardinal's hat upon your head."

Soon after this Ximenes was removed to the Convent of Salzeda, of which he was shortly made guardian.

Meanwhile, in the kingdom of Spain wonderful events were taking place, wars and rumors of war relating to the succession, till at last Ferdinand and Isabella were firmly seated upon the throne—they, unto whom belongs the glorious title of "*Los Reyes Catolicos,*" or "their Catholic Majesties." Happy was Spain in the rule of such sovereigns, and in the glorious combination of such a queen as Isabella and such a prelate as Ximenes. But we anticipate. While the conquest of Granada was taking place, and the defeat of the Moors in Spain, Ximenes was still an humble monk in a remote Observantine convent.

But the queen, who had been fortunate enough to have for confessor the admirable and saintly Ferdinand de Talavera, now made Archbishop of Granada, determined, by the advice of Cardinal Mendoza, to choose Ximenes to replace him. She was, however, desirous of seeing this man, of whom fame already spoke so loudly. Cardinal Mendoza brought him, under some pretence, into the presence of the queen, who was charmed with his modest yet dignified appearance, his candor, his piety, and noble sentiments. When, a day or two after, his appointment as Royal Confessor was made known to him, he at first refused the honor. By the queen's special command he, however, accepted it, upon condition that he would be allowed to live at his convent, and only come to court when his presence was absolutely required.*

He was spoken of even then by contemporaries as

---

* Dr. Hefele's Life of Ximenes, chap. iii. pp. 28-29.

"equal in wisdom to St. Augustine, in austerity of life to St. Jerome, and in zeal to St. Ambrose." A courtier of the day* speaks of him thus:

"A man of great sanctity," he says, "has come from the depths of a lonesome solitude; he is wasted away by his austerities, and resembles the ancient anchorites, St. Paul and St. Hilarion."

During all this time Ximenes was occupied in reforming abuses which had crept into his Order. His zeal was untiring; accompanied by his secretary, Brother Francisco Ruyz, he visited all the monasteries on foot, only occasionally in case of illness mounting upon a mule. As far as possible he adhered to the spirit of the rule, which prescribed that they should support themselves by begging. It is related that his secretary upon one occasion said to him, laughing:

"Most Reverend Father, you will certainly be the cause of our dying of hunger! God gives to every one his particular talent. Do you meditate and pray for me, while I am begging for you."

It was about this time, too, that he ardently desired permission of the queen and his superiors to become an apostle among the Moors. But a holy woman, one of those called *Beatæ*, declared to him that it was the will of God he should remain in Spain, where a glorious career was reserved for him. It is needless to follow the Franciscan in all the trials attendant upon the reforms he desired to make, and in which the queen earnestly assisted him. He had, in fact, been chosen Provincial of his Order, with a view to the correction of abuses

A new path was, however, marked out for him. Cardinal Mendoza, Archbishop of Toledo, died in 1495, and left vacant the richest and most important See in the

---

* Alvarez, in a letter to Peter Martyr.

whole of Spain. So important was it, that this archbishop was regarded as being second only to the king in power and influence. It is said that Mendoza named Ximenes, both to the Papal authorities and their Majesties, as his fitting successor. Be this as it may, on Good Friday of the same year, when the Franciscan appeared in the queen's presence, after having heard her confession, she said to him, at the same time presenting the Papal Bulls:

"Reverend Father, you will see by these letters what are the commands of his Holiness." Ximenes kissed the documents respectfully, but on opening them, and observing the superscription: "To our venerable brother, Francisco Ximenes de Cisneros, Archbishop-elect of Toledo," he turned deadly pale, and immediately left the room without taking leave of the queen. Isabella merely said:

"Allow me to see what his Holiness has written to you." Ximenes, however, had rushed out in haste to seek his companion Francisco Ruyz, saying : "Come, brother, we must leave here without delay."*

When the queen sent two of her head chamberlains to his convent in Madrid, to inform him officially of his new dignity, he was far on his way to Ocaña. In fine, the queen was compelled to write to the Pope concerning Ximenes' refusal to accept the archbishopric, and the Pope was compelled to send him a Papal brief commanding him in virtue of obedience, before he would consent to undertake these new and great responsibilities.

He was then almost sixty years of age, and he shrank from the burden laid upon him. Earthly honors had no

---

* Dr. Hefele's Life of Ximenes, p. 40. Fléchier, 35, 36, 37. Gomez, 10, 11. Robles, 76, 77.

charms for him, and it was with marked reluctance that he allowed himself to be consecrated, at a convent of his Order at Tarazona, in presence of the king and queen. After the consecration, he came, according to custom, to kiss the hands of the king and queen. In doing so he used these characteristic words:

"I come to kiss the hands of your Majesties, not because they have raised me to the first See in Spain, but because I hope they will assist me in supporting the burden which they have placed upon my shoulders."

We are told by various biographers that the king and queen were deeply moved, and that they as well as all the grandees of the court kissed the bishop's consecrated hands, and knelt to receive his blessing. After this he was conducted with all due state to his palace."*

Public events, however, required his presence at the court or at Alcalá, so that it was not until two years afterwards, 1497, that he took possession of his Cathedral of Toledo. He would willingly have entered at night and in silence, but was forced to submit to the desire of the people for a public demonstration.

That glorious scene is before us. We, too, are present, and mingle with the breathless multitude. They hail the name of Ximenes with acclamation. They behold him, with scarcely repressed enthusiasm, as he treads with unwilling feet that new path of glory opening before him. We are in the Cathedral, that gorgeous monument of Spanish piety and munificence; the naves, five in number, are decorated with a mingled beauty and magnificence worthy the earthly dwelling of the King of kings. In the middle or grand nave is the *retablo*, or high altar, of massive carvings and dark panelling, on which rare paintings with golden backgrounds catch

---

* Hefele, p. 39.

every gleam and glint of sunlight. How the brilliance of innumerable tapers sparkles and glows amid the dull gold of that curious old *retablo!* how the alabaster tombs of the dead sovereigns* gleam with unearthly whiteness! how the polished jasper columns reflect the light from below! Gorgeous embroidered banners are everywhere unfurled; the gloom of the Cathedral is warm with mellow light from the painted windows, and their heavy clusters of emeralds, rubies, and sapphires form a picture of light and shadow, rich and glorious as the colors of an oriental sunset. There was a dead pause, and a burst of triumphant, indescribable music from the organs on either side of the choir. It filled the vast edifice to repletion; it thundered through nave and chancel; it woke each slumbering echo, and it fell upon the hearts of the worshippers, rousing them to almost irrepressible enthusiasm. O God! how grandly was Thy name glorified on that thrice-hallowed day! O Ximenes, how even thy glory was annihilated in presence of the Most High!

The procession entered the church. Breathless, the awe-stricken multitude looked upon the face of one who, henceforth, held Spain's mightiest destinies in his hand. Among all that noble array of sovereigns and nobles and prelates and ministers, we discern the tall, spare figure, austere countenance, and lofty mien of the new Grand Chancellor of Spain. The rest fade almost to insignificance—even the princely and chivalrous Ferdinand, the fair and gentle Isabella, called by some the most beautiful woman of her day. There is a visible thrill of enthusiasm among the people. The organ's deep voice again breaks the momentary stillness with a crash; the procession reaches the high altar; the archbishop falls

---

* Don Alvar de Luna and his wife.

prostrate on the marble steps, first to acknowledge the littleness of human things.

Arising, he takes, in a firm and unwavering voice, the solemn oath to maintain all the rights and laws of the Cathedral of Toledo. This done, Don Francisco seats himself for the first time in the great carved chair, rising like a throne above the rows of stalls within the choir. During the concluding ceremonies he sits with bowed head, as if the weight of human glory were oppressive to him. Scarcely is the celebration ended when he escapes into the cloisters. There fresh breezes come from the mountains of Castilia; there gentle sights of nature with her varied charms meet the eye through those dull gray arches; and there, sweetest of all, reigns peace, deep peace, the peace of God.

Such scenes as this remind us of the saying of a modern author,* that "from whatever side the Middle Ages are viewed, they present an aspect of unapproachable grandeur."

After his elevation to this great dignity, Ximenes continued to lead the simple and penitential life of a poor Franciscan friar. He still appeared publicly in the habit of his Order, went everywhere on foot or riding on a mule, and permitted not a trace of state or splendor about his dwelling. At length the Pope was obliged to interfere. The habits of the times, the manners of the people, accustomed to associate authority with outward ceremony, forbade this simplicity of life in a man of exalted station. The archbishop complied with the instructions of the Pope: he appeared before the public in rich garments, while wearing underneath a hair shirt; he spread his table on state occasions sumptuously, but continued to partake himself of such food as was used

---

* Alzog., Church Hist., vol. ii. p. 1066.

by the humblest friars of his Order; provided luxurious couches for his guests, but slept himself on a board. This latter fact, which he kept strenuously secret, was accidentally discovered by his servant. So appalling were the austerities he practised, that it is said the Pope was again obliged to counsel moderation.

At the moment of his accession to power, Don Francisco began a long series of benefits to the Church and State, which ended only with his death. To enumerate them within our present limits seems, indeed, a hopeless task. But we shall endeavor to point out faithfully and conscientiously his chief claims to the reverence and gratitude of humanity. We have already referred to his simple and austere mode of life, but cannot refrain from dwelling a moment longer on those private virtues which throw into such strong relief the grandeur of his public character. He was wont to offer up the sacrifice of the mass every day, and to assist as often as possible at the offices of the Church. In one corner of the mighty realm he commanded, cathedral, palace, kingdom, was a "small, dim chapel." This was his favorite place of prayer. In its cloistral seclusion he found the rest and peace he had once so loved at Our Lady of Castañar. He wore at his wrist a small crucifix, which from time to time during the day he drew out and looked upon most lovingly. He deemed it a preservation from sin. He kept himself surrounded by learned and pious men, with whom he could discourse on the things of God, and he made an annual retreat in a convent of his Order to renew and strengthen his fervor.

He applied himself seriously to reforms among the clergy and religious Orders. He held Synods at Alcantara and Alcalá, where he laid down salutary rules for the guidance of his priests. The various details of these assemblies do not enter into the purpose of our sketch, but those who are versed in the ecclesiastical history of Spain at this period will understand the importance of the measures adopted by Ximenes for the preservation of good order and discipline throughout the kingdom. Suffice it to say, that by these reforms alone he merits the gratitude and respect of all true Spaniards and Catholics. We must necessarily omit many particulars which might be of interest to our readers, such as the great Archbishop's address to his clergy, reminding them of his unworthiness, and asking the co-operation of their prayers, as also any detailed account of the opposition which met him everywhere, and the trials which he had to endure. For the great man did not escape the common penalty of greatness. His reforms were opposed on every side, his actions criticised, his motives questioned. All this he bore with heroic fortitude. When urged to discover and punish the authors of the libels circulated against him, he replied, "When a man is in power, and has nothing wherewith to reproach himself, the wisest course he can pursue is to permit the people to enjoy the poor consolation of avenging their wrongs by words."

As an instance of the justice and firmness which characterized his administration, we may relate the following incident which took place soon after his elevation. He was petitioned to confirm Don Pedro de Mendoza in the government of Cazorla. Now this Don Pedro was the brother of the late Cardinal, who had been in some sort Ximenes's protector. Those who advanced the petition referred to his obligations to the deceased prelate, and, moreover, urged the queen's desire. But Ximenes calmly replied that, as Chancellor of Spain, he acknowledged no private ties; that his sovereign might send him back to his convent, whither he was willing to depart on the instant, but that no personal considerations should ever operate with him in distributing the honors of the Church. Soon after, however, having found Don Pedro worthy, he confirmed him in his office. Every day the palace gates were thronged with mendicants, and at an appointed hour the good Archbishop appeared among them, reading petitions, distributing alms, and giving to every one a patient and kindly hearing. Little wonder that his name is still revered in his Cathedral city, remaining forever dear to its humblest inhabitants.

Busy, indeed, was his life, for, besides his ecclesiastical reforms, he undertook to inquire into the course of justice, and replace all unworthy judges by men of tried integrity and personal merit. He was the constant adviser of the royal consorts upon the most intimate affairs of state, some of which in the course of our narrative we may have occasion to mention incidentally.

Shortly after his accession he began to devote himself to the chief aim of his existence, namely, the conversion of the Moors. Patiently, untiringly, perseveringly he labored, sparing himself no personal toil. It is said that he himself made fifty thousand converts. Among many means which he employed to attain this end, we may mention his custom of inviting the chief Moorish priests, or *alfaquis*, to his palace, where he discussed with them the mysteries of faith, and often succeeded in convincing them. The conversion of the alfaquis led to the conversion of the Moorish people. One day of triumph at last is recorded for Ximenes, and bursting again the bond of time and space, we shall assist thereat in spirit. A mighty multitude is assembled; there is a sound of martial music, and the great Archbishop appears. Wherefore has he come? Wherefore do the trumpets sound those strains of exultation? Is it some kingdom conquered? Do sad-faced captives from foreign shores follow in the train of the conqueror? The kingdom conquered is the souls of men, and the captives are those who bend to the sweet yoke of Jesus Christ. Four thousand souls, purchased by the agony of a God, are baptized unto Christ. Ah, noble Ximenes! our hearts are throbbing with yours; while the multitude are swaying like a mighty and resistless sea, drums beat, trumpets sound, cannons boom, and the Archbishop pours upon each dusky forehead the life-giving waters of the first sacrament. The Koran and the paradise of the houris is lost to them, but heaven is their inheritance and God their portion forever. There is a sound, too, which startles the air of that dim and dusky Granada—the peal of joyful bells. The clangor awakes mingled feelings in the souls of the Moors, for those voices, long silent, tell of the downfall of their race. Well might they name Ximenes "Alfaqui Campanero," for he it was who had again introduced the bells into Granada, and contributed more than any other to implant there the Christian faith.*

But when the last of the four thousand Moorish converts had been baptized, another ceremony still remained to be performed. A fire is enkindled: the smoke rises in dusky cloud-racks, as an offering in the sight of the Most High, and the flames close around great piles of volumes containing the delusive doctrines of Mahomet.† Moorish men and matrons and maidens are witnesses of the deed. We look in vain for one expression of regret when they behold the treasured Koran cast into the flames. Yet it was once their only hope; once yielded them unmixed delight. Now they turn away from it; they need it not: the Gospel, the parables of Jesus, the inspired wisdom of the Doctor of the Gentiles, is their inexhaustible store. Bravely they have left the broad and flowery

---

* The doctrines of Mahomet forbade the ringing of bells.
† *Dublin University Magazine* for 1854.

path upon which they had trodden, and entered upon the narrow road to life eternal. All around them their new brethren in Christ are trampling its rocks and thorns and brambles under their feet, with Ximenes valiantly leading the van.

When we are upon the subject of these Moorish conversions, it may be well to take a brief glance at the misrepresentation and injustice to which the great Cardinal has been exposed in this regard. Protestant historians have shamefully maligned him, the while they themselves do justice to his resplendent virtues and glorious qualities of head and heart. A recent writer * aptly remarks " that none but a Catholic can fully appreciate Ximenes." The very severity with which he is charged was a necessary outcome of the times in which he lived. The measures that might have been applied with complete success in the nineteenth century would have fallen far short of their object in the sixteenth. Another learned author † remarks, "that to be just to the Middle Ages we must judge them by the principles and ideas of those times, and not of our own." And what we have said of him applies to that formidable and much-belied institution, the Spanish Inquisition. It has been said, and with justice, that perhaps no institution connected with the Catholic Church, save and except the Society of Jesus, has been so hated, denounced, abused, and calumniated by Protestants and infidels as the Inquisition.‡ But when we consider that our chief means of information upon this subject are taken from writers hostile to the Church, and that the famous Llorente, its principal historian, himself admits that he destroyed all documents relating to it,

---

* Dalton, in his Preface to Hefele's Ximenes.
† Alzog, Ch. Hist., vol. iv. p. 197.
‡ Dalton, Preface to Hefele's Ximenes.

we must look with the greatest distrust upon all assertions made with regard to this celebrated tribunal. We must also consider, in the words of a learned historian, "that in the middle ages, when the two powers, Church and State, were expected by the people to work in harmony together, a policy towards heretics was pursued, and a personal surveillance was exercised over them, which led to the establishment of the Inquisition, an institution which has been the object of more misrepresentation and erroneous judgment than any other known to history."*
We have touched thus briefly upon an important subject upon which, were time and space at our command, we would gladly dwell, because in 1507 Ximenes was appointed Grand Inquisitor of Leon and Castile. The Archbishop accepted the office, for his clear mind discerned that violence and disorder prevailed at the time in all those countries where this tribunal was not established. The heretics of those days were in nearly all countries, but more especially Spain, the enemies of the existing government. The unconverted Moors forever remained the dangerous foes of their Christian masters. It is an undoubted fact that the primary ends of the Inquisition were good, and that wherever abuses crept in, it was through the fault of individuals or of the civil authorities. In such cases the Pope frequently interfered with the whole weight of his influence, and gave asylum to many of its victims at Rome. As to Ximenes, we have the testimony of the before-named Llorente, a chronicler who is the avowed enemy, to use his own expression, "of whatever savors of the leaven of ultramontanism," to prove with what moderation the Cardinal filled this post.

"Ximenes," he says, "endeavored to lessen the severity

---

* Alzog's Hist. of the Universal Church, vol. ii., p. 668.

of the Inquisition, deposed bad functionaries, and pardoned many accused persons."

Mildly, however, as he may have performed the duties of his office, and grossly as the severity practised by that tribunal has been exaggerated by anti-Catholic writers, we love to look upon the brighter side of the Moorish conversions in Spain. There is a peculiar softness and beauty in the picture of Ximenes and Talavera side by side teaching catechism to the Moorish children and converts, or in that of the devotion and affection displayed by Zegri, a converted Moorish priest, to the Grand Inquisitor.

In this year, 1507, Pope Julius II. sent the Cardinal's hat to Ximenes, with the title of Cardinal of Spain. The news of this nomination was received with the greatest enthusiasm by the sovereigns and people of Spain. But as for the new Cardinal, the burden of earthly honors only weighed him down, only clogged the ardent spirit that in the height of glory would fain have returned to the calm obscurity of the cloister, or longed that the too solid flesh might be dissolved, and he be with Christ. Still, under the Cardinal's robes he wore a hair shirt and the habit of St. Francis; still, he lived upon one frugal meal a day, and slept upon a plank, the while he labored in the heat and burthen of the day, and toiled in the rugged places of this earthly life.

Alone amid thousands, he towered above his fellow-men in solitary grandeur, "a soaring solitude of woods and snows all steeped in golden light." His gaze was fixed upon the domes of the far-off city; the distance was hourly lessening, and through the gates of pearl came to him at intervals strains from the choral of the spheres. What mattered it, therefore, if the way were long, and the pilgrim's feet bleeding from the thorns and briars and brambles that line the narrow road.

Meanwhile he busied himself with works of public utility. An oppressive tax called the Alcavala weighed upon the people. To redress this grievance the Grand Chancellor did all that lay within his power. A famine threatened the land, and Ximenes erected public granaries at Toledo, Alcalá, and Torrelaguna, and had them filled at his own expense. But of his numerous foundations we shall speak more particularly hereafter. The hearts of the people were filled with the deepest gratitude, and they studied how they might best preserve his memory. A memorial of the benefit he had thus conferred upon his country was engraved upon the walls of the senate chamber, and in one of the public squares.

In this interval many important public events had taken place, especially those connected with the partition of Naples, the sending of Peter Martyr as envoy to the Sultan, who threatened the kingdom of Spain as a reprisal for what he had been led to regard as Spanish cruelty towards the Moors. This mission was entirely successful. There were also various outbreaks among the unconverted Moors inhabiting the Sierras, and many other affairs of state, in which Ximenes gave all possible support to his sovereigns. Some two or three years before his elevation to the cardinalate he was seized with a sévere fit of illness, during which he experienced the greatest kindness and attention from the king and queen. At their request and by the command of his physician, he allowed himself to be removed from the Alhambra to the royal summer residence at Xeneralifa. But his malady showed no signs of abating, till Francisca, a Moorish convert, who had married some one in the Archbishop's service, brought thither an old woman of eighty, who succeeded in curing Ximenes by the use of powerful herbs and ointments. In eight days he was able to breathe the pure air of the river Dano, and soon after to return to Alcalá.*

An interesting account is given of the reception of the Archduke Philip and his consort Joanna, in the city of Toledo, on their arrival in Spain. It was in the month of May, and nature and art alike combined to adorn the quaint old capital. The Archbishop, in full pontifical robes, met the young couple at the entrance to the cathedral, and offered them a magnificent cross " resplendent with gold and precious stones," which they knelt before and respectfully kissed. Some days later occurred the ceremony of offering homage. This was also celebrated in the cathedral, where Cardinal Diego Hurtado Mendoza, nephew of the former Cardinal of that name, officiated. He first advanced to offer his homage, followed by Ximenes, all the various dignitaries of the Church, and the civil authorities.

It is recorded that on the birthday of Joanna's son, afterwards Ferdinand I., Ximenes having met a criminal on his way to the gallows, rushed to obtain his pardon from the queen. But this is only one of many incidents related as to the personal benevolence of the Cardinal. A great sorrow was, however, in preparation for Ximenes. The queen's health began to fail, and at times she was confined to her bed for days together. It was then that an Italian noble told Ferdinand " that he had come to Spain to see a woman who from her bed of sickness ruled the world." Many foreigners in fact flocked thither to see her, and one of them, Vianelli, relates the following anecdote of Ximenes. This Venetian possessed a ring which he offered for sale to Ximenes. The latter inquired its price. He was told 5000 ducats.

---

* Hefele, p. 81. Gomez, Book II.

"With such a sum," said he, "it would be infinitely better to do good to five thousand poor people than to possess all the diamonds of India."

But about this time he received a most valuable present. A Franciscan monk came on an embassy from the Sultan to their Majesties. He brought with him a stone from the Holy Sepulchre, which he caused to be divided into five altar stones—one for the Pope, one for the Queen of Spain, one for King Emmanuel of Portugal, one for Cardinal Carvajal, and the last for Ximenes. The Archbishop vowed never to use any other stone upon which to say Mass during his life, and resolutely kept his word. After his death it was preserved in the Cathedral of Toledo.

When he took leave of the queen she said to him, "I hope very shortly to be able to follow you to Toledo." But these were her last words to him. In November, 1504, three years before Ximenes was made cardinal, a terrible blow was dealt to the Spanish nation. The royal-hearted Isabella died—the type, model, and most excellent pattern of a sovereign. It is not here the place to speak her panegyric—a panegyric spoken alike by Protestant and Catholic historians. Her reign was rendered illustrious by the simple fact that in it shone three such men as Columbus, the discoverer of America; Cordova, surnamed "El gran Capitano;" and Ximenes, the great Cardinal. The death of Isabella was a source of great grief to the Archbishop, for apart from the personal esteem and affection with which he regarded her she had always assisted him in his schemes for the promotion of science and art. Isabella's love for learning was indeed only surpassed by that of Ximenes.

In the struggles which followed upon the death of Isabella, Ximenes bore a prominent part. He always took the side of Ferdinand against the unjust pretensions of Philip, who had married Joanna, heiress to the throne; but he was treated with the greatest respect and deference by both claimants for the crown. He was for a time entrusted with the administration of affairs in conjunction with several of the principal nobles even before the death of Philip, and during the absence of the king in Italy. As a statesman he was far-seeing, sagacious, and just, and held by many writers, both ancient and modern, to have far surpassed Richelieu. It was in fact through the intervention of Ximenes that a reconciliation was brought about between Philip, who was now sovereign of Spain, and Ferdinand, who had been named in the queen's will "sole regent of Castile" till her grandson Charles should come of age.

On the occasion of their meeting, Ximenes accompanied Philip, who came with the greatest pomp and ceremony, whilst Ferdinand, on the other hand, appeared simply apparelled and attended. During their interview Ximenes kept all the courtiers away, wishing that the two sovereigns might come to a full understanding, and saying to the attendants,

"I will myself stand sentinel at the door."

Ximenes' presence was now frequently required at Court, where he exercised a most salutary influence upon Philip, advised him against evil counsellors, and moreover succeeded in putting an end to long and sanguinary feuds between such houses as the Benavante and Mendoza.

After the death of Philip, he, aware of the total incapacity of the queen, made strenuous efforts to induce Ferdinand to return, but for some time without avail. During this interregnum, despite the unsettled and undisciplined state of the country, the childish and foolish interference of the demented queen and the intrigues of the nobles, Ximenes governed the country with wisdom and discretion.

Though age and disease and his herculean labors had begun to tell upon the once vigorous frame of the Cardinal, he still toiled unremittingly. He formed the citizens into a well-trained and powerful militia, which, without interfering with their various employments, gave to Spain an honest, moral, and trustworthy force of 30,000 men, far surpassing in every respect the corrupt and degraded soldiery in other countries where standing armies were in existence.

Various outbreaks on the part of the Moors also induced him to carry the war into Africa, where he hoped to effect the double purpose of defending Spain from their future incursions, and carrying the light of the Gospel among them. The nation, like frightened children, had come to the Cardinal's feet, and the Cardinal had fitted out an expedition at his own expense. He gave the command to Pietro Navarro, a rough soldier but skilful general. A fleet of eighty vessels sailed from Carthagena, and Ximenes went with it to encourage the soldiers by his presence. In 1609 occurred the memorable battle of Oran. The Spanish troops landed on the African shore May 17th, and at evening of the following day the town of Oran was theirs. Before the army marched up to the walls, the Cardinal, in full pontifical robes, mounted on a superb charger, and preceded by a Franciscan bearing the Episcopal cross, harangued the soldiers, exhorting them in a glowing address by all that they held dearest, home, country, faith, and God, to combat bravely, reminding them that the contest was, as it were, between Christ and Mahomet, between true religion and infidelity. Immediately after he retired to the oratory of San Miguel, in the adjoining fortress, and prostrating himself upon the altar steps, like another Joshua, uplifted his hands in supplication. On the following day Oran was carried by assault, and the Cardinal entered the gates, preceded by the clergy chanting the Psalm, "Non nobis"—"Not unto us, O Lord! but unto Thy name be glory given." His generous heart was rejoiced by the liberation of three hundred Christian captives, but seeing the number of dead lying on the ground, he burst into tears, exclaiming:

"They were indeed infidels, but they might have become Christians. By their death they have deprived me of the principal advantage of the victory we have gained over them."*

We are assured by many biographers that "Ximenes possessed all the requisite qualities of a general—an invincible courage and an admirable prudence united with a mind fruitful in resources."† Ferdinand appears to have been of this opinion, for he gave the entire command of the expedition into the Cardinal's hands, which gave rise to the contemptuous saying on the part of the grandees, that

"The world was turned upside down; and that while the great captain (Cordova) was telling his beads in Valladolid, the Franciscan Father was preparing for battles and sieges."

At the siege of Oran, Sousa, a captain of the Cardinal's guard, planted the standard of his master on the highest tower of the fortifications, crying,

"Santiago y Ximenes."

At Alcalá, Ximenes was received with the greatest honor on his return from Africa. But we are told that

---

* *Dublin University Magazine* for 1854. Hefele and other biographers.

† Hefele. Gomez.

the students and professors at the university were astonished to hear him speak rather of learning and art than of wars and conquests. One of them made some allusion to his wan and worn appearance, to which Ximenes replied, his pale face glowing with wonderful ardor :

"You do not know, Fernando, the strength and vigor which God has given me. Had my army been faithful to me, pale and emaciated as you see me, I should have hastened at this moment to plant the Cross of Christ in all the chief cities of Africa." It is related that the affection which he always felt for the town of Oran was truly touching. He spoke of it as "the dear Christian oasis in a desert of infidelity." Long after his death the Moors had a legend among them, that a gigantic figure in a Franciscan habit and cardinal's hat was seen to urge the Spaniards on to victory.

In 1516 Ferdinand also died and went to his rest, after having first appointed Ximenes regent—an appointment which was confirmed by the Archduke Charles, afterwards the Emperor Charles V., who was then in Flanders, and could not at present be declared king, as his mother was still alive. The Cardinal was now eighty years of age, and it would have seemed might have been allowed to enter into repose in the peaceful land of Beulah, that poetic region of the perpetual songs of birds and the ceaseless bloom of flowers, the country that skirts the dismal river beyond which are the streets of gold and the amaranthine walls of the Eternal City. But henceforth Ximenes labored still more unweariedly. He was shortly called upon to put down a conspiracy which had arisen among some of the most influential lords against the power of Charles. It was at this time, and in consequence of this insurrection, that the seat of government was transferred to Madrid, which afterwards became capital of the kingdom. At this time, too,

Ximenes received a letter from Charles, in which occurs the following passage referring to the will of his grandfather, Ferdinand:

"The most excellent clause we have found in the Testament is that by which you, Most Reverend Sir, are, during our absence, entrusted with the government of the kingdom and the administration of justice. Indeed, Most Reverend Sir, if this had not been already done we could, considering your integrity, wisdom, and zeal for God and ourselves, not have selected for this office a man who would give greater satisfaction to our conscience and in whose hands the weal of our kingdoms could be safer." *

Ximenes experienced much opposition at the hands of the Grand Constable, the Infantado, and many other of the principal nobles. When exaggerated reports came to his ears of the great uprising which was in preparation, he said calmly,

"These men have only words, not money, to raise a revolt."

And an anecdote, which does not, however, seem to be very well authenticated, is related, that when some of these nobles waited on him to know his intentions respecting the government of the kingdom, he led them to a window, and showing the soldiers and artillery, said,

"Behold the powers by which I govern Castile, by the will of the king, my lord and master!"

He was soon after compelled to send a force, under the Duke de Najara, against Jean d'Albret, the exiled King of Navarre, who, aided by the King of France, was seeking to recover his territory. After a short but decisive struggle the Navarrese were totally defeated, and

---

* Peter Martyr, Ep. 569. Gomez, p. 1073. Hefele, 459.

d'Albret was compelled to retire into the Province of Bearn. We are told that the Castilians were fully satisfied with the measures employed by him for the safety of their kingdom. Scarcely was the danger passed when intrigues were discovered between France and Portugal to the detriment of Spain Hadrian, to whom the treasonable documents were handed in the absence of Ximenes, was frightened by their contents, and sent them post haste to the regent. Ximenes read them through carefully, and said,

"Tell Hadrian that he may rest in peace. I undertake to face the danger."

A serious revolt at Malaga was by his wisdom and prudence terminated amicably. He at first exhorted the insurgents to return to their allegiance, but finding remonstrance useless, despatched Don Antonio Cueva with a force of 6000 infantry and 400 horse against the rebellious town, which submitted without bloodshed. A second insurrection at Arevalo was likewise quickly put down, Ximenes obstinately refusing to give up to Queen Germaine the fortified towns which she demanded. After the contest, Ximenes hastened to obtain pardon from the king for the chief rebel, Count Gutierre Velasquez of Cuellar. He next sent a body of eight thousand men with the requisite vessels against Horac Barbarossa, a daring and successful pirate, who had succeeded in rousing a portion of the Saracens against their Spanish masters. Owing to the incompetency of the generals, this expedition, however, completely failed. But his services to Spain during the period of administration, as indeed during the whole course of his long life, were so many and so varied, that they would easily fill volumes. The reforms that he accomplished, the bad functionaries that he deposed, the exemplary men that he placed in office, his military expeditions, his abolishing of oppressive taxes, would be tedious to enumerate. With a momentary glance at his part in the American missions, we will devote the remaining pages of our sketch to his principal foundations, and more especially those two, so dear to fame, the Complutensian Polyglot and the University of Alcalá.

It will be remembered that Columbus appeared before the King and Queen of Spain, somewhere about the time when Ximenes was entering upon his glorious career as confessor to the queen. So that with the earlier missions sent out to evangelize the Indians of the New World the Cardinal had little or nothing to do, though some few years afterwards a number of priests were undoubtedly despatched there by his advice and direction. It was not, however, till he became Regent of Castile that he was enabled to actively co-operate in the conversion of the aborigines. He then appointed Las Casas, with three chosen monks of the Jeronymite Order, to labor among the Indians. To them he gave very precise commands as to the treatment of the natives; bade the monks impress upon these poor people that they were special objects of solicitude to the Regent of Castile and the Spanish Government; commanded them to procure the erection of villages for the Indians, in each of which there must be a church and school. These villages were to be erected in the neighborhood of mines, wherein the natives were to be employed. In fact the wisdom and foresight of these detailed instructions for the treatment of savages in a foreign land strike us with astonishment. Some years later fourteen Franciscan monks went thither, one of whom was brother to the King of Scotland. Ximenes gave them every facility for their voyage, and urged them to persevere in their holy undertaking.

About this time negro slaves were in great request in

the colonies, and it was represented to Ximenes that if this trade were permitted it would be of the greatest advantage to Spain, and a source of great wealth to the kingdom. But Ximenes sternly forbade it, exerted all his influence against it, and issued an edict forbidding all importation of negro slaves.*

Among the events which marked his regency was the total overthrow of the rebellious nobles under the Duke of Alva and Giron. The town of Villadefredes, where the insurgents had shut themselves up, was burned by order of Sarmento, who conducted the siege. Giron, his son Roderick, and others, were found guilty of high treason, but were afterwards pardoned at the solicitation of Ximenes. In the celebrated troubles about the Priorate of Consuegra, which belonged to the Order of St. John of Jerusalem, and which the Duke of Alva claimed for his son against Antonio Zuniga, who had been for years Grand Master, Charles wrote to Ximenes from Flanders to support Zuniga in his authority. To the great terror of the nobles and grandees, Ximenes therefore seized upon the Priory by force of arms. When Fonseca, one of the principal nobles, remonstrated with him, representing the danger of a revolt, Ximenes replied:

"Be composed, Fonseca. I will so arrange matters that everything shall end well."

And they did end well, for Alva was induced to accept the king's terms, which he had hitherto so steadfastly refused to do.

Just after a visit which the Cardinal had paid to Torrelaguna, his native place, in August, 1517, when he passed on to Bozeguillas, a mountainous region, it is said that an attempt was made to poison him. A masked

---

* Hefele, p. 514.

rider called out to the Provincial of the Franciscans and others on the way to Ximenes:

"If you are going to the Cardinal, hasten yourselves, and warn him not to eat of the large trout—it is poisoned. If you come too late, urge him to prepare for death, for he will not be able to overcome the poison."

The Cardinal would not, however, believe this, and said:

"If I really am poisoned, it is by a letter received from Flanders a few days ago, the sand of which has considerably affected my eyes; yet even this I do not believe."

It was reported, however, that Francisco Carillo, who first tasted of whatever was cooked, fell seriously ill.

It was very shortly after Ximenes' elevation to the archiepiscopal See of Toledo that we find him beginning to think seriously of founding and endowing out of the revenues of his new office a centre of learning and the arts. He had already, like Isabella, done much to bring the then infant art of printing into repute, having given prizes for the best workmanship, and invited printers into the principal towns. Isabella, and following her example most of the grandees of Spain, had shown favor and support in the most lavish manner to the University of Salamanca. Moreover, various archbishops had founded schools at Granada, Seville, and Toledo; but it was reserved for Ximenes to found at Alcalá what is called by Spaniards "the eighth wonder of the world." He chose a site upon the banks of the Henares, where the pure fresh breezes came blowing down from the grand old Sierras, and where the beautiful and varied Castilian landscape was in its full perfection. This was the ancient Complutum and the present Alcalá de Henares.

The College of San Ildefenso, so named from the titular saint of the Cathedral of Toledo, formed the nucleus of the new university. The date of its commencement seems to be about 1508 or 1510. Seven students then came thither from Salamanca. It was enacted that the college should consist of thirty-three professors, in honor of the thirty-three years of our Saviour's earthly life, and twelve priests were added in honor of the twelve apostles. These latter, however, were simply charged with the chaplaincy of the institution, and took no part in the teaching. The professors, it was ordained, were to be distinguished from the other members of the university by a long red, closely fitting robe, with a scarf of the same color thrown over the left shoulder, and falling in folds to the ankle.*

Besides this head college, Ximenes founded the following useful institutions in connection therewith. Thus, for instance, the two boarding-schools of St. Eugenius and St. Isidore, where forty-two scholars were supported for three years free of all expense; two others, those of St. Balbina and St. Catherine, for students in philosophy; a building for students who fell ill, this latter being under the invocation of the Blessed Virgin; again another for poor theological students and a few students in medicine; a sixth, called "the Little School," for twelve Franciscan scholars; and the College of Three Languages, in honor of St. Jerome, for thirty scholars. The university met with great favor, both from the Papal Government, which attached special privileges to it; also from the king. It is related that the illustrious Francis I. of France once paid a visit to the university, and cried out in admiration:

"Your Ximenes has undertaken and accomplished a work which I myself could not attempt. The University of Paris, the pride of my kingdom, is the work of a line of

---

* Gomez. Hefele,

sovereigns; but Ximenes alone has founded one like it."

Another important foundation made by the Cardinal was the Convent de San Juan, to which he joined a house of charity for the special protection of poor girls, under the invocation of Santa Isabel. Here they could remain for some years, under the guidance of a spiritual mother, with certain rules drawn up for their direction. At the expiration of this given time they had the choice of marrying or entering a religious life.

Ximenes was besides one of the chief patrons of the hospital for poor invalids, which also was intended to provide for destitute widows and orphans, and many other works of mercy. He founded in all four hospitals, eight monasteries, and twelve churches.

To Ximenes is mainly due the preservation of the Mozarabic or Gothic Liturgy, which, a biographer remarks, is "so venerable for its antiquity and deep piety." He collected the various manuscripts appertaining to this rite and had them carefully revised by Mozarabic priests. He likewise founded, in his own cathedral, a Mozarabic chapel of rare and curious design, and also a college of thirteen priests to perpetuate these rites. He is said to have spent large sums of money in the printing of breviaries and missals.

But we have now come to what many regard as his chief benefits to Spain and to mankind. We mean his Polyglot edition of the Bible, the first which had been attempted and which is named the Complutensian, from Complutum or Alcalá, where this gigantic work was executed. Prescott, who certainly cannot be suspected of partiality towards the Cardinal, declares this Bible to be "a noble monument of piety, learning, and munificence, which entitles its author to the gratitude of the whole Christian world." His object, Ximenes himself says, was to "revive the hitherto dormant study of the Sacred Scriptures." He collected together for this purpose men the most erudite that the kingdom afforded, amongst whom were three learned Jews, converts to Christianity. The whole expenses of this magnificent undertaking were born by Ximenes; sometimes he was obliged to purchase, at great cost, manuscripts of the Old or New Testaments. He received the greatest assistance and encouragement from Pope Leo X., forever the generous patron of learning and art. Even before he was made Pope, while he was still Cardinal, we are led to suppose from the dates that he sent valuable manuscripts to Ximenes, whom he loved and honored. Ximenes dedicated this great work to the Pope, and on its completion returned him public thanks for assistance rendered. Wonderful sight, indeed, to the panegyrists of modern progress to see a Grand Inquisitor of Spain, years before the so-called Reformation had begun, in those dark middle ages, the parent and foster-mother of ignorance, giving public thanks to a Pope for assistance rendered in bringing out the first Polyglot edition of the Bible.

Whilst the learned men whom he had chosen labored at their stupendous task they were personally superintended by Ximenes, who urged them frequently as follows:

"Lose no time, my friends," would he say to them, "in the prosecution of our glorious task, lest in the casualties of life you should lose your patron, or I have to lament the loss of those whose services are of greater price in my eyes than wealth or worldly honors."*

The first volume was finished after twelve years of labor; the last some three years later. Six hundred

---

* See Quintanilla, Gomez, and other Spanish authorities, as well as Hefele.

copies were then struck off. The German printer, Arnauld William Brocar, sent his son, John Brocar, to announce the good tidings to Ximenes. John Brocar was clad in festal garments and his face was very joyful. The Cardinal, on receiving the intelligence, cried out:

"I give thee thanks, O Lord! that Thou hast enabled me to bring to the desired end the great work which I undertook."

To those around him he exclaimed :

"Of the many arduous duties which I have performed for the benefit of my country, there is nothing, my friends, on which you ought to congratulate me more than on the completion of this edition of the Bible, which now opens to us the sacred fountains of religion when they are most needed." *

We may mention in this connection that the Cardinal had likewise caused to be printed many cheap editions of Lives of the Saints and other edifying works. Amongst these was the life of St. Thomas à Becket, to whom he had a special devotion ; the Letters of St. Catherine of Sienna, the Ladder of Perfection, by St. John Climacus; Meditations on the Life of Christ, by a Carthusian, Landulph; besides many others. His idea was to stop the spread of immoral publications by supplying good reading in their place. Being anxious to promote classical knowledge, he also gave a commission to some learned men to prepare a complete edition of Aristotle ; but his death occurring soon after, put an end to this enterprise.

The Polyglot Bible was, indeed, a fitting close to the life of the great Cardinal. Four months afterwards he died. He lived long enough to experience the ingratitude of kings. Charles, who, in defiance of his faithful minister's will, had caused himself to be proclaimed king, though his

---

* Canon Dalton, in his Preface to Hefele. Feller. Hefele,

mother, Joanna, was still alive, became gradually estranged from Ximenes. Urged by those Flemish favorites and unworthy courtiers, against whom the Regent had so often warned him, he wrote a cold and unfeeling letter to the Cardinal, intimating that his services as Regent were no longer required. Some chroniclers have declared that this letter hastened his death, but the truth is he never received it. The grand old man was already upon the verge of the grave, and the announcement was simply made to the Royal Senate.

For the end was approaching. Already Ximenes stood upon the shores of the dark river; faintly he heard the dipping of the boatman's oars; brighter and brighter gleamed the gates of pearl, upon which his longing eyes had been fixed during all those years of labor and triumph; for the glory and fame and honor of the highest position in the Court had never obscured their vision. The Promised Land drew near; the world receded, and the jasper domes of the heavenly city grew distinct to his failing sight. At last the strong heart ceased to beat— the noble generous heart, which, historians assure us, "did more for Spain than all the kings that ever reigned." At last the giant intellect ceased to plan and execute plans for the welfare of the people whom he so much loved. The thorns and briars of the strait way were left behind, and swift through the narrow gate his spirit passed. That mighty soul, with one great gasp of joy, freed from the earthiness of earth, entered into life eternal. At the hour of death he spoke to his servants "of the instability of all earthly things, and of the infinite mercies of God." He begged of God the pardon of his sins, implored the special intercession of the saints, and received the Viaticum with deep and tender piety. The Prayers for the Dying were read, after which the Cardinal passed away calmly, with the words, "In Te, Domine, speravi,"

—In Thee, O Lord ! have I hoped,—on his lips. He was buried amid the tumultuous grief of the people. Sobs and tears of human sorrow accompanied him to his last resting-place, where he lay down joyfully, content to leave the kingdom which he had so long governed, to struggle for itself, and the world to its long strife and turmoil. Contrary to his orders for a simple and unostentatious funeral, the remains were conveyed, " amidst the blaze of innumerable torches," to the Monastery of St. Mary, founded by him, where a funeral service was celebrated. Near " Burgos the students of the university erected a mortuary chapel," where bishops, priests, nobles, and grandees assisted at the Matins for the dead. A monument of marble was erected over his remains in his own cathedral church, and fifty-eight years after "a magnificent enclosure of bronze was placed around it, upon which were represented the principal events of Ximenes' life."

Our necessarily imperfect glance at this character of unparalleled grandeur is concluded, and it but remains for us to sum up in as few words as possible some opinions upon this the most extraordinary man of his day, and to form our own estimate of his life and works. Even his personal appearance is vividly before us. That tall, spare figure, strongly and powerfully built; the forehead high, broad, and deeply wrinkled; the eyes deep-set, clear, and penetrating; the face long; the nose likewise long, thin, and aquiline. In presence of the multitudinous testimony, exalting him above all the statesmen or prelates of his age, it may be well to quote the following significant opinion, which is enunciated by more than one biographer. Robertson, in his Life of Charles V., says that,

" In the whole history of the world, Ximenes is the only Prime Minister who was revered by his contemporaries as a saint, and to whom the people over whom he ruled ascribed, even while living, the power of working miracles." Arnao, a modern Spaniard, says,

"Ximenes knew how to unite in his person the virtues of the most pious monk, of the most zealous bishop, and the most accomplished statesman. Spain," he adds, "passed under him through the most prosperous and happy phase of her history. Would that another Ximenes were born to her in the nineteenth century!" The Duke of Alva, Ximenes' most bitter political opponent, acknowledged, after the Cardinal's death, that "he was one of the most remarkable of men, a true old Spanish heroic character." The Padre Quintanilla, a Spanish monk, is so profuse in his praise, that it seems almost like exaggeration; while Gomez, Flechier, and innumerable Spanish authors, exalt him to the highest. Dr. Hefele, the learned German, to whose able work on the great Ximenes we are so much indebted, himself draws a parallel between Richelieu and Ximenes, which is altogether to the advantage of the latter. Canon Dalton, in the Preface to his translation of Hefele's Ximenes, says: "As a statesman he was far superior to Richelieu, as a prelate he was the model of bishops; as a monk, full of the spirit of his Order; as a patron of learning, unsurpassed. Not only was he irreproachable in his morals, kind and generous to the poor, severe to himself alone, but zealous beyond conception for the advancement of the Catholic faith, a father to his clergy and canons of Toledo, devoted to the cause of the Holy See, forgiving and even kind to his enemies." "If," adds he, "I can inspire my readers with the same love and admiration for the character of Ximenes which I feel myself, my labor will be fully repaid,"—words which we may apply with full justice to our humble analysis of the character of this truly heroic man. Throughout Spain, he was even in his lifetime popularly regarded as a saint; many miracles are ascribed to him, and in some ancient martyrologies his name is still enrolled. But as we have no decision of the Church upon this point, we may well be content to regard him as what he was—the master spirit of Spain. Whether as Friar, Prelate, or Minister, it must be conceded that he has reached a pinnacle of greatness to which few can aspire. As an humble Franciscan monk, we see him full of the Spirit of God, practising almost unparalleled austerities. Under the Cardinal's robe we find him still wearing his habit of St. Francis and a rough hair shirt; still detached from the world, still full of zeal for the things of God, frugal and penitential in his diet, sleeping upon a plank, his tranquil mind undisturbed by the splendor and luxury of a court. As a statesman he stands out prominent in history as a reformer of abuses, the organizer of a superior military system, the man who increased tenfold the maritime power of Spain; who paid off the national debt, who removed oppressive taxes, and who opposed the introduction of negro slavery in America. A constant generous patron of all that was noble and good and beautiful of science and art, and even of agriculture, for he caused books upon this subject to be printed and promulgated. A patriot who spent twenty millions in the service of his country; and of all the noble revenues which his high offices brought in to him, left not a farthing to any private friend or kinsman. In a word, the liberal protector of the poor, at once the friend of liberty and the supporter of established government, the founder of a University and the compiler of a Polyglot Bible.

His character as a priest was never sullied by even an unworthy accusation, though the bitterest enemies of the Church have written about him. His virtues were all of the grandest; his very faults those which often accompany the truest greatness. His word was inviolable; his

heroic generosity in forgiving personal enemies, an example to the nation; and his perfect unworldliness amid the splendors of a luxurious court, a model to the world. He shunned the honors which were forced upon him, and despised the luxury that surrounded him. The very severity, bordering upon harshness, of which his enemies accuse him, was the quality which enabled him to hold the helm of state amid all the storms of those troublous times. Besides, it was so constantly obviated by his charity, generosity, and benevolence, that we can scarcely make it a subject of complaint. Purest and noblest among the pure and noble, where shall we find his equal? The fulness of the Holy Spirit descending upon him made him superior to any contemporary, and, as his biographer tells us, produced in him "that hunger and thirst after justice" which ceased only with his death. This man of indomitable will, fiery ardor, all-grasping intellect and sublime faith, has slept for ages beneath the marble of that noble temple which he himself founded.*
Its painted windows cast their warm glow upon his tomb, where it stands, in the dark hush and stately grandeur of the proud edifice, an edifice which serves as a fitting monument to as grand and pure a spirit as death ever freed from mortal thrall and immortality ushered through the gates of the grave into the glory of the Eternal City.

The moonlight spell of the dim old city which held us in thrall is dissolved, our task in Toledo is done, and we turn away from its dusky, mediæval splendor and the contemplation of that great life, which in those so-called dark ages shed such lustre upon it.

Before we pass from its gates we cast a hasty glance upon the curious old Church of San Juan de los Reyes,

---

* The Church of San Ildefonso, attached to the University of Alcalá.

built by Ferdinand and Isabella. Upon its reddish tinged façade hang the chains of the Christian captives freed at the fall of Granada; statues of kings and heroes in various attitudes adorn its tawny exterior—kings and heroes famous once in the history of the country, but whose bodies have long since mouldered into dust beneath the cathedrals of the land. We leave behind us the narrow streets, the picturesque oddness of the brightly painted houses, the heavy iron balconies and barred windows, giving them the appearance of miniature fortresses; and we bid farewell to the vast cathedral where, with organ peal, amid the waving of banners and the rich gloom of painted windows, the humble Franciscan first took his place as Archbishop of Toledo—that cathedral, its curious Mozarabic Chapel, and its beautiful one of the Madonna, where, amid a gorgeous mingling of jasper, porphyry, and other precious marbles, Our Lady is enthroned as with Eastern magnificence. According to the Spanish custom, her robe is of rich velvet, adorned with costly jewels, and her crown so resplendent with priceless gems that it reminds us of the splendor of that crown bestowed upon her by Christ, her Son, "to the particular glory of all the Saints."

The splendid pageant fades from our sight, with the last view of the ruined Alcazar, upon which, in the days of the great and good Cardinal, time had scarcely laid its vandal hand. We bid a lingering farewell to the beauties of fair Castilia, to her olive groves and gardens of myrtle, to her silvery streams and dark Sierras. In their midst we leave, as in a worthy setting, the noble, the heroic, the mighty Francisco Cisneros de Ximenes, Cardinal of Spain.

Painter, Poet, Architect, and Sculptor.

O Sovereign Masters of the Pencil's might,
Its depths of shadow, and its blaze of light;
Children of Italy! who stand alone
And unapproached, midst regions all your own.

. . . .

Thou, the inspired One, whose gigantic mind
Lived in some sphere to thee alone assigned;
Who, from the past, the future and the unseen
Could call up forms of more than earthly mien,
Unrivalled Angelo.

HEMANS.

Michael Angelo,

PAINTER, POET, ARCHITECT, AND SCULPTOR.

WHAT a world of historic associations cluster about the name which, in the golden days of Leo X. and down through the lifetimes of successive popes, cast lustre upon all Italy and added new laurels to Eternal Rome. The sound of that magic name brings present to the view Rome of the Curule Throne, Rome of the Tribunes, Rome of the Emperors, Rome of the Mighty Pantheon, and Rome of the Popes. In a mist of memories comes she to the sight, empurpled with the royal mantle of her rulers, empurpled with the crimson of her victims' blood, empurpled with the purple of her hills, empurpled with the twilight shadows enshrouding the Campagna, till they melt in golden light over the yellow Tiber.

Centuries ago a mighty monarch laid at the feet of the Sovereign Pontiff one small portion of this vast world to be the visible Kingdom of Christ upon earth. It was the homage of a generous heart, a trophy of his faith, a pledge of his thanksgiving. For, as ages rolled away, the heathen gods of the idolatrous Romans, who had so long swayed the world, fell, one by one, with hideous clamor, and the old race of heroes, who had swept the world with their conquests, vanished forever from mortal ken. But, meanwhile, the vicegerents of

Christ, the pastors of the faithful, were unknown to the greater part of men. Beneath the palaces of the Cæsars, beneath the temples of their gods, deep in the bowels of the earth, ran dark and tortuous vaults or caverns, where, in the still and solemn midnight, when the symbolic silence of sleep had fallen upon the world, a few faithful hearts gathered around their chief. Tapers illumined the darkness, an altar of sacrifice was raised, the Lamb, a victim of Propitiation, was offered, and the Bread which is the Life of the world distributed to the first Christians. Grand and sublime the chants of praise died away in innumerable echoes among the black arches overhead, or in the sinuous windings of the gloomy Catacombs; silvery and soft the incense floated upwards to the Eternal Throne, filling the dark vaults with sweet aroma; and the white-haired Pontiff, kneeling, upraised his hands in supplication for the people.

But in the fulness of time this newer, grander, most imperishable of monarchies, emerged from this subterranean darkness and looked forth over the earth, never again to disappear from its green surface till Time shall cast its burden of centuries into Eternity's shoreless ocean. Constantine, flushed with victory, beheld in the heavens the sign of the Crucified; he recognized the mightier Conqueror, and he cast before Him wealth and fame and honor, his alike by birth and conquest. Thenceforth the Christian people shunned no more the light of day, and their chief took his place beside the royal victor. Centuries elapsed, and another mighty king came out of the West, and gave unto the Lord the spoils of victory. These he declared should evermore be held the heritage of God in the person of His Vicar; so that when wars or rumors of wars should agitate the earth, the Church might possess her soul in peace, nor be ever again compelled to celebrate the worship of God beneath the earth. Such was the donation of the magnanimous Charlemagne, the possession of which has never until the present day been disputed to the Church. To-day the Vicar of Christ is a captive; the Church, alas! a victim to the spoiler's wrath.

But in the golden days when Christ smiled upon Italy, His inheritance, and created for her sovereign spirits whose very memory casts a spell over the civilized world, was born in Tuscany, on the 6th of March, 1474, at the Castle of Caprese, Michael Angelo Buonarotti, painter, poet, architect, and sculptor. He was descended from the illustrious family of the Counts of Canossa, who had been in successive generations the defenders and supporters of the Papal See. At the time of the artist's birth his father was *Podestà* or Governor of Chiusi and Caprese. When his term of office had expired he returned to Florence, and sent the infant Angelo to the family villa of Settignano. There he was nursed by a woman who chanced to be the wife of one stone-mason and the daughter of another; to which fact the artist often jestingly alluded, as explaining his taste for the chisel.

While still young, Angelo was sent to a grammar-school in Florence, kept by one Francesco d'Urbino; and here his father wished him to prepare for an honorable career in one of the learned professions. But this dearest wish of the paternal heart was not destined to be gratified. Already mysterious whisperings were calling the student into another world, peopled with rare and exquisite creations; the shades of immortal ones, who in the dust of glorious ages had buried the wondrous productions of their art, lured him on with visions of the infinite, and woke in his soul vague longings which bore him far beyond the earth into a nobler and purer atmosphere. Nature, too, with her thousand charms allured him: the dusky purple of the dying day, the mellow light which with translucent beam illumined the evening-shadowed Arno ; as thereafter the rich colors of Ausonian sunsets, the pearl pallor of her dawns upon the lone Campagna ; the melancholy grandeur of the Seven Hills, the bright and warm and rich luxuriance of Tivolian bowers; the deep shadow of the lofty Soracte, the moonlight on the time-vanquished walls of the Coliseum; the citron-scented groves and olive hills and orange gardens of his native land,—all these spoke to his youthful soul in strange language, thrilled him with passionate joy and pain, filled him with mighty imagery and high imaginings, which sought interpretation and troubled him with uncontrollable longings, never to be laid to rest until he had gained a threefold immortality. Even at this early age Angelo spent every moment he could spare from study in drawing and painting. He soon formed the acquaintance of some artists, amongst whom a certain Francesco Granacci, a pupil of Ghirlandaio, did much to encourage the boy's love for art, and brought him to his master's studio. Thenceforth, neglecting all else, Angelo devoted himself to his favorite pursuits, and with the assistance of Granacci, painted on a panel the story of St. Anthony and the Fishes, from a German print. So desirous was he of imitating nature, that he went to the market to observe the forms of the fish, which he consequently reproduced exactly. Soon afterwards he borrowed a head, and so well succeeded in copying it, that he returned his imitation and retained the model, nor was the deception discovered till he himself exposed it.

His artistic tendencies were a source of great displeasure to his father and other relatives, the profession of painter being held as a degradation. Their interference, however, proved unavailing, and his father was finally induced to place him as a pupil in the school of

Domenico Ghirlandaio, then the most eminent Florentine painter.

Angelo must already have been esteemed as an artist of great promise, for the master, instead of receiving the usual compensation from the pupil, agreed to pay him a small salary. From that time his progress in art was wonderful, though he gained but little from the instruction of a master who was notoriously envious of his pupil's growing reputation. Once, however, it is related that even the envious master was forced to applaud a sketch made by his young disciple. Ghirlandaio had been employed to decorate the Florentine Church of Santa Maria Novella. During his master's absence Angelo drew the scaffolding, desks, the whole apparatus, and a young artist who was at work, and this in so masterly a manner that it called forth universal admiration.

Meanwhile, Lorenzo de Medici had opened a school for the study of sculpture, feeling that its progress had not kept pace with that of painting. A garden in or about the Piazza di San Marco was employed for the purpose and filled with antique sculpture. Bertoldo, a pupil of Donatello, was appointed as keeper. Ghirlandaio was invited to send thither his most promising pupils; and Angelo and his friend Granacci became regular attendants, thus gaining a correct knowledge of the antique.*

The young artist now for the first time attempted modelling in clay, and also tried his apprentice hand at carving in marble. Lorenzo de Medici, in one of his visits to the garden, observed a copy of an old head or mask which Angelo had made. It represented a marble faun,

---

*Vasari's Life of Angelo. Vasari's Ragionamenti. Duffa's Life of Angelo

and Lorenzo jestingly remarked that the teeth were too perfect for so old a faun. Angelo perceiving the justice of the criticism immediately remedied the defect. Lorenzo was so delighted with the alteration that he sent for the father of the artist, and asked him to give up his son, also promising to assist in procuring an office for himself. The father consented, and shortly afterwards we find Lorenzo obtaining a situation in the customs for Lodovico Buonarotti, which was given him, "till something better should turn up." Angelo, who was then sixteen years of age, was received into Lorenzo's household, where he was treated as a son. During his residence there he pursued his studies with the greatest ardor and diligence in the old cloister church of the Carmelites, so rich in treasures of art. From that time dates the artist's friendship with Politiano, the distinguished Greek and Latin scholar, and the composer of elegant verse. At his suggestion, Angelo executed a *basso-rilievo* in marble, representing the battle of Hercules with the Centaurs. It was never completely finished, but years afterwards it caused the artist to declare that he regretted not having devoted himself entirely to sculpture.

In April, 1492, Angelo lost his kind and munificent patron. At Lorenzo's death the artist went home. Pietro de Medici, who now succeeded to the paternal estates, was far inferior to his father in mind and character. Still, he induced Angelo to return to the palace, and placed his former apartments at his disposal. For the amusement of his guests he set him to make a statue of snow for the courtyard of the castle. He was proud of the artist's presence in the house, and was heard to boast that he had two extraordinary persons there—Michael Angelo, and a Spanish running footman, remarkable for beauty of person, and so swift of foot that one riding on horseback could not overtake him.*

Angelo occupied himself at this time in carving a great statue of Hercules, which afterwards became celebrated, and was presented to Francis I. of France. Political disturbances, however, caused him to leave the Medici palace and proceed to Bologna in company with some friends. A law was then in force that a foreigner entering Bologna should have his thumb sealed with red wax. Angelo and his friends having neglected this precaution, were detained in default of a heavy fine, till a member of the Bolognese Government, Signor Aldovrandi, released them and invited the artist to his house Angelo felt that if he accepted the invitation it would seem discourteous to his companions, and upon this plea declined the proffered hospitality. Aldovrandi jestingly remarked, "Then I think I will go with you myself to see the world, since you take such good care of your friends."

Angelo finally consented to remain at the house of his new friend, and occupied himself with marble statues for the Church of San Domenico: one, a San Petronio; the other, a kneeling angel bearing a branch for candles in the hand. After some months, however, he returned to his native city, where he executed a statue of an Infant St. John sleeping, and the celebrated figure of Cupid, so perfect an imitation of Grecian art, that he was induced to stain it such a color as it would have been if buried for ages. A man who had suggested the deception to Angelo now sent it to Rome, where the taste for antiquities was then a mania. The Cupid was greatly sought after, and brought a very large price from Cardinal San Giorgio; though the man who had practised the imposi-

---

* Pondivi.

tion, and not Angelo, was the gainer by the transaction. However, when it became known that the statue was not an antique, the Cardinal was naturally indignant, and sent to Florence to learn further particulars. The result was that the man who had sold it was arrested, and obliged to refund the money.

On the invitation of Cardinal San Giorgio Angelo went to Rome, where he made a statue of Bacchus, one of Cupid, and a figure of the Virgin and the Dead Christ, called in Italian a *Pietà*. This was the first of his which gained real celebrity. The beholder is at once impressed by a certain grandeur and simplicity, and a tender beauty of expression. It is now used as an altarpiece in the chapel of La Vergine Maria della Febbre in St. Peter's, and has been extensively copied in marble and bronze. Concerning this piece of sculpture the following anecdote is told. Angelo on one occasion entered the church, and found a number of persons standing in admiration before the *Pietà*. A stranger inquired the name of the sculptor, and Christofori Solari, commonly called *Il Gobbo*, who chanced to be present, answered, "One of our countrymen, a Milanese." Angelo heard but did not contradict the assertion. That night he returned thither and cut his name under the group, so that no such mistake might again occur.

His next work was a cartoon of "St. Francis Receiving the Stigmata;" but about this time he left Rome, and returned to Florence, on the invitation of Pietro Soderini, a liberal patron of the arts and a warm admirer of Angelo, who had just been called to the office of Gonfaloniere of Florence. While in his native city, Angelo executed a colossal figure of David for the square in front of the Palazzo Vecchio. His patron being brought to see it, or so the story goes, declared that the nose was too large. The artist explained on scientific principles why it should be so; but the critic was not convinced till Angelo, stepping upon a ladder, seized a chisel, and pretended to alter the nose, letting the dust, as it were from the marble, fall to the ground. Soderini was much flattered, and exclaimed, "Now I am better pleased; you have given it life."

It was through the Gonfaloniere that he received the commission for the famous cartoon which was to compete with that of Lionardo da Vinci. Angelo chose a scene in the war between the Florentines and Pisans, and Lionardo a battle of cavalry. In the former "all is life and movement," says Mrs. Jameson, "and the subject affords ample opportunity for the great facility of the artist in designing the human figure, for the Florentine soldiers are bathing in the Arno when the call to battle comes. Up the steep banks they rush, buckling on their armor and preparing for combat. There are thirty or more life-sized figures, drawn with black chalk, relieved with white." "The Cartoon of Pisa," says Alzog, "displays every variety of attitude and action, great anatomical knowledge, and admirable skill in foreshortening." This work was received with universal applause, and justly regarded as the grandest which Angelo had yet executed. It was a stupendous design, instinct with life and animation, the full power of the human frame being portrayed with consummate ability. Yet it lacks the sublimity of conception so perceptible in his religious masterpieces.

That of Lionardo da Vinci was also executed with wonderful power, and was, for certain reasons, preferred. Neither of the designs were ever carried out, political changes interfering with their execution, and Angelo was called to Rome by Julius II., who had just succeeded to the tiara. His cartoon was destroyed, it is said, by the malice of Baccio Bandinelli, who tore it to pieces. So that of this magnificent conception but one small copy remains.

The reigning Pope, Julius, was eminently a lover of learning and the arts, both of which he most liberally patronized. Hence it is little wonder that he immediately summoned Angelo to the Vatican, sending an order for a hundred ducats to defray his travelling expenses. Of this Pope an eminent biographer has said, "The character of Julius is one of incomparable grandeur. He well deserved the most magnificent sepulchral monument of the prince of artists." It was now upon his arrival in Rome that Angelo began the design for the celebrated mausoleum of Julius II., which he never entirely carried out. The plan, as we have it from his biographers, was a parallelogram, with a superstructure of forty statues, some of colossal size; it was to be ornamented with various figures, and *bassi-rilievi* in bronze. If completed, it would have been the most magnificent tribute ever offered to the memory of a man who fostered so many geniuses in the sunshine of his munificence. The plan finished, an appropriate place for its execution had to be chosen, and it was found that the then existing Church of St. Peter's would not suffice. Alterations in the building were suggested, and the project grew and grew till it led to the rebuilding of St. Peter's. Angelo, however, began his work upon the mausoleum, and completed the famous statue of Moses, wherein the inspired lawgiver is represented grasping with one hand his flowing beard, and with the other the tables of the law. So high was Angelo in the favor of the Pope, and so great a regard did the latter feel for him, that a covered bridge, it is said, was erected between the Vatican and the artist's studio, that the Pope might visit him at his pleasure and watch the progress of his works. Such distinction naturally excited bitter envy and hatred against Angelo, and efforts were made to bring about dissensions between him and his patron. It was understood that the sculptor was to apply to the Pope for whatever funds might be necessary in the carrying on of the work. On one occasion Angelo went as usual to the Vatican for this purpose, but was told that the Pontiff could not be seen. Disappointed, but attaching no importance to the circumstance, the artist retired. A short time after, he repeated his visit, and was told that the officer had orders not to admit him. A prelate standing by reproved the officer, asking him if he knew to whom he spoke. "I know him well enough," replied the other, "but it is my duty to obey orders." Angelo, who was of quick temper, was deeply hurt, and sent the following message to the Pope:

"Henceforward, if his Holiness wants me he shall have to seek me in another place."

Hastening home he left orders for his furniture to be sold, and departed at once for Florence. The Pope hearing of it sent five couriers to bring him back, but as he was beyond the papal jurisdiction they could not compel him to return. So he refused decidedly, saying, "That being expelled the antechamber of his Holiness, conscious of not meriting the disgrace, he had taken the only course left him to pursue consistent with the preservation of that character which had hitherto rendered him worthy of his confidence." The Pope sent a message to the Florentine Government to induce Angelo if possible to return to Rome, where he would enjoy, as before, the Pontifical favor. Soderini at length persuaded him to return. Some political matter having brought the Pope to Bologna, Soderini considered the opportunity favorable for a reconciliation between him and the painter. An audience was granted, and when Angelo entered the presence chamber, Pope Julius glanced at him sternly, saying coldly, "Instead of your coming to us, you seem to have expected that we should have attended upon you." Angelo answered respectfully that he had been deeply hurt at what he must regard as his unmerited disgrace, and asked pardon for the past. The Pope then gave him his blessing and restored him to favor.

The artist now executed a statue in bronze of his patron, which when completed was of such severe and imposing aspect that the Pope asked if the sculptor had represented him as blessing or cursing; to which Angelo replied, "Only as threatening the unruly." This was placed in the *façade* of San Petronio. Angelo would have continued his work upon the mausoleum, but the Pope desired that the Sistine Chapel commenced by Sixtus IV. should be decorated. Michael Angelo therefore began that immortal work, and thus set his foot with surer hold upon the mountain height of his limitless immortality. Yet the new work was not to his taste. His success as a sculptor was assured; the great mausoleum, an evidence of his power, would go down to remote posterity. Painting in fresco might prove a failure. It is said his enemies counted upon this, and hoped thus to see him fall from his eminence as the master genius of the age. But the Pope would have him paint the Sistine Chapel, and paint he did.

Centuries have passed since then, and travellers pausing in amaze have no need to ask the name of the wizard who has brought thither the powers of earth and air and hell, who has caught half-veiled glimpses of the glory to come, and transfixed them all upon the walls and ceilings of the Sistine Chapel.

The walls had been adorned by once celebrated artists, and the original design was that they should be whitewashed over, and painted by Angelo. The death of

Julius prevented this portion of the plan from being carried out. So that the ceiling and some of the walls alone bear the touch of the master, and by their refulgence cast into shade the lesser lights which shone with considerable brilliancy when that wondrous ceiling of to-day was a vast white blank.

The ceiling bears various decorations in *chiaro-oscuro*, and is divided into several compartments. Four great divisions and five small ones form the centre. In these we have majestic images of the Creator. He bids light appear upon the darkness; He creates the sun and moon, with outstretched arms, calling them out of chaos and fixing them in their orbits; stretching His Almighty hand over the dark waste of waters, He commands them into certain limits, where, chained by His word, they await the moment of universal annihilation. Last comes the creation of man, the handful of clay, the vital breath therein transfused. His image and likeness stamped thereupon, and dominion imparted over the animal tribes, the crowning touch of the divinity given in the creation of Eve and the fair face of nature is complete.

But a change comes over the blissful garden and its happy inmates. The fall, the glory forever fled, the majesty of innocence thenceforth departed, and the souls of earth's primal dwellers, cursed by the unending curse, are all before us, with the sad story of the expulsion. Out, out into the dreariness, and misery, and sin, and labor and death of the outer world, never to revisit, save in melancholy retrospection, the ever fair, ever verdant, ever radiant garden of Paradise. The hope remaining too is here portrayed in the promise of another Eden, whose joy the heart of man cannot conceive; but the way leading thitherward is through the dark and rugged defile of death.

The artist leads us onward to that awful epoch in the

story of our race. The Deluge, the dark mass of waters, the affrighted earth buried fathoms beneath; and above the surging waters wild, despairing faces, distorted limbs, and all the signs and tokens of strong human agony brought in the fulness of life, face to face with death. As a relief we turn to the sacrifice of Noe, whence the smoke of propitiation ascends from the altar stone to the realms of Eternal clemency; and to the vineyard of the patriarch, where the purple grapes ripen under skies and suns that looked down upon the first inhabitants of a new earth. For the mighty surging of the waters has forever borne the old idolatrous race from the surface of the globe.

All this in the centre of the ceiling. But in the surrounding and intersecting curves are the prophets and sibyls, who, with mystical speech, and eyes fixed upon a far-off Galilean midnight, speak unto men of the birth of the Royal Redeemer. They are brought vividly to life by the artist, seated before us with their mighty scrolls or giant tomes, and impress themselves upon our minds with wonderful individuality. Each one feels the breath of inspiration, and the might of some overmastering power which burst asunder the myriad bonds of time and space, and hurries him onward into a marvellous futurity. Yet the aspect of each is different. Strange forms, too, of beings once, in the old mythological days, supposed to preside over the destinies of kingdom and empire, race and individual, await in the ambient air the message for immortality.

In compartments called *lunettes* is the genealogy of Christ, his direct descent from the royal line of David. With rare, intuitive tenderness and conception of the beautiful, the artist herein portrays each figure in a calm loveliness and restful quietude, contrasting well with the awful sublimity of his proximate productions.

In one corner of the ceiling is the majestic figure of Judith, full of austere and stately beauty, at the moment of her triumph over Holofernes. In the other corners are David vanquishing Goliath, the Punishment of Aman, the Brazen Serpent, and the miraculous deliverance of the people of Israel, pointing as it does to the salvation of mankind by Christ the Redeemer. Upon the pedestals, and as it were supporting the cornice, are forty-eight figures of infants in various attitudes. They are just beneath the entablature of *chiaro-oscuro* which divides the flat part of the ceiling from the coved. Here and there in the ornamentation are fifty figures placed at intervals, and ten medallions representing historical subjects.*

In fancy we behold Angelo during the progress of this marvellous work, pausing with brush upraised; his wondrous intellect and its mighty imaginings spellbound, his great soul dilating upon its conception of the Eternal Creator. His the task to give to immortality an idea of the Infinite, which might bear some proportion to the limitless grandeur of the subject. Through the long hours of day he labors; the morning's early sweetness steals upon him at his work, and evening's peaceful loneliness finds him toiling still; adding new and tender touches of majestic beauty to the countenance of the Incarnate Son of God, perfecting each fold and wrinkle of that seamless garment which the infirm made whole so often kissed with grateful rapture; embodying his thoughts of the Madonna, the holy purity, the divine tenderness, the unutterable beauty of the face which smiled above the crib of Bethlehem, and was furrowed with tears of agony on Calvary; peopling all the air with the angelic hosts, lending new brightness to Cherubim and Seraphim,

---

* Mrs. Jameson. Vasari. Duffa.

new glory to the Thrones and Dominations; picturing the saints with the various insignia of their mission upon earth, or the signs and symbols of the divers dark paths of suffering by which they entered the Kingdom of God.

In twenty months the marvellous work was completed; and a day came of unparalleled triumph for Angelo. The heart of the artist swelled within him as he beheld the multitude who thronged the Sistine Chapel to gaze upon the work which he alone had begun and ended, and into which a portion of his soul had passed. His earnest faith, his adoring love, his reverent devotion, were imaged in that which thrilled all beholders with its grandeur and its loveliness. It was the Feast of all Saints; the Sistine Chapel was resplendent. The Sovereign Pontiff entered in his robes of state and sang High Mass, amid the harmonious thunder of the music and the rejoicings of a multitude. The artist gazed upon his creation, beheld the wonder written upon the upturned faces of the people, and the immortal fire of genius burned strong within him. A great uncontrollable desire possessed him to approach what seemed the unattainable, and produce what his soul, full of an undefinable longing, urged him to accomplish—something which would satisfy his high aspirations, fill the measure of his giant heart's content, and put a final term to the soarings of his all-grasping intellect.

He worshipped before the altar, and gave praise to God, the mighty and the strong, the holy and the just, in whose name he felt he could defy the verdict of the universe, and stand where man for good or evil might not stand. High upon that mountain-top, touching that loftiest pinnacle, breathing that purer air, he need acknowledge no kindred with the world that lay stretched at his feet.

A few short months, however, and an end came to the earthly career of one who had been to the artist the noblest of patrons and stanchest of friends. Pope Julius died in February, 1513, and his loss was not readily supplied to Angelo. Pope Leo X., who succeeded to the pontificate, was an equally munificent patron of the arts; but he encouraged the growing genius of Raphael, and aided him to lay the foundation of his enduring fame. Yet he forwarded the plans of Angelo, and assured him of the undiminished favor and support of the Papal See; but it was not with the old undivided patronage which his predecessor had bestowed. He gave Angelo a commission to adorn the exterior of the Church of San Lorenzo in Florence. This the artist undertook with some reluctance, being desirous of completing the mausoleum of Pope Julius, though, as previously arranged, on a smaller and less expensive scale. He felt this to be a debt which he owed the memory of his benefactor. Pope Leo gave him permission to carry out both works at the same time. But the *façade* of San Lorenzo did not progress very rapidly. Pope Leo had heard great accounts of the marble of Pietra Santa; he had been informed that it was fully equal to that of Carrara. Angelo was ordered to examine the quarries. He reported unfavorably, and represented the great difficulty of transporting it thence. But the Pope was anxious that it should be tried, and hence the work went slowly.

A word may not be out of place here regarding the constant encouragement and support given by the Pontiffs to so many artists who were fostered in the shadow of the Papal throne, and supported out of the abundance of the Papal revenues. What a refutation of the old fable, passed from mouth to mouth since the Reformation, that the Catholic Church is an enemy to the enlightenment and cultivation of the human race! But on such a subject volumes might be written, and still much left unsaid. Julius had been a most liberal patron of art and artists, as we have already seen, and Leo, if possible, surpassed him in this respect. In Hazlitt's edition of Duffa's Angelo, we are told that this they did "from a desire to elevate the common standard of mankind." The reign of Leo, who was of the celebrated family of Medici, is known as the golden age of art and literature.

At his court, artists, poets, and men of letters found shelter, protection, and encouragement. His pontificate was, as it were, the horizon upon which appeared the dawning light of Raphael's fame, glowed the fervid noontide of Angelo's inspired labors, and faded the setting-sun of Lionardo's genius. Yet, of the two latter named, neither accomplished so much during his reign as in that of his predecessor. Angelo was in part to blame; his over-sensitiveness and a certain perversity of disposition led to misunderstandings between himself and the Pope; besides, the delay about the marble, which we have already mentioned, retarded the progress that he might have made. Again, with Lionardo da Vinci, it was due to his own indolent and dilatory habits, in addition to a certain feeling of discontent he knew all too surely that his reign as king of artists was over. Soon after the accession of Leo he departed to France, where he died.

Leo reigned but eight years and eight months. He was succeeded by Adrian VI., during whose pontificate Angelo was principally engaged in Florence, upon the statues intended for the mausoleum of Julius, and upon a library and sacristy to be added to the Church of San Lorenzo. He executed two memorial statues of Dukes Giuliano and Lorenzo of the house of Medici. These were to be placed in the sacristy, which when finished was to serve as a mausoleum for that illustrious family. Adrian died after a pontificate of twenty months, and was succeeded by Clement VII., also a Medici. During his reign Rome was sacked by the soldiers of the Constable de Bourbon, so that Angelo remained principally at Florence, excepting a brief interval passed at Rome, and continued his work upon the Chapel and Library of San Lorenzo. He also completed a statue of Christ for the Roman Church of Santa Maria Sopra Minerva. Italy was now threatened by the all-grasping ambition of Charles V., and it was deemed advisable to fortify Florence. Angelo was appointed military architect, and for the first time distinguished himself in that way by the construction of a fortification upon the eminence of Monte San Miniato, which enabled the city to sustain a siege of nine months. After the fall of the Florentine Republic, Angelo at first concealed himself, but on being offered the most favorable terms by Pope Clement, came forth from his hiding-place, and continued his work upon the statues of the Medici in the Chapel of San Lorenzo, and also executed for the same a statue of the Madonna bearing the Child Jesus in her arms. He was directed by the Pope to prepare a design for the end wall of the Sistine Chapel, and this he did with some reluctance, being anxious to complete the mausoleum of Julius, upon which he was again engaged, under the direction of the Duke d'Urbino.

But in the mean time Clement died, and Paul III., of the Farnese family, became Pope. He was most anxious to proceed with the decoration of the Sistine Chapel, for which Angelo had already prepared cartoons. A new engagement was therefore entered upon with the Duke d'Urbino, by which three statues were to be executed by Angelo, and the remaining three by other artists of his choice. So it was finally completed, and placed in the Church of San Pietro in Vincolo.

Angelo now began upon the west end of the Sistine Chapel that grandest and most stupendous of human creations—his immortal picture of the Last Judgment; so terrible in its conception and execution, so vast in its proportions, so awful in its glimpses of the woe and terror of that dread day of wrath. Prominent amid the mighty throng is the figure of the Messiah, no longer the Redeemer, no longer the Man of Sorrows, no longer the veiled God of the Tabernacle, but mighty, resplendent in His infinite brightness, appalling in His infinite wrath. The artist has portrayed Him, as it were, in uttering the dread sentence of unending woe, " Depart from Me, ye cursed, into everlasting fire." He would seem to crush to annihilation the trembling, shrinking figures, "withering away with the expectation of what is to come." Beside the awful Judge stands Mary, her intercession, at last, unavailing. Mournful, yet radiant with the glory of heaven, she turns compassionate eyes upon the multitude. Surrounding them, in the clouds, are the twelve Apostles, seated on twelve thrones, and a glorious company of the saints and elect. Myriads of angels people the air, and sound on innumerable trumpets their summons to the children of earth. On the one hand are the "just made perfect: their sentence of everlasting joy is passed, and a reflection of the blissful eternity in store for them already mingles with the human terror on their faces. Down into the awful gloom, or more horrid brightness of the abyss, demons are dragging the souls of the damned, and a boat, with a fiend at the helm, is sailing over the awful lake of fire into the fathomless ocean of eternity. It is laden with human beings, the faces of whom are appalling in their eternal despair. The whole idea of the picture is sublime, majestic, terrible; a masterpiece of awful sublimity. Alzog declares this picture to be unique in art. Angelo was next engaged upon the frescoes for the Paolina Chapel, built beside the Sistine, by order of Pope Paul; hence its name. He painted the Conversion of St. Paul and the Crucifixion of St. Peter, the chapel being under the invocation of those saints. These were the last pictures of importance ever painted by him. Thenceforth the artist devoted himself more particularly to architecture. About the same time he began a group of the Madonna del Pietá, bearing the Dead Christ in her lap. It was never completed, and stands in its unfinished state before the high altar of the Church of Santa Croce, Florence.

San Gallo, who had been architect of St. Peter's since the death of Bramante, died in 1546, and Angelo was appointed to succeed him. But the weight of years was beginning to weigh him down, and but for the express command of the Pope, he would have utterly refused the appointment. However, to the lasting glory of his name, he at length consented, as he said, *con grandissimo amore*, but on one condition: this was, that he should receive no renumeration. He simply accepted the office from his desire to accomplish something for the honor of the Most High. Such was the deep faith and earnest piety which characterized the great artist.

Now was begun one of what a historian calls "the splendid triumphs of Christian architecture, which we now gaze upon with amazement, whose very conceptions our minds are unable to grasp, and whose vast proportions bring home to our minds the consciousness of our own inferiority." *

In our present limits we cannot follow Angelo through

---

* Alzog, Ch. Hist., vol. ii.

all the years in which he was engaged upon this grandest of monuments, for so many ages the pride and glory of Christendom. It advanced very rapidly under his direction, and was very near completion at the time of his death. He continued his labors upon it during the pontificate of four popes—Paul III., Julius III., Pius IV., and Pius V.

Age began at length to tell upon this man of iron frame, and still he worked with stern and rugged perseverance, even when he was over eighty years of age. Wearily the hand which was wont to handle the chisel with such giant power drew design after design, some of which were to be completed when he was in dust. Slowly and heavily the step, once firm and buoyant, wended its way to the great square of the basilica. But the fire of inspiration still kindled in his eye, the flame of immortal genius still glowed upon his face, as he beheld that vast creation, which, the dews of age gave warning, it was not for him to complete. Still he labored till the chisel fell from his hand. That mighty soul, still young in its unimpaired vitality, felt that the dawn of immortality was at hand. The hour was come when it should soar beyond the worn-out body, which had toiled in the service of too stern a taskmaster, and grown old while the spirit was still in its vernal youth.

A slow fever attacked him, of which he died in the month of February, 1563, leaving unfinished that monument of the ages which is forevermore connected with his name. As the moment of dissolution approached, he called upon his physician and the members of his household to listen to his words. Then he cried out in a strong, clear voice:

"My soul I resign to God, my body to the earth, and my worldly possessions to my nearest of kin."

He then spoke as follows to those assembled at his

bedside, the solemn dignity and repose of death shadowing his face and lending emphasis to his words:

"In your passage through this life, remember the sufferings of Jesus Christ."*

He spoke no more, and some moments afterwards passed quietly away. So died Michael Angelo, the master genius of his age. The body was dismissed from its long servitude; the soul departed whither its aspirations, too mighty for aught save the Infinite to satisfy, had ever borne it: but Michael Angelo was not dead; he had but entered into life, leaving his memory the heritage of the ages. He had lived eighty-eight years, eleven months, and fifteen days. He was laid to rest in the Church of the Santi Apostoli in Rome, attended by an innumerable multitude of all orders and conditions of men; but, at the instance of the Florentine Government, his remains were afterwards conveyed to the Church of San Lorenzo in his native Florence. There his obsequies were celebrated with great pomp and splendor, such as is usually accorded only to royalty, and a magnificent funeral oration pronounced by Varchi. His body was finally placed in the Church of Santa Croce, where peacefully it awaits the resurrection.

The long and laborious career of the painter, architect, and sculptor being ended, our task is done, save as it behooves us to glance at some of his works which have escaped our attention, and at such fragments of his personal character or professional reputation as our brief limits will permit. During the period preceding his death we find that though principally occupied with the grand work of St. Peter's, he was also employed in many lesser undertakings. He continued the building of the Farnese Palace, begun by San Gallo, and erected

---

* Vasari, vol. iii., p. 304.

a palace upon the Capitoline Hill for the Senator of Rome. He also constructed thereupon two galleries for the reception of sculpture and painting, and ornamented the spot with such antique relics as were still from time to time being discovered among the ruins of ancient Rome. On the summit of this hill stood the Conventual Church of the Ara Cœli, upon the site once occupied by the temple of Jupiter Capitolinus. Winding up this steep eminence and leading directly to the church are stairs, also built by Angelo. In the choir of this cloister church the Capuchin Friars were singing their vespers in the gray hush of evening, when without, among the ruins of ancient Rome, the infidel Gibbon listened dreamily to their chants as he pondered upon the work which he then first thought of writing, " The Decline and Fall of the Roman Empire."

During these later years Angelo also made a design for a gate to the city of Rome. This he executed: it was called the Porta Pia, in honor of Pius V., the reigning pontiff. He also carried out the Pope's idea of turning the Baths of Dioclesian, then in a ruined condition, into a Christian temple. He produced a church which for grandeur and simplicity is unsurpassed in Rome. He began a chapel for Cardinal Santa Fiore; the aged artist lived on, but the patron died, and the completion of the work was delayed, till in course of time Angelo died too. It was afterwards completed by Della Porta. "The four great pillars, the drum, and the double cupola are, however, Angelo's work."

One word more of this stupendous undertaking, which alone would have served to immortalize his name—that mighty basilica, of which the temple of Solomon in all its glory was but as a dim foreshadowing. Beholding it, his other works sink into insignificance; for there his master genius has raised, and as it were suspended in the air, the dome of the Pantheon, placing between the admiring earth and the battlements of heaven the grandest and the loftiest thing that mind of man has ever conceived. Before us rises as in a picture the great square, the stupendous bulk slow moving upward to crown the mighty edifice; and, grandest of all, the figure of the weak old man, directing, commanding, following its motion upward, and falling back exhausted when the dome had reached its resting-place. We must not, however, dwell longer on this work of might, St. Peter's; nor can we consider in detail the grandeur of its outlines, the harmony of its proportions, its stupendous size and breadth and depth, in the immensity of which the soul of man is lost, in the vastness of which the carved angels, six feet in height, seem of the stature of children.

Of his other works we have given the brief and imperfect notice which our space permits. But besides the pieces of sculpture and the paintings here mentioned, there are some few in existence of which considerable doubt is expressed. There are also innumerable designs from his hand, some of which were never carried out, and others put into execution by contemporary artists, such as Venusti and Sebastian del Piombo. Jacopo Puntormo and others have painted some of his designs in oil.

So we have seen that in sculpture Michael Angelo stands unrivalled; his carvings in bronze and marble, from the *Pietà* of his boyhood to the Medici monuments of his old age, all alike bear in their various proportions the stamp and seal of his mighty genius. No sculptor of modern times ever equalled him in perfection of form and symmetry of outline; none excelled him in noble and austere majesty, or in sublime simplicity.

As a painter he has produced "the grandest picture ever painted," that of the Last Judgment; and his ceiling of the Sistine Chapel is unsurpassed in the beauty and variety of the figures and the harmony of the whole. No painter, perhaps, ever felt more deeply the imaginative portion of his art, nor none, perhaps, was endowed with a grander conception of the spiritual and material world. Art was his mistress, the sole, absorbing interest of his life. No toils were too toilsome, no labors too unremitting, when offered at her shrine. Perfection was the end he proposed to himself, and this end he pursued with a stern and rugged perseverance, which inspired him with a certain contempt for the efforts of others and at the same time with a certain diffidence in his own power—a diffidence that refutes the unjust aspersion of pride, so often cast upon him. An anecdote is told that a certain Cardinal, finding him one day among the ruins of ancient Rome, asked him what he was doing, to which he replied, "I am still learning." Among his designs was one of an old man in a go-cart, with the inscription, *Ancora impara*—Still learning. Such was the constant desire of improvement which followed him from boyhood to old age.

Angelo never married, nor does he seem to have ever seriously thought of it. He was never known to have an attachment for one of the opposite sex, except his famous Platonic affection for Vittoria Colonna, Marchioness of Pescara, who for talent, virtue, and piety was the most eminent woman of her time. For her he entertained a most enthusiastic admiration; their friendship was deep and ardent, and at the same time noble and elevating. No doubt can exist that it exerted a marked effect upon the genius and character of the artist.

To Vittoria Colonna many of his poems are addressed, and this brings us to a momentary consideration of Angelo as a poet. He has written numerous sonnets, most of which have been translated, some by Wordsworth; but however well rendered into English, they have necessarily lost that smoothness of rhythm and the exquisite melody which belongs to the beautiful Tuscan tongue. Hazlitt declares those on religious subjects to be the best, and those on love to be "a rude mixture of Platonism and metaphysics."

It is, in fact, true of his every effort, whether in painting, sculpture, or architecture—those of a religious character were always the best. For a deep, earnest faith was the groundwork of all he did; religion his highest inspiration; by its aid he attained an eminence which, perhaps, no other man has ever reached in so many branches of art. He was a sincere and practical Catholic; nor did he consider it inconsistent with his dignity to say his beads, hear Mass often, and frequent the Sacraments. In these things he found the inspiration which made of him the great sculptor, the great painter, and, above all, the great architect.

He was very fond of solitude, preferring the society of his books to that of men. Yet no one ever possessed a more profound knowledge of the world, or was more intimately acquainted with the habits, the ways of thinking, and the various peculiarities of his fellow-men. It may have been the combination of these qualities which gained him the reputation of being both morose and cynical. In temper he was undoubtedly hasty and irascible, and, as his old quarrel with Torregiano sufficiently proves, haughty and sarcastic. On that occasion—it was in the ancient Carmelite Church, whither they had gone to study the frescoes of Massaccio—Torregiano became so enraged by the stinging sarcasms of Angelo, that he seized a mallet and flattened the great man's nose, giving him a mark which he bore till his death. Yet, while his defects of temper made him many enemies, those who knew him best loved him well, for he was generous and kindly and liberal even to a fault. The story of his servant Urbino is a striking illustration of his more endearing qualities. When he felt himself growing old, he asked Urbino one day:

"What will become of you, poor Urbino, if I die?"

"I suppose," answered Urbino, "I must e'en seek another master."

"That shall never be," cried Angelo; and forthwith he made over to him a thousand crowns, which would be a liberal provision in case he survived him; but the servant departed before the master, and during his last illness Angelo watched beside him with all possible care and devotion. When he died, the great artist wrote to Vasari the following touching words:

"My Urbino is dead, to my infinite grief and sorrow. Living he served me truly, and dying he taught me how to die. I now have but the hope of seeing him again in Paradise."

Angelo for some time continued a correspondence with Urbino's widow, expressing the greatest affection for the children, making them various gifts, and in short giving every proof of his sincere attachment to the memory of his humble friend.

The great artist was a close and constant student; he was particularly fond of the study of the Scriptures, and dwelt with delight upon the works of Dante and Petrarch.

His personal character was in all respects above reproach: his honor was unsullied, his life pure and blameless, his disposition kind and generous. Of his faults there is but little to be said, and we have already hinted at them in a preceding paragraph. These faults of temper, petty weaknesses, which made him, indeed, bitter enemies in life, died with him; only his virtues, his lovable qualities, remain to heighten the splendor of his fame.

In conclusion, we have but to quote some opinions held of him by his contemporaries, or by more recent writers upon art. Varchi, in the extravagance of his admiration, says, "Had he been born a native of Scythia, under some barbarous chieftain, instead of in the bright era of Lorenzo the Magnificent, he would still have been Michael Angelo, unique in painting, unparalleled in sculpture, a perfect architect, an admirable poet, and a divine lover." Ariosto thus addresses him, playing upon his name:

> " E quel, ch'a par sculpe, e colora,
> Michel, piu che mortal, angel' divino."*

"His style," says Alzog, the historian, "is characterized by sublimity of conception, nobility of form, and ease and breadth of manner."

Vasari and others also speak of him with enthusiasm, while his great and, perhaps, only rival, the immortal Raphael, frequently exclaimed that "he thanked God for having been born in the time of Michael Angelo." A learned Siennese writer, Claudio Tolemei, declares that by many and great artists he was considered "the master, prince, and deity of design." By the great ones of his time he was held in the highest esteem. Upon one occasion, when he appeared before Pope Julius III., that pontiff received him standing and seated him on his right hand in the presence of a great multitude of cardinals, princes, and prelates. He enjoyed in a marked degree the constant favor and support of the successive popes, under whose reigns he lived and labored, each in turn being his munificent patron.

So we have done, and must leave Michael Angelo at

---

* " Michael, both by painting and sculpture more than mortal, an angel divine."

† Hazlitt's translation of Duffa's Angelo.

rest in the great vault of Santa Croce, where statues of painting, sculpture, and architecture keep watch around his tomb. Through life, like the hero of an ancient legend, he pursued unceasingly his doom of immortality, which would not give him rest. The surging waves of time and death closed over all who had been his contemporaries, while alone he still toiled on. Solemn and drear the waters of the cold, dark sea at last engulfed him; unto his mighty heart came peace; unto his indomitable spirit calm; unto the glory of his genius darkness. But the darkness burst asunder, to the gaze of admiring posterity. Upon a mountain of living flame stands Angelo, with the threefold art he loved crowning him with a diadem of immortal fame. Beholding him thus, we cry aloud: Hail to thee, Angelo, hail, for " Il mondo ha molti re, ed un solo Michel Angelo." *

---

* The saying of the illustrious Aretino, " The world has many kings, and but one Michael Angelo."

Explorer and Founder of Quebec.

Wandering there 'mongst the red men,
I bless'd God in truth and in secret,
That he had not suffered my lot to be with the heathen,
But cast it in France—among a people so Christian;
And then I bethought me, peradventure to me it is given
To lead the vanguard of Truth to the inmost recesses
Of this lost region of souls who know not the Gospel,
And these were the thoughts I had far away in the woodlands,
When I saw the savages arm'd, and heard the roar of their
    war-cry.

MCGEE.

Samuel de Champlain.

EXPLORER AND FOUNDER OF QUEBEC.

THE Canada of to-day is a flourishing dominion, containing many prosperous and populous cities, and many happy homes of more than Saxon comfort. But the Canada of the past fills us with a vision of "forests primeval," dark with the cathedral-like gloom of gnarled oaks olden, white in the spring-time with the blossoms of the acacia, and in their hidden depths rendered almost impassable by the thick interlacings of primitive pines and cedars. Canada of the past was then, as now, the Canada of the swift-rolling St. Lawrence and the dark blue Ottawa; but in those far-off times their waters reflected naught save the forest-mantled mountains, the wild, rugged shores covered with a pathless wilderness of uncultivated woodland. The mariners who dared the swift rapids and steered their barks through the treacherous rocks were Indians, and their vessels birch canoes.

Canada of the past is the battlefield upon which the warriors of the Cross fought and died, and is also the foster-mother of countless heroes. But the heroes to whom we more particularly allude are the missionaries—those fearless men, who, far among the boundless tracts of the country of the Hurons, Iroquois, or Algonquins, beside their rolling streams, upon the bosom of their great lakes, in the heart of their mighty forests, on the mountain-top, in the depths of valleys, in the wigwams, near the dying, at the altar, at the stake, were forever to be found. Lallemant, Brebœuf, ye sainted men of yore, your blood has sanctified the streams and hill-tops, the very air is laden with the memory of your mighty deeds.

At this present stage of our sketch, however, we will not pause to consider these missionaries, and especially the Jesuits, in their true character as the authors or pioneers of early Canadian civilization; nor shall we take time to observe the claims of the Recollet Fathers to the gratitude of the settlers amongst whom they labored even before the Sons of Loyola had set foot upon the soil. In the course of our work we may notice these things as they occur, but meantime shall bring forth such facts as we have found in the archives of the past, all of which clearly prove that even the very presence of the missionaries in Canada was owing to the indefatigable efforts of the illustrious Frenchman, Samuel de Champlain.

He was born at Brouage, in Saintonge, and according to the most authentic accounts, in 1567. The exact date of his birth is, however, a vexed question among his biographers. He sprang from an humble stock—from a race of fishermen, the "toilers of the sea," the dwellers upon her changeful waters. The family seem to have risen somewhat in the social scale, for at the time of Samuel de Champlain's marriage in 1611 his father is mentioned in the contract as Antoine de Champlain, *capitaine de la marine*, or sea-captain.

Champlain, however, inherited a love for the sea, and felt the full witchery of her changing moods and restless motion. The gray mists that rose at dawn from her caverns, like voyagers embarking on a new journey; the gold of the noontide plentifully besprinkling the azure plain of waters; the evening glories that, as a miser conceals his treasure, were hidden at dusk by the avaricious ocean—had each its own peculiar charm for him. But the storm bursting over the seething main, the foam, like white, despairing faces on the surface of the waves, the anger of the sky reflected in the sullen waters, and the war to death between contending elements, possessed a fatal fascination for him, and lured him away to brave their fury where their power was mightiest.

He gives a hint of this feeling in a letter addressed many years later to the queen regent:

"The art of seafaring," he writes, "is that which, since my earliest years, has most strongly attracted me, and impelled me to expose myself during many years of my life to the fury of the ocean waves."

This partiality for a life of adventure did not, however, prevent him from devoting most of his leisure time to study, and the acquiring of that accurate and comprehensive knowledge for which he was afterwards remarkable. We do not find any detailed account of the precise manner in which these early years were passed, but we can readily suppose him to have followed his father's calling, and accompanied him on some of his short voyages. The first accurate information we get of him is when in 1594, or thereabouts, he receives the appointment of *Marechal des logis*, in which position he remains till 1598.

Champlain's uncle, a veteran tar, was at this time famous throughout France as an experienced seaman and a successful pilot, having been once employed as chief pilot to the King of Spain. Somewhere about 1598 he received a commission from Marshal de Brissac to proceed to Spain, piloting thither the Spanish vessels. Champlain, all enthusiasm for a seafaring life, and filled with a craving for adventure, determined if possible to accompany his uncle. He had also an ulterior object, hoping that during his stay in Spain some opportunity might occur for a voyage to the West Indies.

He set sail, therefore, with his uncle, in a vessel called the "Saint Julien," which upon their arrival in Spain was declared to be "a stout craft and a swift sailer," and was retained in the service of the Spanish king. So Champlain remained in Spain, hoping for some fortunate circumstance which should send him over the sea to the new continent. These dreams of future voyages did not, however, prevent him from occupying each moment of his time. He made out charts of every place at which the vessel touched; and drew a plan of the city of Cadiz, as also of San Lucar de Barrameda, at which latter port they made considerable stay. Then it was that his desire of a voyage to the Indies seemed about to be gratified. Porto Rico was threatened by the English; the King of Spain was determined to protect it, and for that purpose thought of sending out a fleet of twenty vessels, including the "Saint Julien." While the vessels were being rigged and put into order for this long and perilous voyage, news came that Porto Rico had surrendered to the English. Champlain felt the disappointment keenly, and feared that his dream would prove indeed a dream.

But Don Francisco Colombe, who had come thither to take command of the Spanish fleet, was about to make a voyage to the West Indies, and being pleased with the "Saint Julien," and aware of her fine sailing powers, determined to take her with him. The sturdy old Provençal tar, Champlain's uncle, who had been in command of her, was needed for other duty, and his nephew, already known as a promising sailor, was appointed in his place.

In the month of January, 1599, Champlain set sail for the South American coast, where he arrived somewhere about the middle of April. Would that we could follow our sailor, afloat upon the boundless ocean, with the restless heart of youth aglow within him, or keep pace with his wanderings through the new and beautiful land, in the delights of which he fairly revelled, visiting all those places in the Antilles and the Spanish territories the fame of which had already crossed the far blue ocean. He speaks of these countries in the following glowing terms:

"No one," he says, "could see, nor desire to see, a more beautiful region than the Kingdom of New Spain; the eye loses itself in wide-spreading plains, over which roam innumerable herds of cattle, for its pastures are always green; it is beautified by grand rivers and streams intersecting the greater part of the kingdom; diversified by magnificent forests of the finest possible trees. But," he continues, "the delight which I experienced from all these beauties was little to what I felt when I beheld the fair city of Mexico."

In his "Voyage Aux Indes," in the first volume of his Works, he gives us the result of his wanderings through these luxuriant regions. He tells us of the people; he describes their manners and customs; he takes careful note of places; he gives us glowing accounts of the exquisite natural scenery and abundant vegetation of these southern countries. So when he returned to Europe he brought the king such details of the Spanish-American territories as might prove of the greatest interest and advantage to Spain.

On his return from America, Champlain remained in his native France, and soon grew in favor with distinguished persons at the French Court, and was granted a pension by the king for faithful and accurate accounts of the New World.

Among the great commanders of the day was the celebrated De Chaste. He had long been revolving in his mind certain great schemes relative to colonization in the unexplored portions of the American continent. Some of these plans he communicated to Champlain, hoping to obtain useful advice and information upon the subject. At last he determined to put his plans into execution, and endeavor to establish a colony in North America, which might lead to the conversion of the aborigines.

The Sieur Chauvin, whom he had at first chosen for the undertaking, died, and De Chaste now entrusted the command of an expedition to Champlain. Due preparation being made, the vessel sailed from Honfleur on the 15th of March. Wind and weather proved sufficiently favorable, though towards the end of the voyage they experienced some rough weather.

They arrived at Tadousac upon the 24th of May. The wild and rugged shore which met their view was lined with savages of the Montagnais and Algonquin tribes. In mute amazement they watched the debarkation of the pale-faces, who had come in their "fire-canoes" across the "Big Sea Water." Pont-Gravé, who accompanied Champlain, had visited this region before, and brought one or two Indians back with him to France. One of these Indians now arose, and made an animated harangue to the savages. In glowing terms, full of the wild hyperbole of his race, he told them of his voyage to the country of the pale-faces; of their king, and of his reception at the court. He told them also that the Great Chief had promised to befriend them, to make an alliance for them with the Iroquois, or, failing that, assist them in their wars.

The Indians listened breathlessly; their perfect gravity undisturbed, and their only sign of interest an occasional "ugh" or "tchee," which they use to express admiration or satisfaction. When the orator had concluded his address, the Grand Sachem arose, and passed round the calumet or peace-pipe, offering it first to Champlain, Pont-Gravé, and to the principal Indian chiefs. This was a declaration of friendship towards the whites.

Making but a short delay at Tadoussac, Champlain sailed up the river to the Great Falls of St. Louis, accompanied by Pont-Gravé and one or two of their crew. Their object was, if possible, to reach the source of the great river, which no European mariner had yet attempted. Up the broad river, past the rugged shores, sombre with the dense forest growth, under the shadows of the hills, sailed our mariners in a frail skiff, which bounded light as a feather over the blue waters. As they approached the Falls the river began to break in foaming waves upon the shore, and before them they beheld the seething rapids dashing over the rocks and sending up volumes of spray. They found further progress impossible, and, as Champlain tells us, "could only observe the difficulties to be overcome, the country, and the length of the river;" while they also learned from the savages all that they could of the habits of the natives, the products of the country, and the source of the great rivers, especially the St. Lawrence.

Pending the conclusion of a treaty with the red men, Champlain sailed down towards Gaspé, to examine the condition of the country thereabouts, and to obtain information of certain mines.

He then returned to France, bringing reports as to the condition of affairs in the New World, and accounts of their voyage. Henry of Navarre was at that time the reigning sovereign, and, inspired by the glowing accounts of the mariners, he became very desirous of possessing a portion of that beautiful region beyond the western wave. Distance lent it that enchantment which hung round the Ultima Thule of the ancients, and pictured it as a land full of beauty and mystery, rich in all material goods.

The king, therefore, resolved to encourage Champlain in his taste for adventure, and to further all schemes which had for their object the colonization of North America. At this juncture De Chaste died, and was succeeded by M. de Monts. This latter had visited the Canadian coast before. He knew the rigor of the climate, and the hardships which would fall to the lot of the daring pioneer who sought to make a home amid its forests. He was anxious to found a settlement in the New World, but was also anxious that it should be in a milder climate. He consulted Champlain upon the subject, and Champlain encouraged him in his views; for, like him, the latter had experienced something of the severity of the Canadian climate, in addition to which he had always felt a sort of yearning for the south.

Back to him came gentle breezes redolent with the rich perfume of the magnolia; back to him came soft southern nights, when the stars of a new hemisphere met in strange and unfamiliar constellations in the blue firmament above him; back to him came the tuneful notes of the bright-plumaged birds of tropic forests; back to him came the rich and wild and marvellous luxuriance of the Southland, haunting him with a yearning to make himself a home under its fervid sky.

With this desire in his mind he rejoiced that his new patron should have resolved to found a settlement not, it is true, whither his fancy would have led him, but at least in a milder climate and under a more congenial sun than that of Canada.

So, when next he visited the land of the setting sun,

his course lay towards the milder and more fertile shores of Acadie. It was still spring when they rounded Cape de la Heve, but the summer had passed before they decided upon a place suitable for their purpose. As they cruised along the Acadian shore, they saw Port Royal, resting like a gem upon the waters, and attracting them by its beautiful scenery and natural advantages. M. de Monts had accompanied the expedition in person. So with Champlain he spent three years amid the "forests primeval," within hearing of "the deep-mouthed ocean" and its incessant roar.

Champlain made several voyages thence to various portions of the continent, and amongst other places of interest visited a part of what is now New England, and especially Maine, then the country of the Etchemins, passing on to where years later the "Mayflower" was to land, and the Pilgrim Fathers, in their sad-colored garments, to set foot upon the soil of their new settlement. He pushed his discoveries in that direction as far south as Cape Cod.

From passages in the "Voyages of Champlain" we catch a glimpse of the life of these first settlers at Port Royal; a life, indeed it was, full of romantic interest, of exceeding peril, of inevitable hardship and privation. Of the second winter of their stay Champlain speaks thus:

"We passed that winter very joyously," writes he, "and made good cheer, by means of the 'Ordre de Bontemps,' which I established, and which every one found very beneficial to his health, and more profitable than all the medicines that could be used. It consisted of a chain which, with divers little ceremonies, we put round the neck of one of our people, appointing him thus for the day our caterer. The next day another took his place, which produced a sort of rivalry as to who should furnish us with the best game."

In 1607 Champlain returned to France, bringing with him, as before, accurate accounts of the countries he had visited and the rivers he had navigated, describing also their residences at Port Royal, as well as a temporary one at the island of Sainte Croix, where they had made a short stay.

Meanwhile M. de Monts had met with various losses and disappointments. The jealousy and the intrigues of others had so successfully militated against him, that he was obliged to abandon the Acadian colony. However, he was not discouraged, but communicated to Champlain a new scheme by which he hoped to found a settlement farther north, in defiance of the biting winds and intense cold of a Canadian winter. He proved to Champlain that the banks of the St. Lawrence offered an unequalled facility for commerce. Besides this, the subject of a north-westerly passage had been much discussed ever since the time of Columbus, and both Champlain and his patron were of opinion that a settlement on the St. Lawrence might also lead to its discovery.

For this purpose two vessels were equipped. Pont-Gravé was appointed to the command, with Champlain as his lieutenant. Champlain had already decided upon Quebec as the site of the future colony. The situation was favorable, and could be easily defended. The origin of the name Quebec seems to be a somewhat disputed point. But the most probable theory is that it was so called by the savages because it was situated in a narrow or contracted part of the river. It, in fact, stood at the confluence of a small stream called the St. Charles and the St. Lawrence.

The little band of colonists landed upon a projecting point of land, and lost no time in preparing temporary dwellings, where the red man had hitherto held undisputed sway. The surroundings were wild and rugged;

high rocks, vast forests of oak and pine, and the great river stretching before and around them. But clearings were soon made, strips of forest disappeared, and houses grew up with almost magical rapidity.

Time went on, and the little colony seemed to prosper under Champlain's fostering care; but envy and jealousy had not been left behind in the Old World, and soon began to show signs of their existence. Among the settlers was a man named Jean Duval, who was noted for his bravery, and had done good service in certain skirmishes with the Indians. Hence he was justly held in esteem by his fellow-colonists. With him originated a plot to assassinate the governor, in whatever manner should be found easiest. Poison and a train of gunpowder were finally resolved upon; but some of the conspirators repenting, divulged the plot, and the leader was hung, and others concerned in it sent to the galleys.

Disease having broken out among the colonists, Champlain searched for the Auneda tree, which had been successfully used by Cartier in combating maladies peculiar to their mode of life. The tree could not be found, and from this circumstance it was supposed that the tribe from whom Cartier had learned the secret, or upon whom he had tried it, were extinct, probably exterminated by hostile nations.

Champlain soon found to his cost that quarrels were frequent among the children of the forest, and the results of such quarrels disastrous to the peace and welfare of the colony. In the vicinity of Quebec were innumerable hordes of savages, whose predatory habits involved them in constant warfare with their enemies, the Iroquois. These tribes hoped everything from the assistance of the whites, and as Champlain was naturally anxious to be on friendly terms with his neighbors, he became involved in a disastrous struggle with the Iroquois, who were the most powerful nation of America. They banded together in a sort of league, which included what was called the Five Nations, and these were subdivided into tribes, called respectively the Bear, the Wolf, and the Tortoise.

Champlain has been by many historians severely blamed for his contests with the Iroquois. But these historians have doubtless overlooked the facts of the case. If he had been on terms of enmity with his neighbors, the safety and even the very existence of the settlement would have been constantly endangered; whereas the Iroquois were a distant tribe, and one that openly professed scorn and hatred for the whites, and in all circumstances proved themselves their unrelenting enemies. Besides this, the Hurons and other adjacent tribes in many instances befriended the colonists, and were from beginning to end stanch and devoted allies of Champlain.

In June of the year 1609, Champlain, together with Pont-Gravé, set out from Tadousac on a voyage of discovery. Their object was to gain further knowledge of the country and the people, their habits and mode of life, and such particulars as might be thereafter useful.

It may be of interest to observe the origin of the struggle between the Iroquois and Algonquin tribes. A tradition of the place, to which too much weight must not however be attached, declares its root to have been in a dispute about the chase. Once the Algonquins went forth to hunt the bear or bison, and returned empty-handed. Seeing this, the Iroquois begged that they might be allowed to try their luck. The Algonquins indignantly refused, and the Iroquois, waiting till night, went forth by the light of the moon, and brought in an abundant supply of game. The vengeful Algonquins bided their time, but when the hunters slept the deep sleep of fatigue and exhaustion they cut off their heads. Henceforth the red tomahawk of war was unsheathed between the nations, and so continued from time immemorial.

When Champlain returned from his voyage the neighboring tribes began to remind him that ten moons had not passed since he had promised to assist them against their deadly foe. Anxious to conciliate them, hoping also to bring about a final reconciliation with the Iroquois, and eager to explore their distant country, Champlain determined to give what help he could to the allies.

So taking with him some twenty or thirty of his men, he set out in company with the savages. In solemn silence they sailed up the Sorel river, and entered that lake now known by the great explorer's name (Lake Champlain). Their birch barks glided swiftly through the still, blue waters, the plashing of the oars in the hands of Indian oarsmen making scarce a ripple on the surface of the lake. Past those beautiful shores which border Lake Champlain, and that noble scenery now so familiar to most of us, they hastened on their mission of war and desolation.

They landed on a portion of the shore adjoining the camp of the Iroquois. Night came down solemnly upon the ancient forests; the wind murmured in weird cadences among the mighty trees; the bright golden stars of a northern firmament glimmered through the branches, and the lake, dark and tranquil, laved the green shores. Camp-fires glowed in the forest darkness, showing the dim outlines of the wigwams, and the dusky forms of Indians with wampum belts and plumes and war-paint. At length the silence was broken; the night-bird fled shrieking to her covert, as the savages chanted their discordant war-songs and danced their hideous dance of death. From either camp opprobrious epithets were hurled at the foe, till each had lashed itself into fury, and the day broke. The sun streaked the East with red, like the war-paint of the savage, and came slowly and reluctantly through the overarching forests down upon the two camps.

The Iroquis advanced with the bearing of conquerors, proud and self-confident. They were about two hundred in number, and being tall and symmetrically formed, presented a fine though uncouth appearance. As had been previously arranged, Champlain stepped forward with one or two of his men, who in fact constituted his whole retinue, the remainder having stayed behind. The Iroquois gazed at him in astonishment and terror. No such adversary had ever before confronted them, and they knew not the best mode of dealing with him. However, they discharged a shower of arrows, but to their dismay the stranger advanced unhurt, and blew smoke and fire out of a war-club in his hand. The loud report of the musket terrified them, and when they glanced around they saw several of their number stretched upon the ground. Clearly, they thought, this man must be a messenger from the Great Spirit.

On the other hand the allies were delighted, and begged Champlain to fire again. The other two Frenchmen stepped forward and discharged their muskets. The Iroquois, completely unmanned, fled in confusion, leaving behind them the killed and wounded, and several prisoners in the hands of the allies.

Champlain was compelled to witness a most appalling spectacle. The savages assembled at night in front of their wigwams, and fastening one of their prisoners to a tree, chanted the death hymn around him. It was simply a detailed account of the tortures to be inflicted. Calmly the victim listened with the grim endurance of his race, nor gave the faintest sign of fear or horror at his fate,

Vainly did Champlain endeavor to save him from an end so appalling; but the savages would not be balked of their prey, and at dawn put him to death with the most inhuman tortures.

Champlain soon after went to France, where he remained but a short time, and returning found the Algonquins and Montagnais impatiently waiting for the coming of the French chief to lead them to battle. He consented on certain conditions, but in this second expedition against the Iroquois found them better prepared, they having erected fortifications, consisting of stakes driven into the ground. Champlain and his allies were finally victorious, and the Iroquois were cut to pieces. In this engagement he received a wound between the ear and neck, which fortunately had no serious consequences.

After a brief interval, Champlain again visited his native land, leaving Du Parc in command at Quebec. The king was dead; certain intrigues relative to the colony were taking place at Brouage, and Champlain remained there some time, arranging the affairs of the settlement. It was during this absence from Quebec that Champlain's marriage contract was signed. With all the weighty matters that occupied his mind, and in spite of the roving, desultory life he had led, he seems to have been not insensible to the influence of the tender passion. His choice was in some respects a singular one. Hélène Boullé, daughter of the king's private secretary, was only twelve years old at the time of her betrothal, which took place in 1611, and had been educated in the rigid tenets of Calvinism. Before her marriage, however, she became a Catholic, and ever afterwards clung with deep and loyal affection to the one true faith. Ardently the child-wife longed to accompany her husband to his far home in the western wilderness. She yearned to share his dangers, and enjoy the unconventional delights of colonial life. Her youthful fancy tinged the great world beyond the ocean with a halo of romance, and lent its poetry to the uncertainties, the perils and the hardships of such an existence. It was, however, deemed advisable for her to remain in France, on account of her extreme youth. Perchance, in the twelve years that elapsed before she joined her husband in the western world, time had dispelled many of these illusions, and caused her to dwell rather on the privations and hardships to be endured, than on the romantic joys of a residence in the wilds.

Champlain returned to America with Pont-Gravé. High winds and rough seas, together with dense fogs, so delayed them that they did not reach Tadousac till the middle of May. He proceeded almost immediately to Sault St. Louis, or the Great Falls, where he was to meet the Algonquins. This was the great trading-post, whither the trappers came in great numbers to trade with the Indians for furs. Then it was that Champlain conceived the design of building a habitation in that region to facilitate intercourse with the savages. He chose a favorable site, which was cleared and made ready for building. He called the spot Place Royale, and from this humble beginning sprang in later years Montreal, the Queen City of the North.

Champlain was at this time much occupied by the question of the evangelization of the heathen tribes. This had always been one of his most cherished designs; and in fact he was frequently heard to declare that " the salvation of one soul is of more value than the conquest of an empire; and that kings ought not to think of extending their authority over idolatrous nations, except for the purpose of subjecting them to Jesus Christ."

On one occasion Champlain questioned a savage as to the religious belief of his nation. He asked the chief if they believed in God. Yes, they believed in one Great

Manitou, or Spirit, who had made all things. Champlain then asked if they believed that God created man. The chief said, "Yes; when the Great Spirit had made everything else, he took a quiver of arrows and stuck them into the ground, and thence sprang men and women." Champlain explained to him that Adam was first created, Eve given as a helpmate; and, in a word, told him all the old story of the beautiful garden and its ravishing delights, amid which man had spent his primal morning. The Indian further said that they believed in one Great Spirit, in his Son, in a Mother, and in the Sun that illumines the earth. He added that God was above all, but that he was no better than he ought to be; that his Son was good, and did much for mankind; that the Mother was bad, and would eat the red man; but that the bright Sun that shone above them was good, and brought great blessings to earth.

Champlain asked if they believed that God had ever come down upon earth, and the savage answered:

"In the legends of our people, it is told that in the far-off time five warriors went yonder to the red home of the setting sun, and as they journeyed they met the Manitou who lives upon the mountain top. And he asked them, saying,

"'Whither go ye?'

"And they answered,

"'To seek for life.'

"And the Great Spirit told them,

"'Ye will find it here.'

"Unheeding, the warriors passed on, and the Great Spirit touched two of them with a stone, and they were turned into stone. Then he asked the other three,

"'Whither go ye?'

"And they answered,

"'To seek for life.'

"'Here will ye find it,' said the Creator; 'go no further.'

"But they heard not, and the Spirit taking a stick turned two of them into sticks. And but one remained.

"'Whither goest thou?' said the Spirit.

"'Onward to the setting sun, that I may seek for life.'

"'Here thou shalt find life. Pass not onwards.'

"And the warrior listened and obeyed. Then the Great Spirit gave him the flesh of bear and bison, and when the brave had feasted, bade him return to his people and tell them of the Manitou, and of what had befallen their brothers."

Again, the savage told him the Great Spirit came to a warrior, who was smoking, and asked him to lend him his pipe. The warrior gave it, and when the Manitou had smoked, he broke it. Then the warrior asked why he had broken the pipe when he knew he had no other. And the Manitou, giving him a new pipe, bade him take it to the Sachem of his tribe, and tell him to "guard and keep it from evil, and while he did so his tribe should want for nothing."

The warrior took it to the chief, and the chief guarded it, and while it remained in his possession all was well; but in an unlucky moment he lost it, and famine came among the tribe.

Champlain asked him if he really believed this fable. And the savage answered,

"It is true, my brother.

Then Champlain told him of God, the Father, Son, and Holy Ghost; of the Redemption; of the Blessed Virgin; of the Saints and Angels, and the country of perpetual joy, far surpassing the happy hunting-grounds, whereon they hoped to rejoin their departed brethren. The savage listened eagerly, and asked how he should pray to the God of the pale-faces.

Champlain soon after sailed for France, hoping to obtain assistance which should enable him to bring out missionaries to labor among the savages and teach them the knowledge of the true God. His noble project did not meet with the encouragement it deserved, and meanwhile some vessels arrived from Quebec. They brought news that the savages in great numbers had come down that year to the Great Falls to meet Champlain; that, not finding him, they loudly expressed their grief and disappointment; while certain enemies of the governor led them to believe that Champlain was dead, and would meet them no more, whether for peace or for war.

During this visit to France, Champlain succeeded in placing the colony under the patronage of the Count de Soissons, a wealthy and influential nobleman, and one whom he rightly judged would advance as far as possible its religious interests. De Soissons died soon after his appointment, and his successor was more occupied with political matters than with the spiritual affairs of savages in the wilds of the western world.

While still in his native country, Champlain was inspired with the hope of finding the long-sought northwesterly passage. A man recently returned from Canada declared that the lake in which the Outaouais had its source discharged itself into the North Sea. He gave an account of a pretended voyage thither, during which he had seen the wrecks of English vessels lying upon the shore. This had some show of probability, as the English were at that time pushing their explorations very far north.

Animated by this hope, Champlain made all necessary preparations, and set sail from the island of St. Helena on the 27th of May, 1613, on a quest as vain as the memorable voyage of the Golden Fleece. Favorable winds soon brought him to the Isle des Allumettes, where dwelt Tessouat, the Great Sachem of the Algonquins.

Champlain was accompanied by one savage and four Frenchmen, amongst whom was De Vignaux, the boastful traveller. The savages received the governor with every mark of joy and respect. Tessouat gave a great banquet in his honor, and invited all the neighboring chiefs. This over, the calumet was smoked, and Champlain began to tell them of his plans, asking their advice and assistance. He told them that he had been mainly induced to attempt the passage by the accounts of De Vignaux, who had pushed his explorations to the far north.

The truth was, De Vignaux had never gone farther than the Isle des Allumettes, and so indignant were the savages at his daring imposition, that Champlain could scarcely restrain them from putting him to death on the spot. Overcome with fear and confusion, the impostor fell on his knees and confessed that he had supposed the perilous nature of the enterprise would have deterred Champlain from attempting it, and that he should have gained a reward for his information, without running any risk of detection.

The voyage, however, was turned to good account; for the savages during Champlain's absence had become alienated from the whites, and even declared their intention of going no more to the trading-posts. The governor, notwithstanding, succeeded in re-establishing the old friendly terms between them and the whites.

On his next voyage to France, Champlain effected his long-cherished design of establishing a powerful company, composed of merchants of Rouen, Saint Malo, and La Rochelle, which greatly contributed to the material prosperity of the infant colony.

Some time after, he finally put into execution another

scheme much nearer to his heart. In the spring of 1615 he sailed for Quebec, bringing with him three fathers and a lay brother of the Order of Recollets—F. Denis Jamay, F. Jean Dolbeau, F. Joseph Le Caron, and Brother Pacifique du Plessis. They landed at Tadousac, and immediately set about the work which had brought them from the genial climate of France to brave the rigors of Canadian winters. Two Jesuits had already made the great voyage, but they had remained at Port Royal, so that to the Recollets belongs the honor of first preaching the gospel to the savages in the vicinity of Quebec, at least since the time of Cartier. Champlain busied himself preparing accommodations for them, and caused a chapel to be speedily erected in a quiet and retired spot.

Father Joseph Le Caron, however, made no stay at Quebec, but hastened to the Great Falls, where numbers of savages were assembled for the fur trade. Soon after, the other religious followed him thither, accompanied by Champlain. He tells us "they were charmed with the vast extent of the river, dotted as it was with beautiful islands, and the fertile shores by which they passed; but most of all at sight of the savages, whom they found possessed of quick intelligence and ready perception."

About five miles from the Falls they met Father Le Caron returning to Quebec for church ornaments, as he intended to pass the winter among the savages. Champlain endeavored to dissuade him from his purpose, urging upon him the terrible hardships to which he would be exposed, the intense severity of the climate, and other similar reasons. Father Le Caron replied " that it was necessary for him to learn the language of the tribes and gain an intimate knowledge of their manners and customs. As for the difficulties to be overcome, he hoped to succeed by the grace of God and the assistance which He would grant him in working for His service and for the propagation of His gospel; that he had freely undertaken the enterprise and would do his utmost to further it; that personal discomforts or hardships were little to a man who had made profession of poverty, and whose only aim was the glory of God and salvation of souls."

Champlain says that, seeing him inspired by such ardent charity, he made no further attempts to turn him from his purpose. Of this saintly missionary the eminent American historian Bancroft speaks in the following terms: "The unambitious Franciscan, Le Caron, the companion of Champlain," he says, "years before the Pilgrims anchored within Cape Cod, had passed into the hunting grounds of the Wyandots, and, bound by his vows to the life of a beggar, had, on foot or paddling a bark canoe, gone onward and still onward, taking alms of the savages, till he reached the rivers of Lake Huron." In this connection the historian goes on to say: "It was neither commercial enterprise nor royal ambition which carried the power of France into the heart of our continent; the motive was 'religion';" and he adds, "The only policy which inspired the French conquests in America was congenial to a Church which cherishes every member of the human race, without regard to lineage or skin." *

To return to our subject. On the banks of the Rivière des Prairies, as chroniclers tell us, on the 24th of June, the Feast of St. John the Baptist, the first Mass since the days of Jacques Cartier was sung by Father Le Caron. The savages were delighted, and assisted thereat with the greatest respect and attention. Champlain was present, his heart full of joy at this promising beginning of the great work in which he was so deeply interested.

---

* Bancroft's U. S., vol. 3, p. 118.

We regret that our present limits forbid us to follow these first missionaries in their work among the tribes, and can only take such occasional glimpses of them as the subject affords.

The savages now declared that unless Champlain would assist them in their war with the Iroquois they would have to discontinue their visits to the trading-posts, as the journey was long, and beset by many perils from the hostility of their foes. The governor took council with Sieur du Ponts and one or two others, and it was agreed that aid must be given, in order to keep up friendly relations with the Indians, and prepare the way for their conversion to Christianity.

Champlain now set forth for the country of the Hurons, where the allies were assembled. It lay along the southern shores of the Georgian Bay, west of Lake Simcoe. In his "Voyages" he gives us a detailed account of his journey through the land of the Algonquins, along the shores of Lake Attigoutatan, which he called the Mer Douce (Gentle Sea), from the tranquillity of its waters. He describes Lake Nipissing, and the country in its vicinity, and finally speaks of his arrival at the village of Carhagouha, which was surrounded by a triple palisade of wood, reaching to the height of thirty-five feet. Here he met Father Le Caron, and on the 12th of May assisted at Mass. He observed on his entrance to the village a large wooden cross, recently erected by the missionary. Before proceeding to Cahiagué, or St. John the Baptist, which was to be the meeting-place of the allies, Champlain visited the various villages of the Huron country, in all of which he was received with the greatest joy. He describes this territory as a vast and beautiful region, in about $44\frac{1}{2}$ degrees of latitude. He declares it to be a country of abundant vegetation and great fertility, with immense fields of Indian corn stretching away into the distance, and besides grain and vegetables, a luxuriant growth of fruit and nut trees, as well as oaks, elms, pines, and cedars. Strawberries and raspberries he found in abundance, and of most excellent flavor. But he tells us that it saddened him to see so many poor creatures without the knowledge of the true God, and subject to no law, either divine or civil.

Early in September the army set out from Cahiagué. Having crossed Lake Ontario, they hid their canoes that the enemy might not find them. They pushed into the very heart of the Iroquois country, and soon came in sight of the enemy's camp. A troop of five hundred Carantouanais warriors were to have met and combined with them in the assault. But as they did not arrive when expected, those under Champlain's command rushed on to the attack with the utmost fury. At nightfall, worn and weary, they desisted from a combat which had been utterly unsuccessful. Council was held, and it was at first proposed to await the coming of the Carantouanais braves; but Champlain, fearing to give the Iroquois time for reinforcements, planned a second attack, which also failed from the total want of discipline among the savages. In this engagement Champlain was severely wounded; and, moreover, when he mentioned to the allies his desire to proceed to Quebec, they, whether from selfish motives or really through necessity, declared that he would have to pass the winter among them, as it was impossible to procure a canoe.

In December, Champlain returned to Carhagouha, whence, accompanied by Father Le Caron, they visited several of the tribes, receiving in every instance a most cordial welcome.

The governor returned to Quebec early in the spring, and thence took passage for France to attend to the affairs of the colony. He urged upon the merchants the necessity for providing against all changes affecting the interests of the settlement,—as, for instance, the arrest of its present patron, the Prince of Condé, which had just taken place. For some time after his return to Quebec he labored steadily to accomplish this result.

As the years went on, dissensions sprang up in the colonial company,—the Huguenot members being desirous to prevent the growth of Catholicity in the new settlement, and the Catholics being equally anxious to forward it. A special agent of either party was instructed to keep it conversant with matters at Tadousac and Quebec. Hence they were anxious to remove Champlain from the command, and, while occupying him in the exploration of the country, to vest the executive authority in Pont-Gravé.

Champlain, being lieutenant-governor of the colony by appointment of the king, refused to give up his rights; he declared that "while he respected Pont-Gravé as a father because of his age, and esteemed him on account of their long friendship, he would not, however, yield him any of his rights," and showed a letter from the king, commanding that Champlain should be furnished with means to conduct the affairs of the colony, and continue his explorations.

Not satisfied with this, he proceeded to France and obtained an order from the Council, investing him with the fullest and most indisputable authority, and commanding the associates to desist from all further interference.

When Champlain returned to Canada he brought with him over the deep and dark blue ocean his fair young bride. With brave heart she dared all its dangers, cheerfully forsaking her native France to share her husband's home in the land of the setting sun. Her brother, Eustace Boullé, was both astonished and delighted at his sister's courage, and received her, as might be expected, with the "heart's right hand of welcome."

Four years passed, during which the young wife strove hard to become inured to the dangers and toils, and privations of a colonial life. By every means in her power she sought to add to the comfort of her husband and brother in their rude western home. But sometimes her strong heart failed her; and visions came of her native land, where the purple grape ripened under genial suns, the blossoms fell abundantly in the early spring-time, and the winter was neither long nor severe. The keen Canadian frosts penetrated to the marrow of her bones; the rude winds chilled her, and the want of many luxuries to which in her Parisian home she had been accustomed began to tell upon her. Perhaps more than all, her brother and husband were frequently away on long expeditions to the distant tribes. During their absence she was alone, and a prey to a thousand fears, not only for herself in her lonely situation, but for her loved ones, who were exposed to the treachery and cruelty of the red-skins.

Taking all these things into consideration, Champlain determined to bring her back to France, and we do not read that she ever rejoined him in the New World. Years after his death she became a religious, under the name of Sister Hélène de Saint Augustin, and ended her days in the gray quiet of the cloister.

During these four years changes had been taking place in the affairs of the colony. Condé had resigned the governorship of the province, and was succeeded by the Duke de Montmorency, who confirmed Champlain in his office. When the governor returned to Quebec, he proceeded to the little chapel of the Recollets, and assisted at a solemn Mass of thanksgiving for his safe arrival. That was a day of great joy in the settlement; flags were displayed, guns fired, cannons discharged, startling the distant forests with their report, while the people openly expressed their joy and exultation, when Champlain took formal possession of the town in the name of his master, the viceroy.

He found the habitation in a most deplorable condition, and at once began the work of repairing it. He also caused the erection of a fort on the St. Lawrence for the greater safety of the town.

Meanwhile, as dissensions were still rife among the members of the colonial company in the Old World and their agents in the New, the Duke de Montmorency founded a new association, and sent out copies of the commissions to Champlain, warning him to try and preserve peace in the colony till the arrival of M. de Caen with the official notification of the changes to be made. The agents of the old society determined to maintain their rights, and adopt what measures seemed to them advisable, at least till the arrival of the official documents. Tumult and disorder prevailed in the city; all attempts to preserve peace proved useless; till Champlain, stationing a few men in the new fort, soon reduced the mutineers to order, and forced them to await in peace the arrival of M. de Caen.

The people assembled, alarmed and indignant. They besought Champlain to proceed to France, and take some means of protecting the colony from measures which were so detrimental to its peace and prosperity. Champlain, unable to go himself, sent as deputy to the king Father George Le Baillif, who succeeded in obtaining an order from the Council uniting the two companies, and putting an end to all further violence.

When Champlain accompanied his wife to France, he remained there a year, consulting with the new viceroy, the Duke de Ventadour, who had succeeded his uncle,

De Montmorency. Champlain proposed to him that Jesuit missionaries should be sent to the colony to assist the Recollet Fathers in their arduous labors. The duke ardently embraced the project, being heartily interested in the evangelization of the natives.

On Champlain's return to Quebec he occupied himself in the building of a new habitation, continued the work upon the fort, and constructed a road from the new fort to the fortress of St. Louis. Near the site of the old building was placed a tablet recording the date upon which the new one had been begun, the name of the viceroy then governing the colony, and that of Champlain, the whole surmounted by the arms of the king.

The new building was to be about eight hundred feet in length, with two wings sixty feet each, and with four towers at the four angles of the structure. It was surrounded by moats and drawbridges. As the work had been delayed by the fact that the workmen were frequently obliged to lay aside their tools and attend to the pasturage of their cattle, Champlain erected large stables at Petit-Cap, having a small dwelling adjoining them and broad pasture-lands stretching around them. By this means the cattle could be cared for by a few persons, and the laborers need no longer leave their work.

As the new fort was too small to be used as a refuge for the people in the event of a surprise, Champlain had it torn down and rebuilt on a much larger scale.

During the winter of 1626-7 a treaty was pending with the Iroquois, and Champlain had great hopes of effecting a reconciliation between them and their ancient foes. Meantime some neighboring Indians, who had suffered great loss from the Iroquois, prevailed upon the Algonquins and other of Champlain's allies to join them in an expedition against the Iroquois, offering them as an inducement the most valuable presents. The allies accepted their proposal, and when news of it came to Champlain he was justly indignant, declaring that he had been always willing to assist them in their just quarrels, but that in an unprovoked attack he would not do so.

The chief admitted his fault, and by his advice Champlain sent his brother-in-law, Eustace Boullé, to Three Rivers to arrange, if possible, an amicable adjustment of the difficulties. In this he was successful, and the savages agreed to discontinue hostilities. Meanwhile M. de Caen had proceeded to the Iroquois country, and returned among the allies with deputies from that people. The Iroquois envoys were seized and put to death, and Champlain expressed his indignation at the treachery of the allies in no measured terms. A council was held; the governor determined if possible to conciliate the Iroquois, and for this purpose sent messengers to them. But so infuriated were they at the murder of their deputies that they put the envoys to death without mercy.

Meantime, two white men had been murdered at Cape Tourmente by a savage to whom they had refused food. Champlain assembled the chiefs of the Montagnais and demanded the surrender of the murderer. The chiefs expressed their regret at the occurrence, but declared that it would be almost impossible to discover the perpetrator of the deed. However, to propitiate Champlain, they soon after conceived the idea of offering him some of the daughters of the tribe to be educated in the Christian religion. The governor had once expressed such a desire, and the savages now resolved to gratify it. Champlain graciously accepted their offer, and chose three of the young squaws, whom he sent to be educated in France.

Just then the fort was wretchedly provisioned; food

and ammunition were alike exhausted, and no boat suitable for the purpose could be found to bring provisions thither. Meantime, three Huguenot brothers, Louis, David, and Thomas Kertk, in the service of England, had vowed to destroy the French colony in Canada. They appeared off Cape Tourmente, and burned the fort newly erected at that point. Champlain fortified the city to the best of his ability, and made every preparation for a vigorous defence. A sloop was sent by the Kertk brothers to demand the surrender of the city. Champlain read the document aloud to the principal inhabitants, and then returned the following characteristic answer:

"If the English care to see us nearer, let them come on, and not threaten us from a distance."

Deceived by this undaunted response, and unaware of the deplorable condition of the little garrison, the enemy retreated, burning all the vessels that lay along the coast.

Some years previous to these events a new element had been introduced into the colony. We refer to the arrival of the Jesuits, that heroic body of men, to whose labors on this alien soil Catholic and Protestant historians have alike borne ample testimony, and of whom Chateaubriand says, "If France so long retained her dominion in the New World against the united efforts of the Iroquois and English, she owed it entirely to the Jesuits." *

We will here digress so much from the direct subject of our sketch as to quote some extracts from the "Relations des Jesuites," which may be of interest to the reader. One of the Fathers, writing to his superior in France about a year after their arrival, which was in

---

. * Chateaubriand, Génie du Christianisme.

1625, mentions the intense cold of the climate, the necessity for travelling on show-shoes, and gives some particulars of the fertility of the soil and the products of the country. He also speaks of the religious belief of the savages, their faith in the immortality of the soul, and their consequent provision for it in the world to come, relating that having asked a savage why they loaded the graves of the dead with all their material goods, the Indian answered,

"Because our brother will need them in the land of shadows, whither he has gone."

The missionary assured him that such was not the case, and as a proof pointed out the grave of a warrior who had been dead some time, and whose possessions were still undisturbed upon his grave. The savage replied that the soul of those things had rejoined the soul of their owner in the shadowy land. He says that the Indians called the sun Jesus; hence, when they heard the whites at prayer they supposed that they were worshipping the sun. This planet, they told him, had a passage made through the earth, and at evening went in at one end to come out next morning at the other.

The Jesuit goes on to say that the whites held their lives on very uncertain tenure among these savages, for not only would they kill a white man who offended them in the slightest degree, but also, if they dreamt of one at night, would kill the first they met in the morning, being most superstitious on the subject of dreams. In several parts of his letter he mentions the invariable support lent by Champlain to the missionaries, and his constant and unvarying kindness to them.

In these early memoirs we find it related that a Huron being asked if his nation would receive some Jesuits into their country, answered that they would most willingly receive them if the **Black-Robes** would be content with a wigwam like theirs, adding that they could not give them a lodge like that of the Recollets in Quebec.

One of the most distinguished missionaries, Father Lalemant, who afterwards died amid excruciating torments at the stake, writes, "Our only hope is that our unworthiness may not prove a bar to the operation of divine grace among the natives, and that the weakness of our frail human will may not be of prejudice to the poor savages." He also announces their intention of placing the new chapel, then in process of erection, under the invocation of "Our Lady of the Angels."

Another of the Fathers describes the appearance of enormous glaciers during the month of May; he says "they shone in the sun like crystal mountain-tops or the spires of churches." He mentions saying Mass on the Feast of the Holy Trinity at Gaspé—the first that had been said in that part of the country. He observes a singular coincidence in the Gospel of the day, which contained the words:

"I give to you all power in heaven and on earth. Go ye, therefore, teaching all nations, baptizing them in the name of the Father, and of the Son, and of the Holy Ghost."

He adds that the savages soon learned to confide in them with childish trustfulness, and relates the following instance. They came to the hut of the missionaries and asked for the captain—a word they had learned from the whites; the Superior came out, and they told him that they were about departing for the hunting-grounds, and wished to leave their treasures with him, promising to return in the moon of the falling leaves to reclaim them. The missionary consented, and they brought their valuables thither with the greatest care, depositing them in the wigwam, and expressing a hope that no thieves would find them. "Yet their treasures," says the writer, "mainly consisted of pieces of broken glass and china."

To return to Quebec, which had been lately saved from falling into the hands of the English by the courage and resolution of Champlain. The scarcity of provisions not only continued, but grew daily more alarming, and a vessel sent out by the company to the relief of the colony unhappily met with the English fleet, and being taken at a disadvantage, was utterly defeated. The Recollet and Jesuit Fathers raised as much grain as possible around their little dwellings, but this was but a drop in the bucket. A certain amount of fish and game were procured from the savages, and Champlain meanwhile devised a scheme which afforded temporary relief. As peas were raised in abundance, the governor had them dried and ground, two large flat stones serving as a mortar. Finding the plan successful, he had a mill erected by which the peas could be crushed in greater quantities. During this life and death struggle for the necessaries of life, envoys were sent from the Abenakis demanding aid against the Iroquois. This was impossible under the circumstances, but, anxious to keep up friendly relations with them, the governor sent Eustace Boullé to assure them that he would help them to the utmost of his ability when times were more favorable, and meantime asking a supply of food. Boullé met M. de Caen's vessel bringing reinforcements to the colony, and as he was returning to Quebec was taken prisoner by the English.

The savages had meantime given Champlain some uneasiness; since the arrest of one of their number on suspicion of murder they kept upon the reserve, and as much as possible aloof from the whites. Hence the governor had no surety as to their peaceful intentions.

Such was the condition of affairs when the English, gaining information of the state of Quebec, again appeared before its walls. A sloop was sent, bearing a white flag at the masthead. The inhabitants of the town were abroad, as the weather was favorable, occupied in the fisheries or at other outdoor labor. Champlain replied to the English flag of truce by hoisting a similar one upon the fort. An English gentleman then came ashore, offering favorable terms from Louis Kertk in the event of capitulation. The governor, knowing resistance to be impossible, acceded, obtaining the most honorable conditions.

On the 19th of July, 1629, the town was ceded to the English, and shortly after Champlain, and all those in any way connected with the government, returned to France. Champlain himself tells us that though treated by the conquerors with the utmost courtesy, he nevertheless "thought every hour a day till he left the city, once the English ensign had been hoisted on the fort."

On the 24th of July he set sail in the vessel commanded by Thomas Kertk. Sorrowfully he left the little colony, in which he had spent the promise of his youth and the vigor of his manhood; he was cheered by one hope alone —that of a speedy return. One circumstance that especially grieved him was the fear that the residence of the English among the savages would have a most pernicious result as regarded their spiritual interests.

Apropos of this we may relate the following anecdote, which probably occurred years later, when the Puritan Fathers held dominion in royal Massachusetts. A governor of Boston, being desirous of conciliating the savages, once offered to send them a minister. The spokesman of the tribe at once replied as follows:

"Your words amaze me; you saw me before my French brothers, yet you and your ministers spoke not to me of prayer or of the Great Spirit. You saw my furs and my beaver skins, and you thought of them alone. If I brought many I was your friend. That was all. One day I lost my way, and sailed in my birch canoe to an Algonquin village, where the French Black-Robe preached of the Great Spirit. I was loaded with skins. The Black-Robe disdained to look at them. He spoke to me at once of the Great Spirit, of Paradise, of hell, and of prayer, which is the only way to heaven. My heart was full of joy; I stayed long to hear the words of truth. His prayer pleased me. I asked him to teach me and to baptize me. Then I went back to my own country and told what had happened to me. They saw I was happy, and wished to be happy too. They set out to the distant tribes to find the Black-Robe. When you saw me if you had told me of prayer I would have learned your prayer, for I knew not what was good. But I have learned the prayer of my French brothers; I love it and will follow it to the end. The Red Man does not want your money and your minister. He will speak to you no more."

This gives us an insight into the cause of Champlain's anxiety for the spiritual welfare of the tribes, and his ardent desire to return to his life-work on the shores of the blue St. Lawrence. The day after the departure of the vessel, one was sighted in the distance, which they readily recognized as that of De Caen. His craft had also recognized theirs as an English vessel, and was evidently seeking to avoid it. But the English captain signalled it to approach. A slight skirmish took place, and as the French seemed to be gaining an advantage, Thomas Kertk, the commander, went down into the hatchways to speak to Champlain. He told him that Emeric de Caen had demanded to see him, and said,

"If the vessel is taken you will die. Tell them to surrender, and I will treat them as well as I have treated you; otherwise, it will be certain ruin for them if the two sloops arrive before the terms of capitulation are signed."

To which Champlain replied as follows:

"It is easy for you to kill me under present circumstances. It will be a most dishonorable proceeding on your part; for by doing so you break the promise made me by your brothers. I am not in command of that vessel; and if I were, I would not hinder those on board from doing their duty."

The French vessel, however, surrendered, and proceeded to Tadousac, sailing thence for Europe early in September. When Kertk's vessel landed at Plymouth news reached it that a treaty of peace had been signed between England and France, and that before the surrender of Quebec. Champlain proceeded to London to apprise the French ambassador there of what had occurred, and to urge upon him the advancement of their interest in the New World. In 1632 the matter was decided by the treaty of Saint Germain-en-Laye, and the fort and city of Quebec were to be restored to their original owners. Champlain occupied himself during his stay in France in preparing a new edition of his voyages for publication. This work contains an account of his journeys through various parts of the American continent, as also the most valuable and accurate description of the places and people in those primitive times.

M. de Caen was appointed governor of Quebec for one year, with the revenues thereunto appertaining, to reimburse him for losses sustained at the taking of the city by the English. M. Plessis du Bouchart was appointed his lieutenant. In 1633 Champlain was reinstated in the command by the new colonial company established by Cardinal Richelieu, and known as the "Cents Associés."

Champlain sailed from Dieppe on the 23d of March with three vessels—the "Saint Pierre," "Saint Jean," and the "Don de Dieu." Two hundred persons, including some Fathers of the Society of Jesus, accompanied him. Joyously he steered his course towards the "land of his heart's hope" Twice during the voyage they were driven ashore by what sailors call a "northwester;" once at Cape Breton and afterwards at St. Bonaventure.

Precisely two months afterwards, on the 23d of May, he landed. The people greeted him with acclamation, and hailed him as the saviour of their country. Flags streamed forth, cannons boomed, bells rang out, and the heart of the colony seemed stirred with a common enthusiasm. The governor had returned to the land of his adoption, never to leave it again.

Soon after the Algonquins came down from Three Rivers to treat with him. Eighteen canoes full landed at Quebec. As the English fleet was still cruising about the coast, Champlain made every effort to dissuade the savages from treating with those on board, justly representing that the French were likely to be the permanent masters of the soil, whereas the English were merely birds of passage. The Indian spokesman declared that they would acknowledge no other allies but the French.

The governor's next undertaking was the establishing of a trading-post on the island of Richelieu, making it more convenient for the Indians of the north, as goods could be easily shipped thither from Quebec.

As Champlain labored untiringly for the material prosperity of the colony, so, too, do we find him watching over its spiritual interests. He devoted himself to the advancement of the Jesuits and the success of their missions, which were already yielding an abundant harvest of souls. He sent out missionaries to the Hurons, and persuaded many of the red men to hear the words of truth. Soon after his return to the colony he erected a chapel under the invocation of Notre Dame de Recouvrance, in gratitude for the recovery of Quebec from the

English, and in accomplishment of a vow. Over the altar he placed a picture representing Our Lady saving a vessel from shipwreck.

In this same year, 1633, we find an account in the "Relation des Jesuites" of Champlain going to visit the Fathers at their humble abode, hearing Mass in their little chapel, and dining with them. It was his first visit after his voyage, and the Fathers were still in a great state of rejoicing at the return of Father Brebœuf, who had come over on the vessel with the governor. A merry little party, therefore, assembled at the board, and as the Father tells us, the savages had fortunately supplied them with bear's flesh, which constituted the meal. As they sat at table Champlain began to laugh, and made the remark that "if people in France saw them eating bear's flesh they would turn away in disgust, whereas it was most savory and delicate."

After dinner the Father took some of the savage children and went down to pay his respects to Captain de Nesle, who commanded the vessel in which Champlain had come over. The little savages sang the Our Father in their native tongue for the captain's entertainment, and then stood by in eager expectation that he would give them some *toutouch-pimi*, as in the Indian dialect they called crackers and cheese. When they were departing the captain had a salute fired in their honor, and at the booming of the cannon the savages were both amazed and terrified.

Champlain was busying himself at this time in the establishment of a mission at Three Rivers, which was to be under the direction of the Jesuits, as the Recollet Fathers had not been permitted to return since the English occupation of Quebec, though they petitioned to be allowed the privilege. The government had concluded that the Jesuits were better suited to the exigencies of these distant settlements. So, as we have said, they were to be the sole laborers in the new field of operation. As soon as suitable preparation was made, they proceeded to Three Rivers, where the results of the new mission were truly marvellous. The missionaries extended their sphere of action to the most distant tribes, and did inconceivable good amongst them; but as for themselves, a Protestant writer, the Rev. Wm. I. Kip, observes, "few of them died the common death of all men." For testimony of their labors let us quote one of our most distinguished authors. "All persons," says Washington Irving, "who are in the least familiar with the early history of the West, know with what pure and untiring zeal the Catholic missionaries pursued the work of conversion among the savages. Before a Virginian had crossed the Blue Ridge, and while Connecticut was still the extreme frontier of New England, more than one man whose youth had been passed among the warm valleys of Languedoc had explored the wilds and caused the hymn of Catholic praise to rise therefrom. The Catholic priest went before the soldier and the trader; from lake to lake, from river to river, the Jesuits pressed on unresting, and, with a power which no other Christians have displayed, won the savages to their faith."*

"Their lives," says another Protestant writer before quoted, "were made up of fearless devotedness and heroic self-sacrifice. The sons of Loyola never retreated, and the mission they founded in a tribe ended only with the extinction of the tribe itself."

"Ibo et non redibo," says Father Jogues when he departed on his last mission to the Mohawks. "If the flesh trembled, the spirit never seemed to falter," says Father Le Petit, speaking of some of the martyrs. Each

---

* Knickerbocker, June, 1838,

one indeed felt that he was "baptized unto death," and that his own blood poured out in the mighty forests of the West would bring down greater blessings on those for whom he died than he could win by the labors of a life." *

If in these last remarks upon the Jesuits we have again seemed to digress from the direct purpose of our sketch, it has been with a view to show how greatly Champlain advanced the religious interests of the colony by the introduction of these zealous missionaries. His aim and theirs were one—to gain souls to the knowledge of God; for, as he himself tells us, he "should esteem it a great sin on his part to neglect the religious instruction of the savages."

But when the harvest was most abundant this noble worker in an alien land was called away, after having given such proofs of a lively faith and ardent charity as to render any comments on his life and character unnecessary. Twenty times he had crossed the ocean for the interests of the colony. Many long cold nights, when the snow was deepest on the ground, he had slept out of doors, with his cloak wrapped around him, during his exploring expeditions to the far northwest. In the time of famine he had shown a manly endurance and a heroic self-sacrifice remarkable in the history of the colony. In matters of government he had displayed a wisdom, prudence, and moderation which gained the love of his people and the unwavering attachment of the savages. For to them the Great Chief was once and forever a friend. He was habitually self-controlled, energetic, and decisive. His great penetration served him well on many occasions, and his frankness and simplicity of manner gained him universal good-will.

---

* Marshall's Christian Missions, vol. ii.

But the wheat was ripe, and the sickle of the reaper was laid thereunto. It was in December he was called away, when the western forests stood bare and bleak on plain and hillside, lighting only into faint reflections of their autumnal beauty when the day was waning and the sun gleamed upon them in deep crimson and gold. The snow was lying softly upon the little city he had founded, the people in their primitive dwellings were making good-cheer for the birthday of the Son of God, when the mariner set out upon his last voyage: the ocean—eternity, the pilot—death. It was announced to the colonists that the governor had surrendered the keys of the fortress to a mightier than he, and the Christian had gone to his eternal home in the city of Christ.

Deep and loud were the lamentations, vehement the people's grief, and grand his obsequies. But in the spring-time the bright stream he had loved flowed again on its way with vernal rejoicing, the blossoming trees he had cultivated loaded the air with perfume, the grain he had sown put forth its tender sprouts, and the people for whom he had toiled were occupied with the thought of his successor.

Once more the savages came down the river when spring had made it navigable, and asked for the chief, their friend, and were told that he would trade with them no more. Solemnly they pointed upwards, saying he had gone to the land of the Great Spirit, beyond the red home of the setting sun.

The colony prospered and flourished since that time, while in Quebec and throughout Canada no name, after that of Jacques Cartier, has been more deservedly revered than that of the Sieur de Champlain. In the foundation of Quebec, in his struggle for her civil and religious interests, and in the prominent part he took in the colonization of Canada, he is unquestionably entitled to the deepest respect, the most tender gratitude, of Canadians. But we have considered him not only as a benefactor of the human race by his important discoveries and indefatigable explorations, but as a Christian and a Catholic. His labors for the conversion of the savages, and his introduction of missionaries amongst the North American Indians, would alone entitle him to the gratitude of posterity. Of his character as a man we have said enough, and shown him in his unimpeachable integrity and manly straightforwardness. And so we leave him.

Soft be his slumbers, tranquil his rest, and lasting his memory in the hearts of the people. Honor to the noble dead! Peace to the hero's ashes!

Oliver Plunkett

Archbishop of Armagh and Primate of Ireland.

> "Another scaffold looms up through the night,
> Another Irish Martyr's hour draws near,
> The cruel crowd are gathering for the sight,
> The July day dawns innocently clear;
> There is no hue of blood along the sky,
> Where the meek martyr waits for light to die."
>
> McGee.

Oliver Plunkett,

Archbishop of Armagh and Primate of Ireland.

> "Which is the culprit in the car of death?
> He of the open brow and folded hands!
> The turbid crowd court every easy breath,
> There is no need on him of gyves or bands,
> Pale, with long bonds and vigils, yet benign,
> He bears upon his breast salvation's sign."*

AMONGST all the countries of Western Europe, there is none, perhaps, so deserving of attention, especially from Catholics, nor so full of romantic interest, as Ireland, from the period of St. Patrick's landing upon her shores down to the present day. Ireland has been described, with great justice, as resembling from afar a country of ruins; and how sadly beautiful is the charm these very ruins lend her! The gray and crumbling walls, thickly covered with lichen and wild ivy, give her scenes a picturesque character, and allow free scope to the imagination, which is constantly at work in a tour throughout this beautiful island, resting in its green light and coolness like a gem upon the surface of the water.

At every step upon our passage we are confronted by the solid masonry and architectural skill displayed in

---

* McGee's "Execution of Archbishop Plunkett."

those early and mysterious fabrications, the ancient round towers, which have stood so firm and immovable while thousands and thousands of years have hastened on in their swift passage to eternity. If we be of a poetic turn of mind we are at once whirled backwards into a very labyrinth of legends and traditions and early speculations. We almost seem to see the gorgeously clad priests of the Sun, in the primal days of Irish history, mounting at dawn to watch for the appearance of the god whom they adored as he slowly emerged from the East, and with lingering reluctance showed himself to his worshippers.

Then the priests announced the glad tidings, and the people with one accord lit their adoring fires, or bent to the ground, in profound veneration before their deity.

Or we, perchance, stop before a cairn or cromlech, and again we are back in the night of time, where the moon shines down on the wondrous beauty of this western isle; and forth from the forests, or across the dusky plains, come a band of Druids, with hoary beards, silvery locks, and flowing garments tossing in the wind. They play upon their Druid harps, they chant their incantations, and they crimson the altar of sacrifice with the blood of a living holocaust, while the moon shows, with pallid distinctness, their weird and solemn faces as they mingle in their awful dance of death.

We begin to perceive other ruins too, which tell us other tales. Ruined abbeys stand solemn and desolate, the prey of Time and his parasites,—the mournful ivy and the encroaching moss,—feeding upon their decay. Portions of the walls still remain, with mullioned windows, bearing remnants of delicate tracery carved by hands long mouldered into dust. The groined arches of the roof have entirely disappeared, so time works its will upon the unprotected walls, within which of yore the priests of the Most High offered up their living holocaust of a God.

We pause in wonder, and we ask: Did the monks voluntarily desert this land of their heart's hope, and leave their stately abbeys to decay? or did the faithless natives of the soil dismantle thus their houses of prayer, drive forth the patient monks who toiled among them, contemn their ancient faith, and the worship of their fathers' God? We hear hasty and indignant denials; the sons of a neighboring island, who in the first centuries came thither in uncouth garb, to seek for light and learning from the Irish monks, early famed for their erudition, returned after the lapse of ages, conquered the country, and trampled under foot the religion which their neighbors had received at Tara and ever since preserved inviolate.

But the natives, undaunted by their presence, practised their faith, even when a terrible persecution broke out under Henry the Eighth and was continued in the reign of his daughter Elizabeth. After a brief interregnum, during which Queen Mary, miscalled "Bloody Mary," occupied the English throne, James I. again made arbitrary laws against his Catholic subjects, and weighed very heavily upon the people of Ireland. The same persecution continued, though with diminished violence, during the reign of the hapless Charles the First, and was renewed with redoubled fury under the iron-hearted usurper of the crown,—the pretended liberator, the real tyrant; the destroyer of monarchical government, the founder of a despotism; the denouncer of Catholic greed for gain, the avaricious despoiler of churches and convents; the great soldier, the canting psalm-singer; the far-seeing statesman, the superstitious trembler at shadows; the protector of the liberties of the people, the despot who drove out the parliament sword in hand: in a word, that greatest of contradictions, Oliver Cromwell, Protector of the Commonwealth of England, consistent from beginning to end of his career in one thing only— cruelty.

He it was who, following out the course traced by Henry the Eighth and his daughter Elizabeth, unroofed the abbeys, left their walls to crumble, and gave the finest portions of the country to a godless, Puritan soldiery, the scum of the goodly land of England. He drove out an O'Neil or an O'Donnell, a Tyrone or Tyrconnell, and gave their estates to a pot-house keeper or a tinker who had donned the sad-colored garments, lengthened his visage, and killed the allotted number of Papists or Cavaliers. The new proprietors took their places where the old lords had ruled right royally and gently over their Irish vassals, who remained devotedly attached to them. Nor did they ever waver in their loyalty; the new masters, not being "to the manor born," lacked all the qualities which had endeared the old chieftains to their people, and above all were without the crowning title to their obedience, hereditary right. Scarcely were they established in their new domains when they set about utilizing the old abbeys, which had been founded by the former owners, or in most cases permitted the church and cloisters to fall into disuse and crumble into decay.

So the glorious race of monks, the guardians of the world's civilization, pondered no more over their dusky tomes, rich with the lore of departed generations, nor inscribed therein the chronicles of the times. Their noble mission, too, of imparting the treasures of knowledge to the children of the people, noble or peasant, rich or poor, was ended; and the places where they had sanctified themselves, by lives of wonderful austerity, angelic purity, and divine charity knew them no more.

The smoke of their evening sacrifice ascended not now to the throne of the Almighty; their matin hymns no longer startled the stilly whiteness of the dawn; their prayers, rising once like aromatic incense to the Most High, for their country, their people, and even their very enemies, were hushed. Nor was it alone their matin and their vesper songs which had once arisen before God; rather it was a lengthened chain of harmony, the music of self-sacrifice and charity towards their fellow-men, which all day long went up from the cloisters, securing for themselves a blessed immortality and for their brethren the fertilizing shower of God's grace.

Driven forth from their silent life of prayer, they still continued to travel from village to village, from town to town, from city to city, preaching the Gospel and endeavoring to keep alive the love and sufferings of their Divine Master in the hearts of the people, giving them bright glimpses of the eternal land whither they were hastening. They constantly preached forgiveness of enemies, the duty of praying for them, and warned the people against harboring resentment towards any one whomsoever; while they exhorted them to keep enkindled in their breasts the divine spark of faith. A price was upon the head of every monk, and yet they hid in hovels or caverns, or burrowed themselves hiding-places in the bowels of the earth, and continued their apostolic mission. A long course of rapine and bloodshed and oppression began to tell upon the people, and if their priests had not then used every effort to sustain and elevate them they might have fallen into hopeless degradation.

It would be fruitless in such a sketch as this to attempt a picture of the condition of the country at that dark hour of despair. No Catholic was permitted to hold even the most trifling office; the possessors of new estates were warned not to employ Catholic laborers; it was a crime for priests or bishops to celebrate their functions; and the few remaining native nobles, who had the power, were constantly endeavoring to conceal the monks, seculars and Jesuits. It became felony, or at the very least *præmunire*, which means the exercise of foreign jurisdiction, to say Mass, administer the Sacraments, or attend the dying. The Remonstrance Act, giving absolute authority to the king, soon followed upon the restoration of Charles II., and every priest and bishop was required to sign it. Many of its articles, however, bordered on heresy, and made it impossible for them to do so. New persecution was the result.

When things were in this condition, Oliver, a scion of the noble house of Plunkett, a near relative of the Earls of Fingall and the Barons of Louth and Dunsany, who was then quite young, showed a strong inclination for the priesthood, and was placed under the care of his relative, Dr. Patrick Plunkett, Abbot of St. Mary's, Dublin, where he remained till he was sixteen.

The college of the Jesuit Fathers in Rome was then attracting the attention of all Europe by the fame of its learning and piety. Thither young Plunkett now resolved to repair, that he might make his studies for the priesthood in such an abode of knowledge and sanctity. Father Scarampo, an Oratorian, came to Ireland on a mission from the Pope, and the Irish youth returned with him to Rome. During his residence there his preceptors predicted great things of him, from his ardent love of study, his earnest application, his noble intellect and brilliant talents; with which he combined many remarkable virtues. When he was finally ordained priest, it was impossible for him to return to his country, whence fearful tidings reached Rome, and he took up his abode with the Jesuit Fathers of San Girolamo della

Caritá. He seems to have been deeply imbued with a love and veneration for that illustrious company founded by the knightly Loyola, and who have been since their foundation the Thundering Legion of the Church.

As we have said, fresh tales of horror came each day from Ireland; rivalling the atrocities of the Roman Emperors who, in the early centuries of the Church, rode in their golden chariots over the hearts and lives and religion of their Christian subjects. So now, in those western islands, a sovereign who had been maintained, as it were, on the charity of Catholic France, and supported to the death by Catholic Ireland, was riding in the chariot of his love of ease over the dearest liberties of his Catholic subjects, particularly in Ireland.

Priests were imprisoned, exiled, forced to seek refuge under the earth or in the vaults of cemeteries, and to celebrate their sublime and ancient religious rites in caves and shanties, anywhere but in the broad and open light of day. Only six bishops remained of the Irish Episcopate, and of these three were exiled, and two at least of the other three were enfeebled by old age or bedridden.*

At this crisis the celebrated Edmund O'Reilly, Archbishop of Armagh and Primate of all Ireland, who had been for years an exile from his native country, under sentence of perpetual banishment, died in France. The Sovereign Pontiff, Clement IX., aware of the troublous state of Ireland and the perilous condition of the Irish Church, began to look about for some one worthy to be his successor, at the same time possessed of the heroic courage, zeal, and judgment required in that dangerous position. The Sacred Congregation, too, interested themselves in the matter, and various persons were

---

* Hist. of Remonstrance, or Crolly's Life of Plunkett.

named as being worthy of the dignity. At last the Pope, who had followed the young Irishman's career with considerable interest, exclaimed:

"Why are we discussing uncertainties, when certainty is before our eyes? Behold in the city of Rome itself Oliver Plunkett, a man of long experience, tried virtue, and consummate learning! Him, by my apostolic authority, I appoint Archbishop of Armagh and Primate of Ireland."

Thus it was that the pupil of the Jesuits was appointed to the highest position in the Irish Church. For twelve years he had been Professor of Theology in the celebrated College of the Propaganda, where he would probably have preferred to remain but that he knew his country needed her sons sorely; the Master of the vineyard required many laborers; and in tears and humility of spirit he prepared for the onerous ministry, which he at once, and unhesitatingly, accepted. It was not, however, deemed prudent to have him consecrated at Rome, hence his consecration took place in Brussels, where he was vested with the fullest authority for the administration of spiritual affairs in Ireland.

Once he was Archbishop, he never for a moment entertained the thought of remaining abroad, though he knew that his return to Ireland was attended with the greatest danger. He set sail for his native land after years of absence, and as the vessel heaved and plunged upon the stormy waters of the Channel old longings began to crowd upon him: green spots which in boyhood he had loved; peaceful loughs, wherein he had seen the beautiful sky of Erin mirrored, haunted his waking thoughts or came to him in dreams; memories of the old Abbey Church, where he had first worshipped God, and in the surrounding alleys of which he had played, or of the *Soggarth Aroon*, whose kindly smile and encouraging word had been among his childhood's pleasures. All these things came back to him, and he yearned more and more for a glimpse of the green island of his birth, where "the round towers of other days" were reflected in sparkling waters.

He knew, indeed, that his native land was desolate; her people scattered; her homes broken up; her fires cold upon the hospitable hearths; her priests hunted like wild beasts; her bishops a target for the rage of the enemy; yet he longed to be there, to see her once more, to share her misfortunes, to labor among her people, and to find a grave somewhere on her kindred soil.

We do not find the exact date of his arrival in Ireland mentioned by any of his biographers; but this may be readily accounted for by the fact that he was obliged to enter the country, as it were, by stealth, and afterwards remain concealed for a considerable time. During the period of his concealment Lord-Lieutenant Robarts declared to Lord Conway that he had information from the king that two persons, one of whom was Oliver Plunkett, had arrived from Rome and were lurking in the country to do mischief. Lord Conway, acting on his orders, wrote to his brother-in-law, Sir George Rawdon, telling him that "it would be an acceptable service if he could dexterously seek out the Primate and his companion, and apprehend them."

However, this Lord Robarts, who is described as having been "a stanch Presbyterian, sour and cynical, just in his administration, but vicious under the appearance of virtue; and stiff, obstinate, proud, jealous, and in every way intractable," and who particularly distinguished himself by his hatred of Catholicity, was succeeded, soon after the Primate's arrival, by Lord Berkeley, under whose government the Catholics enjoyed considerable liberty, and were enabled to regain a slight foothold in the country. By this short respite Dr. Plunkett profited to advance the spiritual interests of his flock.

During this first year of his Primacy, he held two ordinations, in which several young men were enrolled in the service of the Church, where they were sadly needed; for death and persecution and transportation had thinned the ranks of the clergy, and that fearless and patient body of men were reduced to a very small number. Under Lord Berkeley, Catholics were permitted to inhabit and trade in the towns, to be elected members of corporate bodies, and to hold commissions as justices of the peace. The venerable Archbishop of Dublin, the illustrious Peter Talbot, now publicly celebrated High Mass, at which the Puritans were exceeding wroth. Encouraged by the leniency of Berkeley's administration, the brave lords and gentlemen who had fought valiantly for the restoration of the king, and as their reward had seen Cromwellian adventurers confirmed, by a strange inconsistency on the part of Charles, in the lands and estates confiscated from the Catholic gentry by Cromwell, now ventured to lay a petition before his Majesty, begging him to take cognizance of their grievances. For this purpose they sent Colonel Richard Talbot, brother of the Archbishop, to London, to negotiate the matter, which called forth fierce opposition from the English Puritans, who then controlled the Parliament.

But in spite of the protestations of Ormonde, who was a bitter enemy of the Catholic cause, the king appointed a commissioner to inquire into their petition. The commissioner was Sir Heinige Finch, who, partly influenced by Ormonde and partly by his own intolerant spirit, returned an unfavorable report. The matter was dismissed, resulting chiefly in the recall of Berkeley, who was considered too lenient in his views, and the appointment of Essex. The latter was not by any means of a cruel or sanguinary disposition; but he was entirely controlled by the English Puritans, whom he feared above all things to offend.

The Parliament now met and induced the king to rescind any acts of indulgence towards Papists or other dissenters; every person who did not take the oath of the king's supremacy was declared incapable of holding any civil or military office; it was decreed that all Catholic priests should be banished, convents and monasteries dissolved; and the arrest of Colonel Talbot was demanded because he had dared to act as agent for the Catholic party. Orders were given to the Lord-Lieutenant to persecute Papists and encourage planters and Protestants.

Meanwhile let us take a glance at the private life of the great Archbishop. He dwelt in a small thatched house of humble exterior, which, as he mentions himself on his trial, was scarcely seven feet high. In his little library he studied, as was his delight, the sacred writings, the works of the early Fathers, and dwelt lovingly upon the history of his country. Visions rose before him, overpassing the bounds of time and space: Tara, the mighty palace of the ancient kings, where king and warrior, and chief and brehon listened entranced to the voice of the minstrel, singing in rude verse the lofty deeds of the remoter heroes, and rewarded with cup or chain of gold; where the priests of the Sun beheld from the green heights of Tara the first rising of their god, and bowed down in adoration. The Primate, even during the troublous times we have described, wrote his "Song of Tara," which has not been entirely preserved, but in which we can imagine he expresses his thoughts on the poetic traditions that hang like a golden haze above the verdant Tara. That hill of predilection, where the apostle of Erin, coming from the shores of ancient Gaul, spake in the Gaelic tongue, and gave to the Irish kings and chieftains there assembled the same faith which the chosen twelve preached of old in Galilee. With one accord the nation laid its superstitions at the feet of Patrick, quenched their sacrificial fires, and turned from the pale sun they had adored to the eternal Sun of Justice, which was henceforth to light their green shores and illumine their dusky hills.

Every venerable tradition, every glimpse of light thrown on the dimly lettered pages of the past, all the ancient glory, every prophetic word or sign, seeming to point to new greatness hidden in the future, was seized upon by the Primate with delight, and stored deep in his heart's recesses. He read over and over again the "Annals of the Four Masters," and felt a real affection for the authors, because of the patient love with which they had gleaned in the harvest-field of Ireland's history, and filled with their garnered sheafs the granary of their country.

This patriotism, this love of native land, seems to have been a prominent feature in the character of Oliver Plunkett, and a sentiment which he would fain keep alive in the breast of every Irishman, side by side with their love for the ancient faith and their pride in it. But he desired that this patriotism should be pure and exalted, never separated from that religious spirit, and always under its control; for he knew that without it, patriots too often rush on to their own destruction.

Thus we catch a glimpse of the Primate in the few hours of leisure or repose that occurred in his laborious life, which was spent in alleviating the miseries of the people, corporal as well as spiritual. Aided by his one servant, the only retinue that this good man permitted himself, he visited the poor, the needy, the distressed, and gave to them cheerfully out of his threescore pounds of yearly income. He made long and frequent journeys into various parts of the country, and on these expeditions his food was usually a piece of oaten bread. Writing to Rome in December, 1673, he says:

"During this past year I have confirmed forty-eight thousand six hundred and sixty-five souls."

This one item gives us some idea of his herculean labors. He travelled, in fact, through every part of Ulster, preaching, instructing the people, and administering Sacraments. "These Sacraments," his biographer tells us, "were often administered under the broad canopy of heaven, pastor and flock alike exposed to wind and rain." *

He occupied himself in a special manner in reforming abuses which had crept in among the clergy. A contemporary writer assures us that these evils, engendered by years of bloodshed and disorder, during which the dioceses were without chief pastors, touched only a very small portion of the priesthood. The Archbishop ordained so many priests that, we are informed, the number of the clergy was doubled between the years 1665 and 1672, while most, if not all, of the vacant bishoprics were filled. He writes again to the Sacred Congregation:

"The past two months have been spent in a fatiguing and most laborious visitation of my diocese, of which I shall shortly give a full account to your Excellency. The distillation of my eyes, which was fatally increased by the laborious visitations in the northern districts, scarcely allows me to write or read letters, even as large as a snuff-box. Still it does not impede my tongue from preaching both in the English and Irish languages."

The Prelate also labored successfully to settle certain

---

* Moran's Memoirs of Plunkett, p. 63.

misunderstandings which had grown out of the famous Remonstrance Act. As far-seeing as he was wise and prudent, he was well aware that the present lull was only the prelude to a more violent storm, and therefore lost not a moment in preparing for it. He believed that in the critical condition of affairs, the clergy, while working energetically to keep alive the spirit of faith among the people, and incite them to the heroic fortitude which would enable them to work out their salvation in the midst of many tribulations, should at the same time endeavor to hold themselves aloof from all interference in public or political affairs. For the regulation of matters appertaining to the spiritual welfare of the kingdom he convened a synod at Armagh in 1670, where many important matters were discussed.

Arthur, Lord Essex, was now, as we have said, appointed viceroy of Ireland, and being too much under the control of the Puritans to show the least indulgence towards Catholics, did not, however, persecute them. We are told that he was a personal friend of the Primate, whose talents and prudence he held in the highest esteem, describing him in a letter to the Protestant Bishop Burnet as "a wise and sober man, fond of living quietly, and in due subjection to the government."

However, his administration was short. In 1677 the Duke of Ormonde became lord-lieutenant, and once more a bloody persecution raged against Catholics. The English people were excited to a sort of frenzy by the pretended Popish plots of Tongue and Oates. These plots were never for an instant credited by enlightened or sensible people, but were frequently used by clear-sighted men to advance their own purposes. Amongst these men was the perfidious Duke of Ormonde. He adopted the severest measures against Catholics, affecting to believe them guilty, while in his private correspondence he treated these charges with contempt and utter disbelief.

He caused Talbot, Archbishop of Dublin, to be arrested on a charge of complicity in the plots, one of which was supposed to be an attempt on Ormonde's life; yet he privately declared that "Talbot was in a dying way, and the Irish in no condition to raise an insurrection." Talbot had only lately ventured back from exile- and on his arrest was indeed, as Ormonde expressed it, "in a dying way;" he lingered two years in prison, suffering excruciating agony, and then found his release where Ormonde's tyranny could never again reach him.

The viceroy's next step was to issue an edict by which he commanded all bishops and ecclesiastical dignitaries, holding their authority from Rome, as well as all Jesuits and other priests, regular and secular, to depart from the kingdom before the 20th of November; and that all convents, seminaries, Popish schools and societies, should be at once suppressed. After the date mentioned it was declared felony for any bishop, priest, or monk to exercise his ministry; and a proclamation followed by which a reward was offered for the discovery of every commissioned officer, trooper, or foot-soldier who attended Mass.

Tho Catholic laity were also disarmed, and the justices of the peace were commanded to make diligent search for arms, to seek out bishops, regular clergy, and their abettors, relievers, or harborers, and to labor for the suppression of Mass-houses and meetings for Popish service.* A proclamation was also issued declaring that no Catholic should come into the Castle of Dublin or any other fort or citadel without a special order from the government; that fairs should only be held in cer-

---

* See Carte, or Cox's Reign of Charles II.

tain specified towns; that no persons of the Romish religion should be permitted to reside in those towns who had not for twelve months past resided there; and that all of said religion were forbidden to meet in large numbers by day or night, or to bear arms. Orders were also sent to remove the Popish inhabitants from certain towns, except a few classes of persons necessary to the town; these orders were obeyed, and the Catholic inhabitants, who were numerous in such places, were at once expelled. Ormonde also declared that the kindred and relations of all notorious outlaws or tories then at large should be imprisoned and kept in close confinement till the arrest or death of the said tories; that when any Popish priest was in a parish where murder or other crimes were committed he should be cast into prison, and if the offender were not discovered be transported over the seas. These intolerant measures were devised for the protection of Protestants alarmed by the Popish plots in England, a country where the Catholics were in the alarming ascendency of one to every hundred Protestants.

The persecution now began to rage with the greatest fury against bishops and priests. Yet if it had not been for their wise counsels and their preaching of the maxims of the Gospel, the poor people, driven to bay, would have turned upon their ungrateful and cowardly oppressors. From the bishops and priests, in their dungeon, or exile, or even on the scaffold, came the golden lessons of endurance and forgiveness, which the poor oppressed people treasured in their hearts and practised in their daily lives. With truly apostolic zeal did the great Archbishop labor among them, continuing to exercise his ministry at the imminent peril of his life. Must a soul go before its Creator unconsoled, unstrengthened by the prayers and sacraments of the Church because the law forbade it? Over the bed of sickness and of death bent Oliver Plunkett, calm and unconcerned, gentle and consoling, as though no statute had ever been passed which bade him fear for his own life and liberty. Many a passage into eternity he smoothed; to many a broken heart he whispered words of peace and comfort; in many a vault and cave he offered Mass and preached the word of God. Fearless, undaunted, gentle as a lamb and bold as a lion, he trod the earth, beloved by his people and respected by his very enemies.

What a spectacle is the one undivided Church, with its hosts of self-denying confessors, angelic virgins, and heroic martyrs, meeting in all times and places, throughout the world's history, with persecution and imprisonment and death! Dying upon the common battle-field of the Church, in the service of one leader, not vainly did Christ promise that the gates of hell should not prevail, and that He should Himself be with His Church all days, even to the consummation of the world.

Meanwhile Oliver Plunkett was preparing by his holiness and austerity of life for a martyr's death. But so exact was he in every duty, so mild, so forbearing, so meek, so full of sweetness and charity, so diligent a promoter of public order and virtue, so zealous and withal so prudent, that, although the Act of Banishment had been passed, even Lord Ormonde was loth to have him arrested, and allowed him to remain at liberty for a year after the proclamation of the Act. He withdrew from his customary abode to a smaller and more retired house in Castletown-Bellew, near Drogheda, but absolutely refused to leave his diocese, much less the country, though the storm was lowering over his devoted head.

On the 6th of December, 1679, officers were sent to apprehend him. He was found, as usual, in his little retreat, where he spent his leisure hours in prayer and study,

Learning their errand, he at once arose and advanced to meet his captors, addressing them with the utmost gentleness and courtesy. They then arrested and committed him to Newgate prison, Dublin, on a charge of *præmunire.*

About this time a proclamation was issued by which a free pardon was offered to all criminals, no matter what their offences, if they would discover persons directly or indirectly concerned in the Popish plots that had stricken the kingdom of Great Britain with such terror. Let us picture to ourselves the result of such a proclamation : robbers, murderers, the most infamous criminals were let loose upon the community, to swear away the lives of good and saintly men who had at heart the true interests of their country and the peace of the kingdom.

Such witnesses, and notably two or three whom Archbishop Plunkett had been obliged to reprimand for their scandalous lives, now, incited by the double motive of gain and revenge, trumped up a charge of treason against him while he was in prison.

At the instigation of Hetherington, as reliable historians assure us, a certain Edmund Murphy proffered evidence of the Archbishop's treasonable proceedings. Most of the witnesses against Dr. Plunkett and other supposed conspirators were themselves in constant correspondence with the tories, and their active aiders and abettors. Murphy, being in prison for these treasonable practices, was discharged in order to become prosecutor, for the king, of Oliver Plunkett, Primate of Armagh. John Moyer, who was also convicted of like offences, showed his good-will towards the government in a similar way.

It is curious to observe the Duke of Ormonde's testimony in regard to the utter worthlessness of these witnesses. He declares it in various letters to his son, the Earl of Arran.* Yet such creatures as he described them to be were permitted to swear away one of the gentlest, purest, and noblest lives in the British realm. This nobleman also very frankly admits in one letter that witnesses were "being brought over from Ireland to give testimony in these plots of which they openly profess to know nothing," † and this was undoubtedly the case, the material for their evidence being manufactured by Hetherington and others, after their arrival in England.‡ It seems almost impossible to understand the perfidy and pusillanimity of which Lord Ormonde was guilty in taking so active a part in a persecution which he knew to be both unjust and unnecessary. The illustrious Charles James Fox declares that "the proceedings of the Popish plots must always be considered as an indelible disgrace to the English nation, in which king, parliament, judges, juries, witnesses, and prosecutors have all their respective, though certainly not equal, shares. Witnesses of such a character as not to deserve credit in the most trifling cause upon the most immaterial facts gave evidence so incredible, or, to speak more plainly, so impossible to be true, that it ought not to have been believed if it had come from the mouth of Cato." §

These testimonies from the pen of an eminent Protestant will enable us to form some idea of the iniquitous proceedings by which the great and good Oliver Plunkett, of "whose innocence," the same writer tells us, "no doubt could be entertained," was tried and condemned to death, his only crime having been, as the attorney-general, Sir Robert Sawyer, expressed it, that he was "an over-zealous Papist."

---

* See Carte, ii. † Carte, ii. p. 105, where the letter can be found.
‡ Carte, ii. p. 517. § Fox's Historical Works.

Meanwhile the wretched Murphy declared to the Duke of Ormonde that he had information to give of the treasonable dealings of the Primate, and the matter was brought for examination before the Privy Council at Dublin, and proved to be totally false and absurd.

Yet the good Archbishop remained in prison. We can picture him to ourselves within his narrow cell, still humbler and more dingy than the poor little library of his thatched house. We can see him sitting on the wooden bench, reading his Breviary by the dim light, or praying, with his soft, dark eyes looking out through the grated window over the fair green face and misty hills of the land he loved. We can almost hear him addressing his jailer, gently and cheerfully, when he brought him the rude prison fare.

Happy and contented was he in his little cell, where he served God in peace and lowliness, undisturbed by the great troublous world that was working out its own ends. Only one consideration troubled him: he could no longer go about among the people, preaching with fervent heart and ardent speech, in fulfilment of his apostolic mission. He could not now divide his threescore pounds a year, with the poor and needy and distressed; he could ordain no more priests to take the place of those who had fallen by the wayside.

But if he could not provide for all these wants as he had done, there still remained to him the sovereign remedy for all evils—that of prayer. Hence to prayer he betook himself. Readily may we suppose that oftentimes when the jailer entered and found him kneeling before the crucifix, with a rapt expression upon his face and the softened light from the grating falling like a halo around him, the man started back in fear, feeling that this indeed was a servant of God.

Meanwhile the witnesses whose testimony against him

had been so scornfully rejected by the authorities in Ireland hastened to London, where they were received with the greatest favor as loyal subjects—they who had been imprisoned for dealings with the tories, and were by profession tories, robbers, and spies, giving information to both parties when successively in power. An opportunity for the display of their loyalty was now presented in the arrest of the Archbishop. He was brought to trial in Dublin, where no twelve men, either Protestants or Catholics, could be found to sit as a jury upon his case; so high was the character he bore as priest and citizen. Therefore it was necessary that the English authorities should provide loyal witnesses to testify to his treasonable practices, and that this time the trial should be in England.

On the 3d of May, 1681, during the Easter term, Dr. Plunkett was again arraigned, but as he had not a single witness for his defence he petitioned that the trial should be postponed till Michaelmas, when he would endeavor to produce the required evidence. This was refused, but he was allowed a period of five weeks or thereabouts, till Trinity term. This time he knew would be of no avail whatsoever, for the witnesses were in Ireland, some of them a hundred miles from Dublin, and there were no railroads nor steamboats. The servants whom he sent over to Ireland, after being two days at sea, were obliged to cast back again and go thence to Holyhead, so that their passage to Dublin occupied thirteen or fourteen days. When they did reach their journey's end the authorities refused to give them the records of conviction showing the character of the opposing witnesses without an order from England, and the Catholics who were to give evidence in the Primate's behalf were afraid to go thither without a pass.

So on the 8th of June, 1681, the day of his trial, his

witnesses had only come as far as Coventry. On the preceding day he moved that his trial should be put off for twelve days more till the end of the term, that the witnesses might have time to appear, but this was absolutely refused, both then and on the following day when he again made application. Yet he declared "that the records, which were almost at hand, would have proved that some of the witnesses who appeared against him were indicted and found guilty of high crimes, some were imprisoned for robberies, and some were infamous people," adding "that if they only allowed him a few days to bring his witnesses and records he would defy earth and hell to convict him." He further said that "no man in Ireland would believe the charge against him, so absurd and impossible was it, even if he were himself to declare that he was guilty of it."

It would seem from the conduct of his prosecutors, on this occasion, that they desired to bring a defenceless man alone and unsupported to the bar of justice. They would seem to have been afraid lest his innocence, of which they were themselves persuaded, would be made clear and manifest, as it had already been in Dublin, where he was known.

However that be, on the 8th of June, 1681, Oliver Plunkett was summoned before the Supreme Court of Justice, to answer to a charge of high treason, whereas he had been arrested only for *præmunire*. The court was crowded, and the excitement was intense when the usher ordered the prisoner to be introduced. There was a moment's pause: a man prematurely old and worn entered, attended only by his jailers. He was simply attired in his cassock, wearing the pastoral cross conspicuously upon his breast. So unruffled was the majesty of his mien, so calm the dignity with which he confronted them, that in spite of their gorgeous apparel his prosecutors sank into insignificance. Such a scene was frequently witnessed of old in the Roman forum. The implacable judges, the defenceless victims whose white hairs might have won compassion, and the lictors with their axes whetted for the sacrifice.

It may be well to remark that, had Dr. Plunkett foreseen his trial before leaving Ireland, he would have made arrangements for the production of witnesses; but he was under the impression that having been tried in Dublin he could not be tried in England for the same offence.

He was brought into court amid a profound silence, sworn, and pleaded not guilty. After which, the proclamation being read by the clerk of the crown, the Primate proceeded to explain the unavoidable delay in the arrival of his witnesses, and begged the court to believe he had made every effort to produce them, and that he had been under the impression he could not be tried in England, concluding with the touching words:

"I am come here where no jury knows me nor the quality of my adversaries. If I had been in Ireland I would have put myself upon my trial, without any witnesses, before any Protestant jury that knew them and me. When the orders went over that I should be tried in Ireland, and that no Roman Catholic should be on the jury, so it was in both the grand and other jury; yet there when I came to my trial, after I was arraigned, no one appeared. This is manifest upon the record and can be proved."

To which the Chief Justice having answered that he had not been prosecuted there for this offence, the Archbishop replied: "But, my lord, here is no jury that knows me or the quality of my adversaries, for they are not a jury of the neighborhood that knows them. . . . Though I cannot harbor, nor will not, nor ought not, the least conceit of hard measure or injustice, yet since I have not full time to bring my records and witnesses all together, I cannot make my defence. . . . Therefore I beseech your lordship that I may have time to bring my records and witnesses, and then I will defy all that is upon the earth and under the earth to say anything against me."

To which the Chief Justice answered:

"Look you, Mr. Plunkett: it is in vain for you to talk and make this discourse here now; you know when a man is indicted for felony or treason it is not usual to give such time. . . . We can't furnish you with witnesses; you must look to get witnesses for yourself."

And more to the same effect. The Archbishop again asked for time, if only till the end of the term, saying:

"I am then in imminent danger of my life if I cannot get ten days to have my witnesses over. I desire I may have but to the 21st of this month, and then if they do not come you may go on."

However, his further pleading was in vain, and he was asked if he took exception to the jury, to which he replied by asking if it was this same jury who condemned the five Jesuits. To which the Chief Justice said, "What if they have? that is no exception;" whereupon they were sworn in, and the clerk of the crown commanded the prisoner to hold up his hand, and the jury to hearken to his charge. He proceeded to declare, in the usual formula, that the Archbishop was "a traitor against the sovereign Charles II.; that he was seduced by the instigation of the devil, not having in his heart the fear of God, from the cordial love and obedience he owed the king; that he was contriving with all his might against the peace and tranquillity of the kingdom of Ireland and that of England, stirring up war and rebellion against the king, and working in parts beyond the seas to subvert the power of and depose the aforesaid sovereign and put him to death; as also to bring destruction on the true worship of God in the kingdom of Ireland, by law established, and there had used the superstition of the Romish Church.

"And to fulfil and accomplish his said wicked treasons, Oliver Plunkett did, in parts beyond the seas, maliciously, devilishly, and traitorously assemble with divers other traitors unknown to bring destruction upon the crown and government of the kingdom, and compass the death of the king, and did for these purposes unlawfully, maliciously, and devilishly collect, pay, and expend divers sums of money."

This was the sum and substance of his indictment, to which he pleaded "not guilty." According to the cruel custom of those times, no lawyer was permitted to conduct the defence of a criminal, and as Oliver Plunkett had not a single witness to give testimony, he stood alone against three judges who scarcely allowed him to speak without interruption, six of the most eminent lawyers in England, and a host of perjured witnesses; and that in a strange country where his spotless character was unknown. One of the lawyers, Mr. Heath, then commented on the indictment, and called upon the judge and jury to find the prisoner guilty if the points aforesaid could be proved. Sergeant Maynard spoke somewhat to the same effect, and the Attorney-General began his speech by making the following observation: that "the character this gentleman bears as Primate, under a foreign and usurped jurisdiction, will be a great inducement to you to give credit to that evidence we shall produce before you;" and declared that "the title of Primate had been given him merely as a reward for his offer to raise 60,000 men in Ireland for the Pope's service, and to subvert the government."*

---

* The judges were Sir Francis Pemberton, Lord Chief Justice, Justice Dolbein, and Justice Jones; the lawyers, the Attorney-General (Sir Robert Sawyer), the Solicitor-General, Sergeants Jeffries and Maynard, Sir F. Withins, and Mr. Heath.

The various witnesses were now called, all of them being men of notoriously infamous and depraved character, and those among them who were ecclesiastics a stain upon the name they bore of priests or friars, and actuated chiefly by revenge against the Primate, who had been forced to suspend and excommunicate them for their evil lives and the scandal they occasioned. They all made the same statements, their lesson having been readily learned: that he had collected money for treasonable purposes, was in collusion with the king of France, who was to send men to Carlingford for the conquest of England and establishment of the Roman Catholic religion; that it was well understood in Ireland (the witness being evidently in the confidence of the dignitaries of the Church) that Dr. Plunkett had been appointed by the Pope in preference to other candidates because he had expressed himself more capable of managing affairs with the king of France; that he had sent letters by Neal O'Neal to Baldeschi, the Pope's Secretary, and to the Bishop of Aix and Principe Colonna, that they might solicit help from foreign powers for France; that he had exacted money from the clergy of Ireland for the purpose of introducing the French; that he had commissioned Captain O'Neal to demand aid from the French king; that he had written to Cardinal de Bouillon, exhorting him to impress on the Catholic powers that they should not war with each other, but unite in defence of their persecuted brethren in Ireland; that he had commissioned one of the witnesses, Hugh Duffy, to raise men in the provinces; that he had fixed upon Carlingford as the best place of invasion for the French; that he had assisted at certain meetings in the county of Meath, and exhorted those present to take up arms."

When Edward Murphy was produced he contradicted all his previous calumnies against the Primate, and even endeavored to throw discredit on the witnesses who preceded him, and finally made an attempt to rush out of court. However, he was seized and brought back, but refused to corroborate what he had before deposed, in consequence of which he was committed to Newgate. This Murphy was one of the unfortunate men whom the Archbishop had censured and excommunicated, and was in fact, like the other witnesses, a base apostate, of notoriously bad character. He seems, however, to have had some scruple at last, as we find by his singular conduct on the trial.*

When the witnesses were all examined a stranger handed in a paper containing the names of David Fitzgerald, Eustace Commines, and Paul Gorman, and the Chief Justice at once demanded whence it came.

"I was told," said the stranger, "that these were good witnesses for Dr. Plunkett, and I gave him the names."

"Where are they?" asked the Chief Justice.

"They are hard by," was the answer.

Then the Attorney-General asked for Eustace Commines, who, it seems, had given evidence against the prisoner. Paul Gorman was brought in, and the Primate himself asked him "if Mr. Moyer did allure and entice him to swear against his cause," but Gorman, becoming frightened, denied this. He, however, declared that Moyer had told him "if there was law or justice in Ireland, he would show Mr. Plunkett his share of it," and added that, as he had a soul to save, he never heard of any misdemeanor on the part of the prisoner. The Chief Justice then asked if Mr. Plunkett sent for him, and the prisoner at once replied:

---

*The witnesses against Dr. Plunkett were Florence MacMoyer, John Moyer, Hugh Duffy, Henry O'Neal, Neal O'Neal, Hanlon, Edmund Murphy, John McClare, and Owen Murphy, one or two of whom were Franciscan friars who had been expelled the Order.

"I never sent for him."

Gorman then said to the Archbishop, in allusion to his previous declaration of having come from Ireland to reveal plots:

"It was not against you; they knew I had nothing against you. I thought you did more good in Ireland than hurt; so I declared."

The Chief Justice asked the prisoner if he had any more witnesses, and Dr. Plunkett answered:

"I have no more witnesses, my lord."

The Chief Justice then made an address to the jury, reminding them that the evidence was strong against the prisoner, and that he had nothing to say in his behalf, except that his witnesses had not yet come over.

"I can say nothing to it," said Plunkett, "but give my own protestation that there is not one word of this said against me true, but all plain romance. I never had any communication with any French minister, cardinal or other."

The jury withdrew for a quarter of an hour, and returning gave the verdict:

"Oliver Plunkett, hold up thy hand. How say you, is he guilty of high treason, whereof he stands indicted or not guilty?"

The foreman answered:

"Guilty!"

And the Archbishop said:

"Deo Gratias!" (Thanks be to God!)

The prisoner was removed from court, and on Wednesday, the 15th of June, 1681, was brought back again to hear his sentence. The clerk asked him what he had to say for himself why sentence of death should not be pronounced.

The Archbishop in a long address, which in our present space cannot be given, pointed out the utter absurdity and improbability of many of the charges against him, and the falsehood of all of them, alluding to the fact of having been tried for treason when he was arrested for *præmunire*.

The Chief Justice in reply made a rude and most brutal address to the prisoner, in which he declared his religion to be "ten times worse than all the heathenish superstitions." Such gross discourtesy and want of humanity is almost without a parallel.

Plunkett responded that the witnesses against him were apostates and renegades whom he had endeavored to correct for seven years, and who therefore bore him malice; he also made the following declaration, which he afterwards repeated in his dying attestation:

"If I were a man that had no care of my conscience in this matter, and did not think of God Almighty, or conscience, or heaven, or hell, I might have saved my life, for I was offered it by divers people here, so I would but confess my own guilt and accuse others. But, my lord, I had rather die ten thousand deaths than wrongfully accuse anybody, or take away one farthing of any man's goods, one day of his liberty, or one minute of his life."

The Chief Justice said he was sorry to see him persist in the principles of that religion, and the Primate again replied:

"They are those principles that even Almighty God cannot dispense withal."

After which the Chief Justice spoke as follows:

"Well, however, the judgment which we must give you is that which the law says and speaks. And therefore you must go from hence to the place whence you came, that is, to Newgate, and thence you shall be drawn through the city of London to Tyburn; there you shall be hanged by the neck, but cut down before you are dead, your bowels shall be taken out and burnt before your face, your head shall be cut off, and your body divided into four quarters, to be disposed of as his Majesty pleases; and I pray God to have mercy upon your soul."

The Archbishop asked leave for a servant and a few friends to visit him, which was granted. But the Chief Justice recommended him to receive a visit from some minister, to which the prisoner replied:

"My lord, if you please, there are some in prison that never were indicted on account of any crime, and they will do my business very well; for they will do it according to the rites of our own Church, which is the ancient usage; they cannot do it better, and I would not alter it now."

He formally declared that he was innocent of all treasons laid to his charge, and referred them for his character to the Lord Chancellor of Ireland,* Lord Berkeley, Lord Essex, and Lord Ormonde. He was led away, and the court adjourned. It is unnecessary to make any comments on these most unjust and iniquitous proceedings. We shall, however, quote from the Protestant Bishop Burnet, who says:

"Plunkett, the Popish Primate of Armagh, was at this time brought to his trial. Some bad Irish priests and others of that nation, hearing that England was at that time disposed to hearken to good swearers, thought themselves well qualified for the office; so they came over to swear. . . . The witnesses were brutal and profligate men; yet the Earl of Shaftesbury cherished them much, and what they said was believed by the Parliament; so that they have come over in whole companies. Lord Essex told me that this Plunkett was a wise and sober

---

* The Lord Chancellor was Rev. Michael Boyle, Protestant Primate of Ireland.

man, who was for living quietly and in due submission to the government, without engaging into intrigues of state. Some of these witnesses had been censured by him for their evil behavior; and they drew others to swear as they had directed. They had appeared the winter before upon a bill offered to the grand jury; but, as the foreman of the jury, who was a zealous Protestant, told me, they contradicted one another so evidently that they would not find the bill. But now they laid the story better together, and Plunkett was condemned."

In the Chronicle of Sir Richard Baker we find the following: "He [Dr. Plunkett] was a worthy and good man, who, notwithstanding his high title, was in a very mean state of life, having nothing to subsist on but the contributions of a few poor clergy of his religion in the province of Ulster, who, having little themselves, could not spare much to him. In these low circumstances he lived, though meanly, quietly and contentedly, meddling with nothing but the concerns of his function, and dissuading all about him from entering into any turbulent or factious intrigues."

He goes on to speak of the witnesses, whom he says were "profligate wretches, some of whom Plunkett had censured for their wickedness; so, partly out of revenge and partly to keep themselves in business, they charged a plot upon that innocent, quiet man, so that he was sent for over and brought to trial."* Both this author and another Protestant historian, Eachard, mention that Essex applied to the king to obtain the pardon of Plunkett. Says Eachard:

"The Earl of Essex was himself so sensible of the poor man's hardship that he generously applied to the king

---

* Chronicle of Sir Richard Baker, continued to the death of King George I.

for pardon, and told his Majesty the witnesses must needs be perjured; for these things sworn against him could not possibly be true."* And the Chronicle of Sir Richard Baker gives the king's reply: "Why did you not declare this, then, at the trial? It would have done him some good then; but I dare pardon nobody;" and ended by saying, "His blood be upon your head, and not upon mine." †

On the day following that on which he had received his sentence Dr. Plunkett wrote thus to Father Corker, in the most beautiful and touching language:

"DEAR SIR: I am obliged to you for the favour and charity of the 20th, and for all your former benevolence; and whereas I cannot in this country remunerate you, with God's grace I hope to be grateful in that kingdom which is properly our country. And truly God gave me, though unworthy of it, that grace to have a courage fearless of death.‡ I have many sins to answer for before the Supreme Judge of the high bench, where no false witnesses can have audience. But as for the bench yesterday, I am not guilty of any crime there objected to me; I would I could be so clear at the bench of the All-powerful. *Ut, ut sit*, there is one comfort, that He cannot be deceived, because He is omniscious and knows all secrets, even of hearts; and cannot deceive, because all goodness; so that I may be sure of a fair trial, and will get time sufficient to call witnesses, nay, the Judge will bring them in a moment if there will be need of any. You and your comrade's prayers will be powerful advocates at that bench. Here none are admitted for

"Your affectionate friend,
"OLIVER PLUNKETT."

---

* Eachard, Hist. England, vol. iii. p. 631. † Ibid.
‡ " Fortem animum mortis terrore carentem."

From this time forward the Primate seems to have been most tranquil and happy. All the cares and trials he had known in the exercise of his arduous ministry were soon to be laid down in one great burden at the foot of the scaffold. At its summit he was to receive a martyr's crown and a swift and unutterably blissful entrance into that glorious immortality of which no human soul, howsoever exalted, can conceive even the slightest portion. Eye hath not seen, ear hath not heard, nor hath it entered into the heart of man to conceive the ineffable glory which awaited the martyr beyond the tomb. Well done, thou good and faithful servant; enter into the joy of the Lord; possess the kingdom prepared for you from the foundation of the world.

In the time of waiting he knelt all day long before the Image of the Crucified wrapt in holy contemplation, supplicating Jesus, the Lamb of Calvary, to strengthen him for the sacrifice. His figure was worn and emaciated with suffering and austerity; upon his face shone glimpses from the eternal light towards which he was hastening. Father Corker, who was his confessor and attended him in his last moments, thus speaks of his life in prison:

" He was kept, as you know, closely confined, secluded from all conversation save that of his keepers, until his arraignment; therefore I can only inform you of what I learned, as it were by chance, from the mouths of the said keepers: that he fasted three or four days a week with nothing but bread; that he appeared always modestly cheerful, without any anguish or concern at his danger or strait confinement; that by his sweet and pious demeanor he attracted an esteem and reverence from those few that came near him. But his trial being ended, and he condemned, his man had leave to wait on him alone or in his chamber, by whose means we had intercourse by letters to each other. And now it was I clearly perceived in him the Spirit of God and those lovely fruits of the Holy Ghost, charity, joy, peace, etc., transparent in his soul. And not only I, but many other Catholics who came to receive his benediction and were eye-witnesses (a favor not denied to us), there appeared in his words, actions, and countenance something so divinely elevated, such a composed mixture of cheerfulness, constancy, love, sweetness, and candor, as manifestly denoted the divine goodness had made him fit for a victim and destined him for heaven. None saw or came near him but received new comfort, new fervor, new desires to please, serve, and suffer for Christ Jesus, by his very presence. Concerning the manner and state of his prayer, he seemed most devoted to Catholic sentences taken out of Scripture, the divine office and missal, which he made me procure for him three months before he died: upon these sentences he let his soul dilate in love, following herein the sweet impulse and dictates of the Holy Ghost, and reading his prayers, writ rather in his heart than in his book, according to that 'unctio ejus docet vos de omnibus' (1 St John ii. 27).

"For this reason, I suppose, it was that when with great humility he sent me his last speech to correct, he also writ me word that he would not at the place of execution make use of any set form of prayer except the Our Father, Hail Mary, Creed, the psalm *Miserere*, and 'Into thy hands, O Lord, I commend my spirit,' etc., and for the rest he would breathe forth his soul in such prayers and ejaculations as God Almighty should then inspire him withal. He continually endeavored to improve and advance himself in the purity of divine love, and by consequence also in contrition for his sins past, of his deficiency in both which this humble soul complained to me as the only thing that troubled him.

"This love had extinguished in him all fear of death.

The very night before he died, being now as it were at heart's ease, he went to bed at eleven o'clock, and slept quietly and soundly till four in the morning, at which time his man, who lay in the room with him, awakened him; so little concern had he upon his spirit, or rather so much had the loveliness of the end beautified the horror of the passage to it. After he certainly knew God Almighty had chosen him to the crown and dignity of martyrdom, he continually studied how to divest himself of himself and become more and more an entire, pleasing, and perfect holocaust; to which end, as he gave up his soul with all its faculties to the conduct of God, so, for God's sake, he resigned the care and disposal of his body to unworthy me, etc.

"But I neither can nor dare undertake to describe unto you the signal virtues of this blessed martyr. There appeared in him something beyond expression—something more than human; the most savage and hardhearted people were mollified and attendered at his sight; many Protestants, in my hearing, wished their souls in the same state with his. All believed him innocent; and he made Catholics, even the most timorous, in love with death." *

In a letter written about this time to Father Corker he expressed his joy at the prospect of being put to death for the faith, "since," he says, "Ireland, so fertile of saints, has but few martyrs."

But his last night upon earth arrived, and, as the keeper, Richardson, tells us, "he retired as usual and slept soundly." He seemed, in fact, full of joy, anticipating on the morrow a happy release from all that had weighed him down since he returned from his studies in Rome.

"When I came to him this morning," says Richard-

---

* See both these letters in Challoner's Lives.

son, "he was newly awake, having slept all night without any disturbance; when I told him he was to prepare for his execution, he received the message with all quietness of mind, and went to the sledge as unconcerned as if he had been going to a wedding."*

This, then, was his awakening for the last time upon earth. Calmly and tranquilly he rose, his face more peaceful and serene than on the morning when, by the grace of the Holy Ghost, he received the seal of the episcopacy. The Pope had given him an onerous charge, which he was now about to lay down, nobly, grandly, heroically, upon the scaffold at Tyburn. Father Corker relates that "as he passed out of the prison-yard to execution he turned him about to our chamber windows, and with a pleasant aspect and elevated hands gave us his benediction."

An immense multitude had assembled to witness the last act of his truly apostolic life. Blue and cloudless was the sky, bright the golden sun, that shone with equal glory upon the hideous gibbet. It was the morning of the 1st July, 1681, a day never to be forgotten by those who witnessed the execution of that lonely, defenceless man. Slowly and with undisturbed majesty of aspect he mounted the scaffold, and stood in presence of the gaping multitude, who were crowded close together in their desire to see and hear him. An awe fell upon them, something of the hush of fear that crept upon the centurion on Calvary when the darkness came down and he cried, "Indeed, this was a just man!" It was not the sunlight alone which shone upon the Primate's face, but a calm yet glorious light, seeming to proceed from within, illumining his emaciated features, and lending dignity

---

* Memoirs and Reflections of Sir Richard Bulstrode upon the Reign and Government of Kings Charles I. and II.

to his wasted frame. He still wore his cassock, and the pastoral cross. He looked for a moment afar off, as if he were seeking to penetrate the distance that separated him from the green hills and bright streams and golden sunlight of Ireland, praying, as he would thenceforth pray at the throne of God, that the ancient faith of their brave forefathers might forever be preserved among the people, however fierce the storm of persecution. He looked upon the multitude at the foot of the scaffold, and the overmastering joy and gladness upon his face told of the longing by which he had been consumed to be with Christ. After a moment's scrutiny of their upturned faces he spoke as follows:

"I have some few days past abided my trial at the King's Bench, and now very soon I must hold up my hand at the King of kings' bench, and appear before a Judge who cannot be deceived by false witnesses nor corrupt allegations, for He knoweth the secrets of hearts, neither can He deceive any, or give an unjust sentence, or be misled by respect of persons; He being all goodness, and a most just Judge, will infallibly decree an eternal reward for all good works, and condign punishment for the smallest transgressions against His commandments. Which being a most certain and undoubted truth, it would be a wicked act and contrary to my perpetual welfare that I should now, by declaring anything contrary to truth, commit a detestable sin, for which, within a very short time, I must receive sentence of everlasting damnation; after which there is no reprieve nor hope of pardon. I will, therefore, confess the truth without any equivocation, and make use of the words according to their accustomed signification; assuring you, moreover, that I am of that certain persuasion that no power, not only upon earth, but also in heaven, can dispense me or give me leave to make a false protestation; and I protest upon the word of a dying man, and as I hope for salvation at the hands of the Supreme Judge, I will declare the naked truth with all candor and sincerity; and that my affairs may be better known to all the world.

"It is to be observed that I have been accused in Ireland of treason and *præmunire*, and that there I was arraigned and brought to my trial; but the prosecutors (men of flagitious and infamous lives), perceiving that I had records and witnesses who would evidently convict them and clearly show my innocence and their wickedness, voluntarily absented themselves, and came to this city to procure that I should be brought hither to my trial (where the crimes objected were not committed), where the jury did not know me or the qualities of my accusers, and were not informed of several other circumstances conducing to a fair trial.

"Here, after six months' close imprisonment or thereabouts, I was brought to the bar the 3d of May, and arraigned for a crime for which I was before arraigned in Ireland—a strange resolution; a rare fact, of which you will hardly find a precedent these five hundred years past. But whereas my witnesses and records were in Ireland, the lord chief justice gave me five weeks' time to get them brought hither; but by reason of the uncertainty of the seas, of wind and weather, and of the difficulty of getting copies of records, and bringing many witnesses from several counties in Ireland, and for many other impediments (of which affidavit was made), I could not at the end of five weeks get the records and witnesses brought hither. I therefore begged for twelve days more, that I might be in readiness for my trial, which my lord chief justice denied; and so I was brought to my trial, and exposed, as it were with my hands tied, to those merciless perjurers who did aim at my life by accusing me of these following points."

He then proceeded to answer each of the charges in detail, after which he continued as follows:

"And though I be not guilty of the crimes of which I am accused, yet I believe none ever came to this place who is in such a condition as I am; for if I should even acknowledge (which in conscience I cannot do, because I should belie myself) the chief crimes laid to my charge, no wise man that knows Ireland would believe me. If I should confess that I was able to raise 70,000 men in the districts of which I had care, to wit, in Ulster, nay, even in all Ireland, and to have levied and exacted moneys from the Roman Catholic clergy for their maintenance, and to have proposed Carlingford for the French's landing, all would but laugh at me, it being well known that all the revenues of Ireland, both spiritual and temporal, possessed by his Majesty's subjects are scarce able to raise and maintain an army of 70,000 men. If I will deny all those crimes (as I did and do), yet it may be that some who are not acquainted with the affairs of Ireland will not believe that my denial is grounded upon truth, though I assert it with my last breath.

"I dare mention further, and affirm, that if these points of 70,000 men, etc., had been sworn before any Protestant jury in Ireland, and had been even acknowledged by me at the bar, they would not believe me, no more than if it had been deposed and confessed, by me that I had flown in the air from Dublin to Holyhead. You see, therefore, what condition I am in, and you have heard what protestations I have made of my innocency, and I hope you will believe the words of a dying man.

"And that you may be the more inclined to give me credit, I assure you that a great peer* sent me notice 'that he would save my life if I would accuse others;' but I answered that I never knew of any conspirators in

---

*Probably Shaftesbury.

Ireland but such, as I said before, as were publicly known outlaws, and that to save my life I would not falsely accuse any nor prejudice my own soul. To take away any man's life or goods wrongfully, ill becometh any Christian, especially a man of my calling, being a clergyman of the Catholic Church and also an unworthy prelate, as long as there was any connivance or toleration; and I by preaching, and teaching and statutes, have endeavored to bring the clergy of which I had a care to a due comportment, according to their calling; and though thereby I did but my duty, yet some who would not amend had a prejudice for me, and especially my accusers, to whom I did endeavor to do good. I mean the clergymen; as for the laymen who appeared against me Florence MacMoyer, the two O'Neals, and Hanlon, I was never acquainted with them. But you see how I am requited, and how by false oaths they brought me to this untimely death; which wicked act, being a defect of persons, ought not to reflect upon the Order of St. Francis or upon the Roman Catholic clergy; it being well known that there was a Judas among the Twelve Apostles, and a wicked man called Nicholas among the Seven Deacons; and even as one of the said deacons, to wit, holy Stephen, did pray for those who stoned him to death, so do I for those who with perjuries spill my innocent blood, saying as St. Stephen did, 'O Lord, lay not this sin to them.'

"I do heartily forgive them, and also the judges who, by denying me sufficient time to bring my records and witnesses from Ireland, did expose my life to evident danger. I do also forgive all those who had a hand in bringing me from Ireland to be tried here, where it was morally impossible for me to have a fair trial. I do finally forgive all who did concur, directly or indirectly, to take away my life; and I ask forgiveness of all those whom I have ever offended by thought, word, or deed. I beseech the All-powerful that His Divine Majesty grant our king, queen, the Duke of York, and all the royal family health, long life, and all prosperity in this world, and in the next everlasting felicity.

"Now that I have shown sufficiently, as I think, how innocent I am of any plot or conspiracy, I would I were able with the like truth to clear myself of high crimes committed against the Divine Majesty's commandments (often transgressed by me), for which I am sorry with all my heart; and if I should or could live a thousand years, I have a firm resolution and a strong purpose by your grace, O my God, never to offend you; and I beseech your Divine Majesty, by the merits of Christ, and by the intercession of His blessed Mother and all the holy angels and saints, to forgive me my sins and to grant my soul eternal rest!"

While he read this speech many of the listeners were affected even to tears, and the deepest emotion was manifested, while no man made the least sound which might interrupt him. Then he concluded:

"To the final satisfaction of all persons that have the charity to believe the words of a dying man, I again declare before God, as I hope for salvation, what is contained in this paper is the plain and naked truth, without any equivocation, mental reservation, or secret evasion whatever; taking the words in their usual sense and meaning, as Protestants do when they discourse with all candor and sincerity. To all which I have here subscribed my hand,

"OLIVER PLUNKETT."

Then he turned away, saying the psalm *Miserere*, "*Parce animæ,*" "Into Thy hands, O Lord," etc., and other ejaculations. The attention of the spectators was now fixed upon him in breathless silence; they seemed as if spell-bound, so intense and painful was their interest, so heartfelt their emotion. But the Primate had no further concern with them, with Ireland, with the world; for the last time he had looked upon the earth and sky; for the last time he had addressed the people, not those whom he had loved and amongst whom he had labored: for them it only remained to hear of his death and weep. A thrill went through the people as he gave a preconcerted signal to a disguised priest who was near at hand, and meekly bowing his head, received absolution. Some there were who understood the mystic sign of pardon, others understood it not; but it seemed to all that the heaven whither he was going had already transfigured him with its light. Surely the golden gates were ajar, and a ray of the glory had fallen upon him. An expression of celestial beatitude was upon his face, and the people seemed to feel the presence of the angel who held the crown above the martyr's head. But a moment and heaven would be his; the Adorable Trinity would receive him with love; the Man-God offer him to the Eternal Father as a most precious fruit of His Passion; the Queen of Angels bend down to greet him, and the choirs and thrones and principalities, with the saints and elect, praise God with exceeding praise for the martyr's death.

He commended anew his blessed soul into the hands of Jesus the Redeemer; the cart was drawn away, and the Primate was hanging by the neck. When he seemed insensible he was cut down, quartered, and disembowelled; his bowels were thrown into the fire; but his happy soul had escaped the eternal fire of hell and flown into the bosom of "the Lord God, the strong and patient Judge."

"They doomed him without stain, and here he dies."

His body was begged of the king, and was interred, all but the head and arms, in the churchyard of " St. Giles's in the Fields," within the shadow of the north wall, beside the five noble Sons of Loyola, who had laid down their lives as cheerfully and heroically as he. Upon his coffin was placed a copper-plate bearing the inscription:

"In this tomb resteth the body of the Right Reverend Oliver Plunkett, Archbishop of Armagh and Primate of Ireland, who, in hatred of religion, was accused of high treason by false witnesses, and for the same condemned and executed at Tyburn, his heart and bowels being taken out and cast into the fire. He suffered martyrdom with constancy, the 1st of July, 1681, in the reign of Charles II."

This inscription was written by Father Corker, to whom the Primate had bequeathed his body, as the priest himself mentions, and as is also related by Dodd in his Church History. But his body was not suffered to remain in the quiet corner of St. Giles's; in 1683, when the Crop-eared Plot, as it was called, broke out, the Primate's remains were taken up and conveyed beyond the sea to the Benedictine monastery at Lambspring in Germany,* where they rested for some time, with a handsome monument erected by Father Corker and bearing a Latin inscription.

We have but little more to tell, save that the blood of the martyr seemed to be as an iron wall against the rage of the persecutors. In the very consummation of this act of cruelty and injustice the innocence of the martyr was almost universally admitted, and he himself held up to public veneration. It is declared by some of his contemporaries that by his death he did more for the

---

* Athen. Oxon., p. 221.

Irish Church than he could have done by living a century longer. Yet this does not prevent his execution from being, as a Protestant writer, Goldwin Smith, declares, "a stain on the white ermine of English justice." Bishop Burnet affirms that "he was condemned and suffered very decently, expressing himself in many particulars as became a bishop. He died denying everything that had been sworn against him."[*]

The Primate's right hand was enshrined and kept in the sanctuary; his head was brought from Lambspring to Rome in 1683, and fell into the possession of Cardinal Howard. Dominick Maguire, who had been appointed Dr. Plunkett's successor in the primacy, died soon after, and Dr. Hugh McMahon became Archbishop of Armagh. Being an ardent admirer of his martyred predecessor, he brought with him, on his return to Ireland, the head of Dr. Plunkett, which he had obtained from Cardinal Howard. It was, however, finally given to a convent of Dominican nuns founded at Drogheda, of which Catherine Plunkett, probably a relative of the deceased Prelate, was Prioress. Here, in what is known as the Sienna Convent, the head remains, with a certificate of its genuineness signed by several authorities. It was at first placed in a silver case. "At present it is enshrined in a little ebony temple, at each of the four angles of which is a Corinthian pillar of silver; the sides are also inlaid with silver. There are two doors, one in the front and one in the rear, and inside of each there is a glass plate, through which the head can be seen. On the silver plate in the front door are the Primate's arms, surmounted by a silver mitre. On each angle of the roof is a silver flame, emblematical of martyrdom. The head itself is of a brown color and quite perfect, with the exception

---

[*] vol. I. p. 502.

of the nose, which is slightly injured. It still retains some of the white hair, as we find from De Burgo." *

We have endeavored, as far as the limits of our sketch would permit, to give a faithful picture of the great Archbishop, whose sufferings for the faith and subsequent martyrdom, have placed him in the front rank of those whom the Church holds up to our veneration. While we are conscious of having fallen far short of the greatness of the subject, we are also aware of having labored faithfully and conscientiously to add our mite in bringing before the Catholic public this great and good man, too little known at the present day. Our task is, however, done, and it only remains to take a last general glance at the qualities which would have rendered him illustrious, had the crowning glory of martyrdom never been vouchsafed him, as well as to give a brief description of his personal appearance, which our readers may find interesting. In the various portraits extant of him, as well as in the accounts of biographers, we find him represented at first in the very prime of manhood, and afterwards under the aspect of a prematurely old and sorrow-stricken man. In both are the same high, broad forehead, firm mouth and chin, attesting the mingled strength and gentleness of his character; the large dark eyes, and the unalterable expression of truth, holiness, and purity. But in the later pictures of him we observe the untimely furrows, the worn and sorrowful expression, lending a chastened dignity and an exalted sanctity which well befitted the martyr soon to win his crown. He was not very old at the time of his martyrdom, having been born at Loughrea in or about the year 1631 and suffered death in 1681. In character he united the most consummate prudence with the most

---

* Crolly's Life of Plunkett.

heroic courage; profound learning, with remarkable modesty and simplicity; the purest patriotism with the most unqualified submission to authority; a burning zeal with an untiring gentleness. Patient, full of charity, extraordinarily humble, he seemed to have ever before the eye of his mind that divine Master whom he served. In order that for the contumely he had suffered he might have glory, and for the sorrow a garment of praise, he seemed never to have lost sight of the vision of "light everlasting, infinite brightness, and steadfast peace." To such privileged souls as his, endowed with special gifts and graces, it is given to behold the mansions of that supernal city with something of the distinctness of the just made perfect, while we poor pilgrims perceive it afar off "and darkly as if through a glass." So it is well with him, and may he offer up prayers for us before the eternal altar of the most high God! It is curious, on the other hand, to observe the fate of some of his enemies. On the very day after the Primate's execution the Earl of Shaftesbury was dragged to the Tower amid the execrations of the populace. Many of the witnesses whom he had employed at the trials of his victims offered to give evidence against him, so that he narrowly escaped and fled to Amsterdam, where he died soon after. Oates was convicted of perjury and condemned to perpetual imprisonment, being also deprived of his pension. Rouse and College were hanged. The Dissenters, who had been so active in bringing about his death, were themselves persecuted before the end of the year, the laws against Dissenters being put in force. Most of the witnesses against him were reduced to a condition of the greatest misery, and were universally detested, even by those whom they had formerly aided by their perjuries, and it is said were consumed by the liveliest remorse. One of them, Duffy, prematurely old, worn, and wasted, came years after the Primate's death to Dr. Hugh McMahon, his successor, crying out in agony, "Am I never to have peace? Is there no mercy for me?" Dr. McMahon, in answer, pointed to the martyr's head, and the unhappy wretch fainted. He afterwards did public penance for his sins, and died a penitent. His conversion was no doubt obtained by the prayers of the great and good Primate offered to Christ, who had placed him among the elect.*

---

* We have taken our information principally from the Life of Dr. Plunkett, by Rev. George Crolly; from the Ecclesiastical History of Ireland, by Rev. M. J. Brennan, O.S.F.; from Feller's Biographie Universelle; from Dr. Moran's Memoirs of Plunkett; and from various other sources, Protestant as well as Catholic.

OF CARROLLTON,

Signer of the Declaration of Independence.

In his deportment
Was seen a clear collectedness and ease,
A simple grace and gentle dignity,
That failed not at the first accost to please.

In public strife his spirit glowed with zeal,
For truth and justice, as its warp and woof,
For freedom as its signature and seal.

His life thus sacred from the world, discharged
From vain ambition, and inordinate care,
In virtue exercised, by reverence rare
Lifted, and by humility enlarged
Became a temple and a place of prayer.

TAYLOR.

Charles Carroll of Carrollton.

SIGNER OF THE DECLARATION OF INDEPENDENCE.

It ought to be one of the first objects of a republican people to enshrine the characters of those men to whom their prosperity may be even in part ascribed, and with whose names their national character will be associated.*

NEVER in the history of the world has a more inspiring struggle taken place than that which began by the battle of Lexington, April 19th 1775, and ended by the Treaty of Peace signed at Paris, on the 3d of September, 1783. It is not our purpose to trace out the causes of that revolution, to go back through that long list of oppressive acts, upon the part of the British Government, which finally induced the patriots of the New World to take up arms in the sacred cause of liberty. The soul-thrilling words of Patrick Henry in the Assembly of Virginia, "give me liberty, or give me death," rang like a watchword through the

---

* The Jesuit's Letters—Letter VI. from Inchiquin, dated Washington, p. 65.—These letters are a private correspondence between one Jesuit in America to another in Europe, and were said to have been accidentally brought to light. The ideas therein contained upon Washington, his government and the like, are admirable. The following passage occurs in a note to one of the letters: "No political improvements, no national institutions, no course of policy, no system, however excellent, can tend so much to make a nation happy as the disinterested exertions of individuals, exalted by their superior talents and virtue."

country. From the grand old Potomac sweeping on its way, from the calm shores of Lake Champlain on the north, from the eastern limits of Cape Cod, sounded and resounded that password of freedom. Massachusetts shouted it in triumph from her hill-tops, the mighty West heard it echoed and re-echoed through her pathless prairies, and the broad southern river bore it onward into the depths of the Gulf Stream. "If this be treason," cried he, "make the most of it." The most was made; the Virginia Assembly was forcibly closed. Boston, after its celebrated tea-party, was the next to fall under British displeasure. Her port was closed. But in spite of all the spark had kindled into a flame—a flame never to be extinguished till America was free. The struggle began; messengers bore the news from Boston to Lexington that the British were on their way thither. Every town and village, every tree and fence, afforded shelter to the Americans. The sun of liberty had appeared above the horizon, nor has it yet set, though a hundred years have lent their majesty to the graves of Washington and the patriots of the revolution.

To follow the glorious panorama of battles now opening out before us would be apart from the purpose of our sketch. But it can neither be out of place nor uninteresting to the Catholic reader to observe the part borne by our co-religionists in the struggle for independence. Their exalted patriotism should indeed free us forever from the unjust reproach that no true Catholic can be a loyal citizen. It should rather serve to establish a contrary axiom, that every true Catholic must of necessity be a loyal citizen.*

---

* A Frenchman, Du Bourg, gives the following in his description of America, quoted by J. Carroll Brent in his Biography of Archbishop Carroll: "During the last war which the United States waged

To begin by the foreign aid, which came to assist the colonists in their hour of bitter trial, when, bravely fighting against adverse circumstances, they had little but their confidence in the justice of their cause to save them from despair. Catholic France stood from the outset at the head of the list. The king gave substantial sympathy and assistance under the form of 6,000,000 francs. The queen, that fair and gracious Marie Antoinette, whose tragic death was so soon after to fill all Europe with gloom, took the interests of the colony much to heart. Many noblemen and officers were directly or indirectly encouraged to come out to America and offer their swords to the illustrious Washington. Of these latter we must be content to name the principal ones, and of course begin with Lafayette, the witty and graceful, who fitted out a vessel at his own expense, became aid-de-camp of the generalissimo, and subsequently a major-general in the Continental army. From his own vessel, the "Victory," he writes to his wife:

"From love to me become a good American. The welfare of America is closely bound up with the welfare of all mankind; it is about to become the safe asylum of virtue, tolerance, equality and peaceful liberty." *

Among the women of France he was the hero of the hour, and even the beautiful young queen gave him her admiration. A contemporary was known to say, "It is fortunate for the king that Lafayette did not take it into his head to strip Versailles of its furniture to send to his

---

against England, none were more ardent in their patriotism, none more ready to carry aid wherever it was needed, and none more active in laboring, even with their hands, in the construction of whatever was requisite for the defence, than the Catholics; so that the Protestants were compelled to acknowledge that they were excellent citizens, no less than upright and honorable men."

* Bancroft, vol. ix.

dear America, as his majesty would have been unable to refuse it."

There was D'Estaing, who arrived with his fleet at a moment of vital importance to the cause of independence, and whose assistance conduced so much to the final and famous end of the drama at Yorktown. There was Rochambeau, with his men and his squadron; the Count de Grasse, with his naval force, and a host of other brave soldiers who came to shed their blood if necessary upon this alien soil. This aid from France was never withheld, from the time when that wounded French officer appeared in Philadelphia, and, after repeated intimations that a stranger had arrived in the place, a committee was appointed to see him. They asked him his business; he said, " Gentlemen, if you want arms or ammunition you shall have them; if you want money you shall have it." They asked him his authority. "Gentlemen," he said, drawing his hand across his throat, " I shall take care of my head." He answered no further, and was seen no more in Philadelphia.

Within the last year the descendants of those heroes have been invited to American shores to participate in the celebration and the rejoicings of that far-off victory of Yorktown. What Catholic France did for the welfare of the young republic, Catholic Spain did in the measure of her ability. Though this aid was chiefly in money and goods, it was none the less acceptable, and betrayed none the less the kindly spirit which animated the Spanish people. There are accounts given, too, of services rendered by the Count de Galvez, Spanish governor of Louisiana, and one of the ablest statesmen of that day in Spain. Meanwhile, there was another little country of Europe, the very gem of Catholic States, the national misfortunes of which, and the sufferings of which, endured for religion, have made it the theme of many a ballad and romance. From Poland came the noble and disinterested Casimir Pulaski and Thaddeus Kosciusko. They were both members of ancient and honorable families, who had distinguished themselves by devotion to a hapless and hopeless cause. It was long after the War of Independence that Kosciusko, released from imprisonment by the czar, took back his sword, with the mournful words, "I have no need of a sword. I have no country to defend." He appeared before Washington, and was asked, "What can you do?" "Try me," was his laconic but forcible reply. In common with his compatriot Pulaski, he displayed the same desperate valor and loyalty that both had so often shown on the battle-fields of their native land. To Kosciusko Congress returned a vote of thanks at the end of the war. To Pulaski a monument was erected at Savannah in memory of his gallant deeds. It was at the siege of that city that he fell mortally wounded.*

Last but not least there were innumerable Irishmen who fought in this good fight, and lived to enjoy the ultimate triumph or strewed the ground with their corpses at Valley Forge, at Trenton, at White Plains, Ticonderoga, or Quebec. We do not only refer to Irish officers in the service of France, such as Count Dillon and others of his rank, who claimed from the French king the first and best right to fight against the English. We mean such men as Moylan, brother to the Roman Catholic Bishop of Cork, who organized Moylan's Dragoons, and was aid-de-camp to Washington; as Barry, the dashing and brilliant Barry, the father of the Ameri-

---

* We have made no mention here of the brave German soldiers who likewise had their share in promoting this good cause. The reason is obvious; and indeed these individual Germans were the only non-Catholic people of Europe who evinced any sympathy for the Americans.

can navy, the first naval officer who bore the title of commodore, "saucy Jack Barry, half Irishman, half Yankee," as he described himself, the incorruptible hero, who, when offered by Lord Howe 150,000 guineas and a commission in the royal navy, cried out:

"Not the value nor the command of the whole British fleet could tempt me from the American cause." He was a sincere and devoted Catholic, and, we are told, "practically religious." He left most of his possessions to the Catholic Orphan Asylum, Philadelphia, and lies at rest in St. Joseph's, of that city.

On such soldiers, again, as Colonel Fitzgerald, Washington's favorite aid-de-camp,* and an officer in the old Blue and Buffs, the first volunteer company raised in the South. At the battle of Princeton occurred the following incident: The American troops were on the point of retreating. Washington, placing himself between his men and the enemy, cried out, "Will you give up your general to the enemy?" Fitzgerald, who had taken an order to the rear, returned at this moment. He thus describes it himself:

"On my return," said he, "I perceived the General, immediately between our line and that of the enemy, both lines levelling for the decisive fire that was to decide the fortune of the day. Instantly there was a roar of musketry followed by a shout. It was the shout of victory. On raising my eyes, I discovered the enemy broken and flying, while dimly amid the glimpses of the smoke was seen Washington, alive and unharmed, waving his hat and cheering his comrades to the pursuit. I dashed my rowels into my charger's flanks, and flew to his side, exclaiming, 'Thank God! Your Excel-

---

* Mr. G. Washington Custis and other writers of note mention him at length, as also McGee, in his Irish Settlers, etc., etc.

lency is safe.' I wept like a child for joy."* Of the Irish patriots, who fought for American independence, a well-known writer says : " They may sleep in the silent tomb, but the remembrance of their virtues will be cherished while memory is dear to the American heart." Among other Catholics who played a more or less important part in the history of those stirring times we must not forget the Abbé Nicoli, Tuscan Minister to the Court of Joseph II., who was an enthusiastic "abettor of the insurgents," and did all in his power to persuade the Austrian sovereign to lend them his countenance and assistance. But the latter's conclusive " I am a king by trade," settled the matter. His heart was closed against such generous sentiments, and he would neither receive the American ambassadors, nor permit the subject of the rebellion to be mooted in his presence.† But this was the same Joseph who plotted at once against the Church and the Jesuits.

Nearer the theatre of war was Father Gibault. This eminent and patriotic ecclesiastic was pastor of Vincennes, and was truly devoted to the continental cause. He it was who blessed the arms of the French officers in the service of America, who administered the oath of allegiance to Congress in his church, and who induced the Catholic Indians to take up arms. A distinguished Protestant writer declares that, " the United States were principally indebted to Father Gibault for the accession of the States comprised in the original Northwestern Territory." ‡

It was the Catholic tribes of Maine that most nobly responded to Washington's appeal for assistance, and Orono, a devout Catholic chief, makes quite a romantic

---

* McGee's Irish Settlers. † Bancroft, vol. ix. ‡ Judge Law.

figure in early colonial history, and in the continental army, wherein he held a commission. These good and simple souls made only one stipulation, that they should have a priest with each detachment. We have thus lightly skimmed over a subject which is of the deepest interest and last importance. So noble and so valiantly sustained was, indeed, that wonderful struggle for independence, that we cannot help regarding with the highest admiration, deepest respect, and utmost sympathy, every actor who appeared upon its scenes. Now, among its actors, and more particularly among those gentlemen of birth, education and position, who were called upon to sign the immortal Declaration of Independence, none strikes us more forcibly, nor seems, as it were, to stand out more boldly from the rest, than Charles Carroll of Carrollton.

Charles Carroll came of a good old Irish stock. His grandfather was the first of the family to settle in America. He came thither about the year 1680, and settled at Annapolis in Maryland. A brief glance of the history of Maryland about this time, and for many years before and after, gives us one of the most curious instances of religious intolerance on record. It will be remembered that Lord Baltimore had established at St. Mary's, on the Chesapeake, " the first community in the world in which entire freedom of conscience was a fundamental maxim of law." * " It forms a curious fact in the history of the human mind," continues the same author,† " that exiles from intolerant episcopacy in Virginia ; persecuted dissenters from Puritan New England ; the Swedes, driven by violence from Delaware, and

---

* History of the American Revolution, by a non-Catholic writer, Samuel F. Wilson.

† Ibid.

French Huguenots from Europe, found generous protection and complete freedom of faith in a colony of Catholics.* For some time all went well, some Jesuit fathers, notably Fathers White and Altham, arrived on the shores of the Chesapeake in March, 1570. They offered up the Holy Sacrifice, and marched in procession bearing a large cross. The governor, commissioners and many others took part in this procession, and a site having been chosen, the cross was planted there, with deep and fervent devotion. " They raised the cross, a trophy to Christ the Saviour, humbly chanting, and on bended knees, the Litany of the Cross." These priests afterward went to labor, one among the Patuxent, the other among the Piscataway Indians. But others took their places, and religion was making its first steps in the colony when a revolution broke out in 1644. After that time intolerance had full sway in Maryland, the intolerance of non-Catholics against their Catholic fellow-citizens, who had first procured for them the blessings of religious liberty. This persecution of priests and Catholics had previously existed in most of the other States, but here, in the cradle of freedom, it began now to rear its head. Every possible restraint was put upon Catholics; the exercise of their religion was forbidden them, and they were consequently almost entirely without churches. This state of things continued, and was in full force on the arrival in America of Mr. Carroll, the grandfather of our hero. Some years later, in 1689, he entered the service of Lord Baltimore as his agent, and fulfilled the duties of that office with an honesty and energy which commanded the highest respect. The son of this Charles Carroll married Eliza-

---

* The "curious fact" is not apparent to us. It was only what was to be expected from a colony of devout Catholics.

beth Brookes, and it was their only son who was destined to play so important a part in the history of his country.

Of his earlier years the glimpses given by most biographers are scanty enough. He was born in the year 1737, at that old Manor House built upon the 10,000 acres which Lord Baltimore had granted to his agent. That Manor House in Anne Arundel County, Maryland, had its view of the broad rolling Patuxent, its plantation, and its wide lands attached, and it also had, what in those days the Catholic gentry of sufficient fortune and position were compelled through religious persecution to have, namely—a chapel. This chapel was to supply, in some degree, for the want of a neighboring church, and here the Carroll family on Sundays and holy-days devoutly assembled.

While Charles was still very young he was sent with his cousin John Carroll, afterwards Archbishop of Baltimore, to begin his studies with the Jesuit Fathers at Bohemia Manor. Here these indefatigable religious had established, in the face of trial and danger and discouragement, a small boarding-school, where the youth of the country might be trained in knowledge, virtue and their duties to God and man. It was as a dim foreshadowing of that great College of Georgetown, many years afterwards established by Archbishop Carroll, "on one of the loveliest and most captivating spots on the Potomac."

But many years had to elapse till then; the Carrolls were to see many trials and many changes abroad and in their native land, seas were to roll between, and divers great events, before the one cousin was to found, so to say, the Catholic Church in America, and the other to stand foremost among the defenders of national liberty.

The record of both boys at their elementary school was good, though their stay there was but short. Charles Carroll, at the age of eleven, bade farewell to his native Maryland, which he was not to see for many years, accompanied by his cousin, the future archbishop. It is probable the boy's heart was scarcely mature enough as yet to feel more than a brief and passing sadness at this separation from home, with its sweet and tender associations, from favorite playmates and beloved parents. The next six years were spent with his cousin at the Jesuit College of St. Omer, in France. Here the boy's natural love of learning displayed itself, and that fine and polished intellect of after years began to develop within the walls of that celebrated sanctuary of learning. St. Omer was followed by a year at Rheims, Rheims by two years at the famous College of Louis le Grand, Paris, Paris by Bourges, and Bourges by England. In each of these places, which we shall momentarily regard in detail, highly colored threads of the old romantic life of Continental Europe were woven into the warp and woof of the young man's existence, that existence which was to ripen and grow to old age among strange and troublous scenes in his native country. There was St. Omer, the quaint, quiet, almost mediæval town, Rheims, with its histories of grand pageants and its gorgeous historical memorials, where the gloom of rich cathedrals was brightened by the burnished gold or steel of many mail-clad warriors; where kings came in triumph to bend the head, and receive from the hands of archbishops the gem-studded diadem of France; where the most wondrous event in the world's history was enacted, and the peasant maid, the virgin of Domremy, restored to France her king. Bourges, that living chronicle of olden days, all were to have their effect in making the boy what he afterwards became. But they had all little in common with the newer and more varied phases of life through which the mind of the student passed in those two great centres of civilization, Paris and London. Not that the gay, brilliant life of the French capital could entirely dispel the growing shadows of age that were darkening around that far-famed College of Louis le Grand. The name of those shades was legion ; the poet and the saint, the courtier and the general, the noble and the rich citizen, the gifted and the witty and the learned, all alike passed from its portals into the amphitheatre of life. But they bore with them their *alma mater's* ineffaceable mark ; the something indefinably chivalrous in bearing, indefinably courteous in manner, the scarcely perceptible vein of romance, the remnant of the true old French knightly spirit which the preceptors had encouraged rather than discountenanced. The two years which Charles Carroll spent therein passed rapidly away, but not so their effect. The polished and erudite debater of after days, the patriot and the statesman, bore "its shadow plain to see." After a year more at Bourges the student proceeded to England, specially to continue his law studies at the Inns Temple. It was an abrupt change from Bourges, it was an abrupt change from the royally endowed college where the young gentlemen of France were instructed not only in science and religion, but in all the accomplishments suitable to their rank, fortune and position. The manner of life was totally different, but the young man formed many warm friendships in London during the seven years of his stay there. At the end of that time he thought of returning to America. He returned alone.

His cousin and schoolfellow, John Carroll, had long since entered the novitiate of the Society of Jesus, and was some years previous to this a priest. In 1764 Charles Carroll set sail for home, his heart full of strange and varied emotions. The boy returned a man, with the ripe judgment, scholarly intellect and polished manners which his long absence in foreign countries and his experience of various peoples and places had given him.

The first years of his return home were those in which revolutionary principles began to be rife in the breasts of the colonists. Not that they desired revolution, nor at first even separation from the mother country. But they were growing every day more determined to preserve those inalienable rights and sacred liberties which they had crossed the sea to find. Our hero almost from the first entered with animation into the subject of political freedom. His clear judgment and quick perception saw where the weakness lay in the system of government which the mother country was trying to impose upon the colonies. It was somewhere about 1770 that he became involved in the famous polemical warfare with the eminent lawyer Dulany. It was a question of principle between the people versus Governor Eden. Mr. Carroll's logic in favor of the former was unanswerable. He had precisely the temper of mind to encounter such an antagonist, and the courage of his opinions to maintain the right. In this controversy he assumed the soubriquet of First Citizen, in allusion to a dialogue once published on a similar subject under the names of First and Second Citizens.

There was a softer episode in his life about this time, for it must not be supposed that that old manor house near the Patuxent had not its measure of romance, the golden thread of poetry, to brighten the dark tissue of actual fact.

In 1768 Mr. Carroll married Mary Darnall, a kinswoman of Lord Baltimore. This marriage, contracted under the most auspicious circumstances, with the full approbation of all concerned, was destined to be of brief duration. While the four children born of this union were still quite young, Mrs. Carroll died, and the husband, inconsolable for her loss, devoted himself heart and soul to the affairs of his country. Three of his children, Catherine, Mary, and Charles, remained to become the joy and solace of their afflicted father, but the fourth, Eliza, died in early childhood.

Some years after Mr. Carroll proposed to another Mary Darnall, a cousin of his wife and a rich heiress; he was accepted.

After his triumph in the First Citizen contest he was greeted with acclamation by the citizens of Annapolis. They made a public demonstration in his honor, and tendered him the thanks of the community. He was, in fact, already fast coming into prominence as a bold and fearless patriotic leader. It was about this time that Maryland replied, in answer to Governor Sharpe's message, " that they would not be deterred from joining in constitutional measures for common objects with the legislatures of the other colonies." " We shall not be intimidated," continued they, " by a few sounding phrases from doing what we think to be right."

It was about this time, too, and when the temper of the people was such as we have seen, that Charles Carroll boldly urged upon the naval commander, Stewart, the necessity of resolute action in regard to the tea with which his vessel was loaded. The commander had wavered and wavered, but this word in season decided him. The vessel was burned to the water's edge, and the people of Annapolis thus added their protest to those which had been going up from the other States. Some time before, in a letter to a friend, Mr. Carroll had broadly asserted the determination of the people to resist all such oppressive deeds as the passage of the ever-memorable Stamp Act, and declared that so great was their love of liberty that nothing but an armed force could ever overcome their opposition to the unjust principle of taxation without representation. Some years afterwards he wrote to this same friend the famous and truly inspiring words:

"The British troops, if sent here, will find naught but enemies before and behind them. If we are beaten in the plains we will retire to our mountains and defy them. They will be masters but of the spot on which they encamp. Necessity will force us to exertion, until, tired of combatting in vain against a spirit which victory after victory cannot subdue, your armies will evacuate our soil, and your country retire, an immense loser from the contest." Such was the spirit which animated the man, and when the people of Maryland, somewhere as early as 1773, joined with the other States in a fearless and resolute opposition to the encroachments of the home government, they found an active leader, a polished yet forcible mouthpiece, a courteous yet formidable champion of their views in the subject of our sketch.

Mr. Carroll's eminent public services were at last beginning to make a favorable impression upon those who had hitherto regarded him with the liveliest distrust and even hostility, as a Papist and an emissary of the Jesuits. He was heart and soul devoted to that faith, which had been so carefully fostered in him from infancy upwards. It now bore its fruits in the stand which he took to have the disgraceful statutes of religious intolerance effaced from the Constitution of Maryland. This laudable object he earnestly pursued for some years, and strained every nerve for its accomplishment. "A committee to prepare a declaration of the rights and form of government for this State," had a most zealous and efficient member in our hero. This was a year before the Revolution, consequently in 1775. That their efforts were crowned with the measure of success which they deserved, our after glimpses of the history of Maryland fully prove.

Meantime, strange events were occurring in Europe. There was the bitter and impious warfare against the Jesuits in Portugal which afterwards extended to France and other continental countries. This outbreak drew forth from various archbishops, cardinals and even the popes themselves, an energetic and indignant protest against this unjust and unworthy persecution of a society, which, to quote the Archbishop of Paris, Christopher Beaumont, "is *pious*, because the Council of Trent has so declared it, is *venerable*, as it was styled by the illustrious Bossuet." The Pope, Clement XIII., speaks of it as "an Institute, useful to the Church, long approved by the Apostolic See, honored by the Roman pontiffs and the Council of Trent with imperishable praise." He declared that he shuddered in saying that the men were "by violence dispensed from the observance of those sacred vows they had taken before God's altar." However, the whole pontificate of Clement XIII., and, indeed, that of his predecessor, Benedict, was spent in vainly defending this noble company. During the reign of Clement XIV. such pressure was brought to bear on him that, like "one who sacrifices his most precious goods to allay the fury of the storm,"* he issued his famous Bull "Dominus ac Redemptor," suppressing the Society of Jesus, "its houses, functions and offices."

It would be idle here to bring forward the innumerable proofs of what is so widely known to Catholics, namely, that the Bull, as its very wording suggests, was a mere matter of expediency, which none more deeply

---

* Abbé Darras, Church History, vol. iv.

regretted than the sovereign Pontiff himself. To be assured of this, we need only remember that other, though not so widely known Bull, " Cœlestium Munerum Thesauros:" "It is with joy and happiness that we bestow of the abundance of heavenly treasures upon those who earnestly seek the good of souls, as we reckon among those faithful laborers in the vineyard, the religious of the Society of Jesus. We most assuredly desire to nourish and increase, by spiritual favors, the enterprising and active piety and zeal of those religious." This Bull, indeed, marked the beginning of his pontificate, and served but to bring down upon his head the full fury of the storm.

If we have alluded to this subject here, and if our so doing should seem an unwarrantable digression, the reader must remember that this occurrence had a twofold and apparently contradictory effect upon the Catholics of America. In the first place, the effect was decidedly unfavorable; it deprived them of their most zealous and indefatigable pastors and missionaries, and at a time when both had still to encounter the turmoil of religious strife and the fury of religious intolerance. But, in the second place, it militated favorably upon the infant Church, by bringing out Father Carroll, the Jesuit, to his native land. His arrival, about 1774, was an occasion of lively joy to the Carroll family and to the Catholics of Maryland in general. His after career, as Vicar-Apostolic, Bishop and Archbishop cannot be here considered. But we know that he was the patriarch and pioneer of Catholic faith in Maryland, and, indeed, in his whole vast diocese, which for some time included the thirteen original colonies.

Some two years after Father Carroll's arrival, in the spring of 1776, Charles Carroll was requested to persuade his cousin, the Jesuit, to accompany him on a mission, which was just then being planned to Canada.* It was a diplomatic mission of a delicate nature, and had for its object to persuade the people of Canada to join with the United Colonies in the coming struggle, or, at least, to remain neutral. Charles Carroll, Samuel Chase and Benjamin Franklin were the lay commissioners, and Father Carroll the only clerical. He had consented to co-operate with them to the extent of inducing the Canadians to remain neutral; further than that he declared he could not go, deeming it incompatible with his profession as a minister of the Gospel. On the 2d of April, 1776, they set out from New York, sailed up the Hudson, and continued their voyage from Albany to Montreal, with all the discomforts and hardships which made travelling in those days a species of martyrdom. The voyage lasted a month. The details given of this journey are not numerous. What we principally know of it is, the failure of its object. That which the lay commissioners did among

---

* We subjoin an extract from the Archbishop's letter to his mother: "We have come," he says, "at length to the end of our long and tedious journey, after meeting with several delays on account of the impassable condition of the lakes. We were received here (Montreal) at the landing by General Arnold, and a great body of officers, gentry, etc., and saluted by firing of cannon and other military honors." He goes on to speak at some length of the social civilities offered them, and continues (letter of Archbishop Carroll, from Brent. Biography of Archbishop Carroll, pp. 40–43), describing the journey homeward, speaking of New York as " no more the gay, polite place it used to be esteemed;" but as "almost a desert except for the troops." At Albany they were entertained by General Schuyler. "At Ticonderoga," he says, "we embarked on the great Lake of Champlain. We had a passage of three days and a half. We always came to in the night time. Passengers generally encamp in the woods, making a covering of the boughs of trees, and large fires at their feet. But as we had a good awning to our boat, etc., I chose to sleep on board."

the Canadian people, Father Carroll did among the clergy. But in vain. Many reasons militated against them. In the first place, it was but the year before that the Continental Congress had sent their foolish and insolent protest to Lord North against the passage of the Quebec Act; the Quebec Act being simply legislation to confirm the French Canadian Catholics in the freedom of conscience previously enjoyed under the French régime. The terms in which this remonstrance was couched were, to say the least, bigoted, fanatical and abhorrent to every member of the Catholic Church. The Canadians could not forget, and though Congress offered them the most advantageous terms, and proffered complete and entire freedom in religious matters, the people of Canada were chary of connecting themselves with a country wherein religious intolerance had been so long rampant. It was a spirit which had come out as an evil legacy from the mother country, and a stain which it required the purifying influence of the Revolution to purge out. Added to this there was the conciliatory policy of Governor Guy Carleton, one of the most popular of English Viceroys of that day. To Father Carroll the clergy made the same response that the lay seculars did to the other commissioners; they said they could not encourage their flock to take up arms for a chimerical liberty, when they were even then in possession of all its most solid advantages. Hence, though they were treated with every courtesy, this mission to Canada totally failed. The French Canadian people, indeed, for the most part, and especially in some districts, combatted the Americans during the progress of the war with little enthusiasm. But our space forbids us to enter into such details. The commissioners returned to New York, Father Carroll and Benjamin Franklin first, the others following. From this journey dates a warm friendship between the Jesuit and the philosopher.

Charles Carroll having returned to Maryland, first paying a visit to Washington, then to New York, entered heart and soul into the plans for the coming contest. And it must be remarked that his cousin, the future Archbishop, was a no less sincere and enlightened patriot. It would have been hard indeed for such generous and noble breasts as theirs to remain unmoved. The cry of freedom was going up from the heart of that vast continent, the broad rolling streams of which, the lofty mountains and unconfined vastness of whose prairie lands, seemed incompatible with any other idea than that of liberty. But here let us mark the difference: liberty might look down and smile; there were no bloody massacres to be done in her name, no established order of things to be overthrown, no anarchy to be produced, no injustice, no rapine, no robbery; simply there was to be a just and noble struggle, in which no right of humanity, no sacred authority was to be violated. It was for the defence and freedom of that native land, which had grown dearer and more hallowed from the toils and dangers and hardships suffered there in those sturdy, vigorous pioneer days.

Soon after his return from Canada, Charles Carroll was elected member of the Continental Congress, where, as Bancroft remarks, "the disfranchised Catholics of Maryland saw in him the emblem of their disenthralment."* Proud title this, prouder even that that one which was to follow, for he was none too soon to take his place in that noble phalanx of heroes, the signers of the Declaration of Independence. For 1776 was the immortal year, when freedom offered to the world this spectacle of honest, sincere and enlightened patriots, assembling to frame and affix their signatures to

---

* Bancroft's U. S. Hist., vol. ix.

that imperishable document, which in its significance and its results has had no parallel in history. It was upon the Fourth of July, that day of which John Adams thus speaks in a letter to his wife:

"I am apt to believe that it will be celebrated by succeeding generations as the great Anniversary Festival. It ought to be commemorated as the day of deliverance by solemn acts of devotion to God Almighty. It ought to be solemnized with pomp, shows, games, sports, guns, bells, bonfires and illuminations, from one end of the continent to the other, from this time forward forever."

Of that glorious proclamation, which was that day given forth to the people of the United States, he thus speaks:

"You will think me transported with enthusiasm, but I am not. I am well aware of the toil, the blood, the treasure that it will cost us to maintain this declaration, and support and defend these States. Yet through all the gloom I can see the rights of light and glory; I can see that the end is worth more than all the means, and that posterity will triumph, although you and I may rue, which I hope we shall not."

It was an inspiring moment indeed. The vicinity of the old State House, Philadelphia, was a living mass of breathless, expectant beings. The city streets were crowded; the people were eager and excited. The very bell-ringer, at his post in the belfry of the building, had stationed his son below, bidding him tell him when the Declaration was passed. All morning long he stayed at his post, alternating between hope and fear, and sometimes exclaiming in despair, "They'll never, never do it." About two o'clock the report of the committee was adopted, and it but remained for the signers to affix their names. There was not an instant's irresolution. With brave and lofty determination they advanced each in turn. No writing was clearer or more unfaltering than that of Charles Carroll. The slight incident, which has attached to his name a peculiar and enduring glory, occurred in this wise: As he signed the paper, a voice, said to be that of Benjamin Franklin, spoke out: "There go millions," in allusion to his wealth. But a second voice, said, "No, he cannot be identified; there are many Charles Carrolls."

This decided the patriot. He did not desire safety which could not be shared by his fellows. He advanced again, adding to his signature the significant appendage, "of Carrollton," remarking as he did so, "They cannot mistake me now."

Noble words, noble scene, and worthy of the cause which these men served. Almost at the moment the lad stationed below clapped his hands, crying out to the bell-ringer, "Ring, ring!" There was a peal of joy such as the old man had never put into his bell before, and the wonderful news was proclaimed by that ancient bell which bore upon its sides the strangely appropriate inscription, "Proclaim liberty throughout all the land, to all the inhabitants thereof."

Such booming of cannon as there was after that, such cheering among the people, such lighting of bonfires, such congratulations and such wishing each other joy! Surely they forgot the dark and deadly struggle that had to come. They knew only that they were proclaimed "free, sovereign and independent States." In New York, by order of General Washington, the decree of Congress was read at the head of every brigade in the army. The rejoicings there, as well as throughout the other colonies, were no less cordial and heartfelt. Yet it was only the first scene in a glorious but sanguinary drama.

During the years that followed Mr. Carroll continued to serve his country in the arena of political life. He soon after retired from the Continental Congress, remaining there but two or three years after the Declaration. He, however, divided his time for many years to come between the duties of State Senator in his native Maryland and those of United States Senator in Congress. His labors thenceforth were many and varied. Such men as he were, at this trying crisis of affairs, needed to stand in the breach. His political sagacity, clear judgment, long and varied experience of men and manners, his energy, his devotion to the cause, and his uncompromising honesty made him the man amongst men, to unite with his co-laborers in the formation of a just, solid and harmonious form of government to suit the exigencies of the time and circumstances. Nor did he neglect meanwhile to identify himself closely with the movements of the Catholic party. Soon after the election of Washington to the Presidency, Mr. Carroll, in conjunction with his co-religionists, sent to him the following address, which we do not think it out of place to give here in full.

Address of the Roman Catholics to George Washington, President of the United States:

" SIR:—We have been long impatient to testify our joy and unbounded confidence on your being called, by a unanimous vote, to the first station of a country, in which that unanimity could not have been obtained without the previous merit of unexampled services, of eminent wisdom and unblemished virtue. Our congratulations have not reached you sooner, because our scattered situation prevented the communication and the collecting of those sentiments which warmed every breast. But the delay has furnished us with the opportunity, not merely of presaging the happiness to be expected under your administration, but of bearing testimony to that which we experience already. It is your peculiar talent in war and in peace to afford security to those who commit their protection into your hands. In war, you shield them from the ravages of armed hostility; in peace, you establish public tranquillity, by the justice and moderation, not less than by the vigor of your government. By example, as well as by vigilance, you extend the influence of laws on the manners of our fellow-citizens. You encourage respect for religion, and inculcate, by word and action, that principle on which the welfare of nations so much depends, that a superintending Providence governs the events of the world, and watches over the conduct of men. Your exalted maxims and unwearied attention to the moral and physical improvement of our country have produced already the happiest effects. Under your administration America is animated with zeal for the attainment and encouragement of useful literature; she improves her agriculture, extends her commerce, and acquires with foreign nations a dignity unknown to her before. From these happy events, in which none can feel a warmer interest than ourselves, we derive additional pleasure by recollecting, that you, sir, have been the principal instrument in effecting so rapid a change in our political situation. This prospect of national prosperity is peculiarly pleasing to us on another account, because, whilst our country preserves her freedom and independence, we shall have a well-founded title to claim from her justice, the equal rights of citizenship, as the price of our blood spilt under your eyes, and of our common exertions for her defence, under your auspicious conduct; rights rendered more dear to us by the remembrance of former hardships. When we pray for the preservation of them, where they have been granted, and expect the full extension of them from the justice of those States, which still restrict them, when we solicit the protection of Heaven over our common country, we neither omit, nor can omit, recommending your preservation to the singular care of Divine Providence; because we conceive that no human means are so available to promote the welfare of the United States, or the prolongation of your health and life, in which are included the energy of your example, the wisdom of your counsels, and the persuasive eloquence of your virtues.

"In behalf of the Roman Catholic Clergy,
"J. CARROLL.
"In behalf of the Roman Catholic Laity,
"CHARLES CARROLL of Carrollton,
"DANIEL CARROLL,*
"THOMAS FITZSIMMONS,
"DOMINICK LYNCH."

In reply to this address, Washington wrote as follows:

"*To the Roman Catholics in the United States of America:*

"GENTLEMEN:—While I now receive with much satisfaction your congratulations on my being called, by a unanimous vote, to the first station in my country, I cannot but duly notice your politeness in offering an apology for the unavoidable delay. As that delay has given you an opportunity of realizing, instead of anticipating, the benefits of the general government, you will do me the justice to believe that your testimony of the increase of the public prosperity enhances the pleasure which I should otherwise have experienced from your affectionate address. I feel that my conduct, in war and in peace, has met with more general approbation than could reasonably have been expected; and I find myself disposed to consider that fortunate circumstance, in a great degree, resulting from the able support and extraordinary candor of my fellow-citizens of all denominations.

---

* A cousin of our hero.

"The prospect of national prosperity now before us is truly animating, and ought to excite the exertions of all good men to establish and secure the happiness of their country, in the permanent duration of its freedom and independence. America, under the smiles of a Divine Providence, the protection of a good government, and the cultivation of manners, morals and piety, cannot fail to attain an uncommon degree of eminence, in literature, commerce, agriculture, improvements at home, and respectability abroad. As mankind becomes more liberal, they will be more apt at all times to allow that all those who conduct themselves as worthy members of the community are equally entitled to the protection of civil government. I hope ever to see America among the foremost nations in examples of justice and liberality. And I presume that your fellow-citizens will not forget the patriotic part which you took in the accomplishment of their revolution, or the establishment of their government, or the important assistance which they received from a nation in which the Roman Catholic faith is professed.

"I thank you, gentlemen, for your kind concern for me. While my life and health shall continue, in whatever situation I may be, it shall be my constant endeavor to justify the favorable sentiments which you are pleased to express of my conduct. And may the members of your society in America, animated alone by the pure spirit of Christianity, and still conducting themselves as the faithful subjects of our free government, enjoy every temporal and spiritual felicity.

"G. WASHINGTON."

Now that, as we have said, the new Constitution was in gradual process of completion, Charles Carroll and the other Catholics of Maryland and the United States began to consider the necessity of obtaining some recognition from Congress of their religious rights. The vague and indefinite pronunciamento of Congress in 1775 did not satisfy these true-hearted men, who foresaw a time when rights and liberties, dearer to them, and holier even than those for which they had so freely shed their blood, might be again imperilled. They were resolved to free their posterity from the curse of intolerance, the bitter fruits of which they had themselves tasted. Congress said, in 1775: "As our opposition to the settled plan of the British administration to enslave America will be strengthened by a union of all ranks of men within this province, we do most earnestly recommend that all former differences about religion or politics, and all private animosities and quarrels of every kind, from henceforth cease, and be forever buried in oblivion." This answered its purpose in 1775, but in 1784 the Catholics of America wanted a more explicit and definite acknowledgment of their position. They were aware of their eminent services to the cause of independence, and felt themselves justified, by every title, in demanding recognition from the government. A memorial was consequently drawn up, signed and presented to Congress. Once again we find the name of Charles Carroll of Carrollton, ever foremost in every noble scheme, of his cousin the Archbishop, Dominick Lynch, George Meade, father of the late Major-General Meade of the United States Army, and Thomas Fitzsimmons, who are mentioned as the framers of this document. It was presented to Congress principally through the exertions of Washington. That enlightened patriot and statesman was fully aware of the important services rendered by Catholics to the cause of independence, and of the impolicy of inviting disunion by a renewal of the old spirit of intolerance. His personal esteem for many members of the Catholic party no doubt had its effect. His own body-guard was principally composed of Catholics, and he knew innumerable instances of their courage, patriotism and devotion. For the Carrolls personally it is said that Washington entertained the highest esteem, and when going from place to place, and met, as usual, by a band of patriots, Bishop Carroll's hand was always the first he grasped. The Hon. Mr. Custis, a nephew of Washington's, refers to the Archbishop as follows: "From his exalted worth as a minister of God, his stainless character as a man, and above all, his distinguished services as a patriot of the Revolution, Dr. Carroll stood high, very high, in the esteem and affection of the Pater Patriæ." And as to Charles Carroll, we know that Washington visited him at his manor, and on all occasons treated him with confidence and respect.

The memorial and the efforts of the Catholics resulted in the Third Article of Amendment to the Constitution, namely, that "Congress shall make no law respecting the establishment of religion, or prohibiting the free exercise thereof." Surely an important concession, when seen in the light of past intolerance. Somewhere about the age of sixty-three Mr. Carroll retired from public life. Thenceforth it is our privilege to see him in the calm seclusion of his home, where he devoted his time to private affairs, and the pursuit of elegant learning and classical literature. Need we say that the pupil of St. Omer and of Louis le Grand was an accomplished scholar? He delighted in the study of the classics, finding in them, as it were, a rich mine of intellectual delights, and was known to say, "After the Bible read Cicero."

These latter years of the veteran statesman's life form a charming picture. He dwelt at the old Manor House, which was furnished and appointed with a luxury and comfort to which those early colonial days were no strangers. Speaking of a date much anterior to this an esteemed correspondent * tells us that the larger cities of the colonies "were almost on a par with London, certainly with any other English city, in luxury, dress, etc. You know," he continues, "it was the reports of the English officers, in regard to the elegance of living which they witnessed, which led to the taxation of the colonies, and this, again, to the Revolution. The costumes were those of the English of the same period, certainly not more than a few months behind the extremes of the fashion. Remember, I am speaking of people in good circumstances, which remark extends to *all the patentees or large landholders on their manors or holdings.*"

Of manners, he says, "There was a great deal more dignity than at present. It was yet the era of the Minuet."

"In person," says another correspondent, "Mr. Carroll was slight and rather below the middle size. His face was strongly marked, his eye quick and piercing, his manners easy, affable, and graceful, while in all the elegancies of polite life few men were his superiors." A portrait of him can be seen in the Rotunda at Washington, as also in Independence Hall, Philadelphia, where each of the signers hangs upon the wall, silent for evermore, but still forcibly attesting their convictions.

The Doughoregan Manor, as it now stands, is one of those true old Southern mansions which has been built and added to by several succeeding generations, until at this date it presents a large, wide front. It is beautifully situated in the midst of richly cultivated fields and orchards,

---

* Gen. J. Watts de Peyster. The extract above quoted is from a letter of his to the author, Nov. 5, 1878.

with splendid woods behind, and it is through these woods that a broad and spacious avenue winds up from the Lodge. The several parts of the building now form a pleasing whole. At one end is a pretty little chapel, St. Mary's, the silvery bell of which is heard on Sundays, calling all at the distant " Quarter" to Mass. The chapel seats about three hundred, and is principally for the use of the family and people of the estate, although the neighboring families also attend there. The walls are frescoed, with panels of blue; the windows are of stained glass; the altar is of white marble, brought from Italy by the late Colonel Carroll, father of the present resident and proprietor, Hon. John Lee Carroll. At either side are handsome marble tablets sacred to the memory of deceased members of the family. A white marble slab is likewise let into the floor of the aisle. A very fine painting, " Christ Curing the Sick and Maimed at the Gate of the Temple," hangs over the altar, while to the left, just above the seats occupied by the family, is an exquisite copy of Murillo's Immaculate Conception.

The wing at the other end of the building, corresponding to that in which is the chapel, has a billiard-room, and above are the servants' apartments. The centre and oldest part contains drawing-rooms and dining-rooms, where George Washington and most of the signers were entertained. They are all panelled and hung with family pictures from the very first Carroll down to the last. Other valuable portraits likewise adorn the walls. These rooms, as well as the library, boudoir, hall, and staircase are exactly as they were in the signer's time. The rest of the house is more modern both in style and furniture, but yet all full of quaint and historical remembrances. At front and back are two wide porticos with pillars and floor of gray and white marble. At the back this portico extends the whole length in a wide veranda, and overlooks an exquisite lawn, laid out in terraces, smooth spreading lawns, and flower-beds, but especially beautified by fine old trees, which lift their lofty heads to the heavens. Two giant catalpas and two ancient weeping-willows particularly attract the eye. They are the more deserving of notice that they were planted by the two daughters of Charles Carroll, when they were quite young, and still bear their names, Catherine and Mary. Beyond this lawn the eye loses itself in green meadows and corn-fields, with a background of forest trees.

In front the carriage-drive sweeps round a wide circle, the only ornament of which is four magnificent old trees, locust and elm, besides some palms and Australian ferns in the summer-time. Sloping down beyond the circle is an avenue of locust-trees leading to the " Quarter," which lies below, hidden by a delightful grove. This is quite a village, inhabited by the colored people belonging to the manor, and who, now no longer slaves, still prefer remaining with the old family. In the house are several of the older hands who still remember the signer very well. In his lifetime there were upwards of a thousand slaves upon the estate. At the Manor Mr. Carroll is never known but as " The Signer." Every one, grandchildren, servants, and all, calls him so.*

There is no doubt that the Revolution, and the causes leading thereto, may have put a check upon a luxury, especially in dress, which under the circumstances would have been ill-timed and misplaced. The receptions of Washington may have been graced as often by the homespun garment, as by the exquisitely fine English cloth

---

* The account of the Manor and other valuable information was sent through a kind and valued friend, now residing with the Carroll family, and the letters which appear on page 213 through the courtesy of Hon. John Lee Carroll, to both of whom the author returns thanks.

of other days, and it is not unlikely that the stiff broideries, the plush and brocade, and all the gorgeousness of apparel, which marked the Paris of Louis XV., and found its way to the colonies, may have gradually fallen into discredit and disuse, under a form of government whose boast must henceforth be its simplicity. But we know that under the *régime* of the first two or three Presidents there was a strong flavor of old-world punctiliousness, and courtliness of dress and manners, which democratic theories and even practices were powerless to destroy. Such a flavor remained likewise about the old manor houses, like subtle aromas from long withered herbs, and it lent a poetry and a pomp and a stateliness to the declining years of the venerable patriot, which seem most in harmony with his life and character. He was wealthy for those days, and the appointments of his Manor of Doughoregan were all of the handsomest and most luxurious. His household consisted of some two hundred and eighty-five slaves, the linen and other articles of domestic use were imported direct from England,* as well as the clothing for the family. In such surroundings grew to womanhood the two daughters of Mr. Carroll, one of whom, Mrs. Caton, was the mother of the three beautiful sisters who became historical as "the American graces." Mrs. Patterson, (Mary Caton),† the eldest, who afterwards married the Marquis of Wellesley, brother to the Duke of Wellington, was the handsomest and most celebrated of the graces. It was of her that the Prince Regent, afterwards George the Fourth, exclaimed, "Is it possible that the world can produce so beautiful a woman?" The Marquis was, at the time of his marriage, Lord Lieutenant of Ireland,

---

* Up to the time of the Revolution at least.
† Sister-in-law to the wife of Jerome Bonaparte.

and his young American bride was called upon to preside over a country, where the people were charmed to see "the Lord Lieutenant's lady attending chapel." Strange sight indeed there, whence her ancestors had fled by reason of their faith. She ruled right royally; and, according to an account given by an eye-witness of her first ball at the Castle, appeared "every inch a queen." "Certainly," continued he, "no other court in Europe could have produced a woman of greater elegance or more accomplished manners than the American Queen of the Irish Court." Her sisters, Elizabeth and Louisa Caton, became, respectively, Elizabeth, Lady Stafford, and Louisa, Lady Hervey, afterwards Duchess of Leeds. All England bent before their fresh new beauty, which rested like a crown upon the peerless sisters. But let us observe that contemporaries unanimously describe them as women who, amid all the licentiousness of the time, "stand out in brilliant contrast in all the sweet enchantment of purest womanhood." Their "irreproachable conduct" was no less the subject of admiration than their beauty. Lady Wellesley, who, afterwards became First Lady-in-Waiting at Windsor Castle, in the reign of William the Fourth, when her husband was Comptroller of the Household, was "admired excessively by the king, because of her freedom from all court gallantry."* They were in a word true Catholic ladies, worthy of the race from which they sprung.

Meanwhile, far off there in America, their grandfather was receiving the homage of his fellow-citizens, and going down the decline of years with the serene majesty that "life in its Holy Saturday" lends to such as he. "In the life of Charles Carroll," says a biographer,† "we

---

* For details on this subject, see Harper's Monthly, Sept., 1880.
† L. C. Judson, in his Biography of the Signers of Independence.

have an example worthy the imitation of youth, of manhood, of old age; of the lawyer, the statesman, the patriot and the Christian. His career was guided by virtue and prudence; his every action marked with honesty, frankness and integrity; richly meriting and largely receiving the esteem and veneration of a nation of FREEMEN."

All the distinguished men of his day visited him at Doughoregan, eager to see and to converse with the late relic of a so glorious day; hither came the courtly, grave and gentle Washington, not unwilling to exchange reminiscences with this pillar of the people's rights; hither came the brilliant Lafayette, the hero of the French Court of that day, the admired even of the beautiful queen; hither came foreign ambassadors, and men of note, travelling merely for pleasure; and hither came generals, senators, statesmen and officers, both naval and military, who had had each their part in that fierce and mighty struggle, and now came, in the calmness of peace and prosperity, to speak of it as of a something past. Jefferson, Adams, Hancock, Monroe, Franklin, all met betimes in that ancient drawing-room, and in the courtly parlance, dress and manner of the day, discoursed upon what had been and was to be. The conversation of Mr. Carroll must, indeed, have been of great and varied interest; for besides his store of anecdotes relating to the early colonial times, and the rough pioneer days, memory must have frequently led him backwards to recollections of life in Europe, episodes of his stay at that seat of learning and chivalry, the College of Louis le Grand. We can imagine that often the mention of a name recalled to him scenes in which he had been an actor, or that distinguished men in England or on the Continent were remembered by him as old schoolmates, or fellow-students at law.

In the usual course of human affairs "the sun of glory

shines but on the tomb of greatness." But not so with
Charles Carroll. He received innumerable testimonies
of the esteem in which he was held by his countrymen.
"The good and great made pilgrimages to his dwelling
to behold with their own eyes the venerable political
patriarch of America." Mr. Carroll's home was one of
the great social centres of the day, as we have already
shown; its courtly and cordial hospitality was proverbial;
there wit, intellect and fashion met on equal terms; the
conversations were sprightly and brilliant, yet dignified
and stately. Charles Carroll upon one occasion received a
deputation from the assembled Catholic Bishops of the
First Council of Baltimore. This was a mark of respect
which he appreciated above all others. It touched him
deeply, and appealed to that loyal, generous heart of
his, which had been equally true to his country, his religion and his God. For this model citizen, this incorruptible patriot, was also a model Catholic, a devout
child of Holy Church. He delighted to adorn the
chapel attached to his dwelling, which was richly and
tastefully ornamented.* He was present every day at
the Divine Sacrifice, and usually served Mass himself
until he was over eighty years of age. He jealously
guarded this privilege, and would suffer none to en-
croach upon it, for he held it as his highest honor. His
library was composed in great part of works of piety.
Milner's End of Controversy is spoken of by biographers
as one of his favorite books. Bossuet's History of the
Variations of Protestant Churches, and the Abbé Mc-
Geoghan's History of Ireland, had also a conspicuous
place upon the shelves.

---

* The author remembers hearing the late illustrious Dr. Brownson
describe an occasion upon which he heard Mass in the Carroll Chapel,
at the manor. He spoke of it as most impressive, the family devoutly
assembled, and the colored slaves to form a background.

In June of the year 1824, John Quincy Adams sent him, at the hands of Congress, two fac-simile copies of the original Declaration of Independence. The letter accompanying it so fully displays the sentiments of the American people in his regard, that we transcribe it *verbatim*.

"*To Charles Carroll of Carrollton :*

"SIR : In pursuance of a joint resolution of the two Houses of Congress, a copy of which is hereto annexed, and by direction of the President of the United States, I have the honor of transmitting to you two fac-simile copies of the original Declaration of Independence, engrossed on parchments, conformable to a secret resolution of Congress, of July 19, 1776, to be signed by every member of Congress, and accordingly signed on the 2d day of August of the same year. Of this document, unparalleled in the history of mankind, the original, deposited in this department, exhibits your name as one of the subscribers. The rolls herewith transmitted are exact copies, as exact as the art of engraving can present, of the instrument of itself, as well as of the signers to it. While performing the duty thus assigned me, permit me to felicitate you, and the country, which is reaping the reward of your labors, as well that your hand was affixed to that record of glory, as that after the lapse of nearly half a century, you live to receive this tribute of gratitude from your children, the present fathers of the land.

"With every sentiment of veneration, I have the honor of subscribing myself,

"Your fellow-citizen,

"JOHN QUINCY ADAMS."

This great and good man gives us an admirable epitome of his life, in those words, which have become almost as well known as his famous utterance upon the occasion of the signing of the Declaration:

"I have lived," says he, "to my ninety-sixth year; I have enjoyed continued health; I have been blessed with great wealth, prosperity, and most of the good things which the world can bestow: public approbation, esteem, applause; but what I now look back upon with the greatest satisfaction to myself, is that I have practised the duties of my religion." Grander words these than any he had spoken throughout a long and truly eventful career.

The following extracts from two letters to his son will serve to give a further insight into the truly pious and Christian sentiments which animated this model gentleman.

"April 12, 1821,

"In writing to you I deem it my duty to call your attention to the shortness of this life, the certainty of death, and of that dread judgment which we must all undergo, and on the decision of which a happy or a miserable eternity depends. The impious man said in his heart, 'There is no God.' He would willingly believe there is no God; his passions, the corruption of his heart, would fain persuade him that there is not; the stings of conscience betray the emptiness of the delusion; the heavens proclaim the existence of God, and unperverted reason teaches that He must love virtue and hate vice, and reward the one and punish the other."

"We should not set our hearts too much on anything in this world, since everything in it is so precarious, as health, riches, power, talents, etc., of which disease, revolution, or death can deprive us in a moment. Virtue alone is subject to no vicissitudes. In the hour of death, when the emptiness of all worldly attachments is felt, it alone will console us, and while we live soften the calamities of life and teach us to bear them with resignation and fortitude."

Mr. Carroll gave practical proof of his piety and devotion to the Church by his many generous donations in the cause of religion. His old historic home at Annapolis, round which memories cluster thick as leaves in an autumn forest, he made a present to the Jesuit Fathers, while his old home in Baltimore he bestowed upon a community of nuns. He also gave the ground for the present College of St. Charles, which stands just opposite the Lodge and is used by the Sulpician Fathers as preparatory to their Seminary of St. Sulpice.

What may be called the last public event in his life now approached. America was holding the golden jubilee of her independence, and but three of "the signers" lived, Charles Carroll, Thomas Jefferson, John Adams. Fifty years had passed, with all their vicissitudes, since they had stood in the face of the nation, the mouthpiece of a sacred cause. Children, who were infants then, had grown to manhood; men, who, in the flush of youth, had waited, eager and expectant, the result of that immortal conference, were now bent and grey. But, towering above them all in the majesty of their years and honors, were these venerable three. For the last time. The sun of that July day bore with it the souls of Jefferson and Adams. Charles Carroll was alone. He had outlived them all; he had seen generation after generation pass away. He was the sole relic, the remnant of that hallowed past. On the occasion of the golden jubilee a banquet was given in Charleston, and Bishop England proposed the toast: "To Charles Carroll of Carrollton—in the land from which his grandfather fled in terror, his granddaughter now reigns a queen."

But death, which had long spared this stately figure, came at last. It was in November of the year 1832, He had some time previously returned to his town house, in Lombard Street, Baltimore, so that it was there he passed away. He was attended to the last by his confessor, Father Chanche. His last moments were edifying and impressive in the highest degree, the fitting close to a life spent in the love and fear of God, and the service of his fellows. His household was assembled, children, grandchildren, and even his negro slaves. Seated in a chair, he received the Blessed Sacrament, humbly and reverently, as became the Christian. Though aware that his end was approaching, and already overcome by weakness, he fasted until he had received the Body of his Lord. Immediately after he was laid upon the bed, and did not long survive the change of position. His soul took its flight so tranquilly that the attendants scarcely knew it had gone.

We extract the following from a contemporary article upon his death:* "Carroll is in the tomb. But he shall not wholly die. No. The sceptre of the monarch, the glittering diadem, and the purple of the monarch shall moulder at the solemn mockeries of liberty, and their pageants be forgotten. But not so with the patriarch. Whilst gratitude shall swell the bosom of republics whilst the flag of our own confederacy shall wave on the outward wall of our Capitol, Carroll shall live, not alone on the canvas or in marble bust, but in the memory of virtuous freemen. His name, with that of Hancock, Franklin and Washington, shall in after ages be hymned to the lyre of the minstrel; whilst the muse of history

---

* In the Ave Maria, May, 1881, we find the notice taken from a little paper, The United States Catholic Miscellany, published at the time of Mr. Carroll's death.

shall point to the bright quaternion as the fadeless monument of American wisdom in the cabinet, and valor in the field.

" The devotion of the venerable patriot to the principles of freedom was only equalled by his adherence to the altars of his fathers. The memorable oath of '*Life, Fortune and Sacred Honor*' well attested the one ; as a Catholic, his practical piety and unsullied morality well proved the other. The blended rays of both shed a halo round his name while living ; sweetly tempered the evening of his virtuous life, till, the object of the veneration of twelve millions of freemen, he tranquilly breathes his spirit to his God, and consigns his remains to the tomb of his ancestors."

If the sentiment seem to us exaggerated in its expression, it only proves that he had in truth the nation for his mourners. From one end of the continent to the other poured in testimonies of grief and respect. Church and State alike bewailed his loss ; the Catholic Church in America had lost one of its pioneers and pillars, a true old Catholic gentleman, with the knightly spirit that even in his day had still a certain ascendency strong within him. The pupil of the Jesuits, the student of that home of science and of chivalry, the college of Louis le Grand, the wise statesman and framer of laws, the logical, forcible and elegant writer, the dignified and impressive orator, the ardent patriot, the zealous Catholic had passed away from the shores of his native Maryland, not into the "*æternum exilium*" of the poet, but unto the shores of his new country. He, who had outlived all the others, followed them in turn to a common resting-place, where the nation, with a sob of anguish, threw the earth upon the grave of the " LAST OF THE SIGNERS."

Henri de Larochejaquelein.

The Hero of La Vendee.

> "*Of ancient name, and knightly fame,*
> *And chivalrous degree.*"

> "*Amid the foremost of the embattled train,*
> *Lo! the young hero hails the glowing fight!*
> *And though the troops around him press the plain,*
> *Still fronts the foe, nor brooks inglorious flight.*
> *The young, the old, alike, commingling tears,*
> *His country's heavy grief bedews the grave!*
> *And all his race in verdant lustre wears,*
> *Fame's richest wreath, transmitted by the brave.*
> *Though mixed with earth, imperishable clay,*
> *His name shall live, while glory loves to tell,*
> *True to his country, how he won the day,*
> *How firm the hero stood, how calm he fell!*"
>
> TYRTAEUS.

Henri de Larochejaquelein,

The Hero of La Vendée.

IN the year 1772, at the ancestral castle of Durbelières, near Chatillon-sur-Sèvre, in Poitou, was born Henri de Larochejaquelein. His father was a colonel in the royal Polish artillery, and had no prouder ambition for his son than that he should likewise be a soldier. Hence Henri was early sent to the military school at Sorèze to be taught the arts of war and the whole system of military tactics. At this time he is described as a slight, soldierly, and graceful youth; his frank and gentle face strongly marked by the innate nobility of his soul, no less than by the outward tokens of that nobility to which the accident of birth entitled him. His eyes were the most remarkable feature of his face: dark, and yet intensely bright—bright with that immortal spark which urged him to his high destiny of fame and early death.

He was then sixteen years of age, and time had dealt gently with him. He chased the deer through the green forests of his native Poitou, beside her winding streams and over her broad fields, while friends and comrades looked with envy upon his skilful horsemanship, for which he was even then remarkable.

But the smiling landscape passed from sight. A day of horror had come for France. The leaders of the Revolution had unleashed their bloodhounds, who, fiercely following the scent, rushed abroad through the verdant fields, the pleasant homes, and kingly palaces of regal France. The kingdom of Sully, of Richelieu, of Louis XIV., and of Henry of Navarre was ruled by the lowest and vilest, the feeblest and most irresolute, strong only in cruelty and bloodshed. Robespierre and his execrable associates held the sceptre of St. Louis and sat upon the throne of many a glorious race of kings. The halls wherein the golden-tongued orators, Bourdaloue and Massillon, poured forth words of burning eloquence; the council-chambers in which the Louvois and the Colberts devised great schemes for their country's glory; the armies once led to victory by the Turennes and the Luxembourgs; the cities in which every fair and gracious thing was gathered to enrich and beautify the dwellings of the people; the plains whereon Clovis, heaven-inspired, became heir to a kingdom mightier than that of France,—all were polluted by the presence and the acts of base and unprincipled men.

Human life was as a feather, to be blown from their path by the breath of anger or resentment. Gray-haired sires were trampled in the same dust where childhood and innocence lay weltering in the bright heart's-blood of youth. Vested priests were torn from the sanctuary, and dragged forth to end their blameless lives at the guillotine; churches were entered by bands of armed ruffians, who, in their mad unbelief, saw not the thunderbolts of the Most High trembling above their heads. That land so rich in divine favors was now a prey to these awful workings of woe and terror. Like the men of old in the country of the Gadarenes, her people besought of heaven to withdraw its importunate blessings, and raising their second Babel, the Temple of Reason, as did the degenerate descendants of Adam in times of yore, God sent upon them confusion of speech, and, knowing not each man his brother, they fell upon and slew each other.

Henri de la Larochejaquelein was then, as we have said, about sixteen years of age, when the terrible storm overshadowing his native land drew him forth from childhood's green and sheltered places to take his rank among its foremost defenders. The life of the king was already threatened, and our hero, inspired with the loyalty which had come down to him amongst the heirlooms of his race, hastened to Paris to enroll himself in the Constitutional Guard. But the awful 10th of August came, when Louis, who had still some faithful arms to strike a blow for God, for king, for country, gave himself up by an act of misplaced confidence, with his wife, children, and attendants, into the hands of the National Assembly. "I am come into your midst," he said, "to prevent a great crime." Alas! he could not foresee the future, when the sin of regicide would call down a deeper vengeance upon their heads.

Needless to dwell upon these harrowing scenes; the poor king's trust in the affection of his people; his grief and regret when he heard a discharge of artillery directed against that cruel mob which twenty-four hours later condemned him, with his wife, children, and his sister, Madame Elizabeth, to the prison of the Temple. There he remained for many months; that gentle and gracious king whose grave, sad face, so full of mournful resignation, has come down through the intervening years, haunting France and the world like a pale ghost. And that queen whose hair, once the hue of molten gold, was turned amid those prison horrors into snowy white; whose face, the delight of kings and courts, was now pale and wan with deadly sorrow; whose eyes, once sparkling with hope and delight, had grown dull and sad with the mists of despair; whose step, now heavy and slow, once bounded over Trianon's flowery sod, or trod with graceful dignity the princely halls, which were for her so many paces, from childhood in an Austrian palace, to her death upon a scaffold.

Here, then, was a touching appeal to chivalry, and Larochejaquelein felt that he must be up and doing; must stand among the few loyal ones that formed an outwork round the king—an outwork stanch and true indeed, but too fatally "near the citadel." In Paris, however, his presence was of no avail, and the young hero returned to Poitou, crying:

"I go to my native province, whence they shall hear of me before long."

We may remark incidentally here that never, perhaps, does the history of any conflict present such extremes of nobility and degradation, of vice and exalted sanctity. Never, to our thinking, in the annals of the world, occurs a finer episode than that of the 4th January, 1791, when the ecclesiastical members of the National Assembly were called upon to take the oath of defection. There was a mob, drunk with blood, at the door, crying: "Death to the priests who will not take the oath!" There were human tigers within ready to spring upon their prey. The Convention summoned them individually. The first called was M. de Bonnac, Bishop of Agen.

"Gentlemen," answered he, "the sacrifice of wealth is of little moment to me; but there is one sacrifice which I cannot make—that of your respect and my faith. I should be too sure of losing both did I take the oath required of me."

M. de Saint Aulaire, Bishop of Poitiers, followed.

"Gentlemen," said he, "I am seventy years old. I have spent thirty-three in the episcopate, and I shall not now disgrace myself by taking the oath required by your decrees. I will not swear."

The whole body of the clergymen on the right loudly applauded his words. The Convention then summoned them collectively as follows:

"Let those ecclesiastics who have not yet taken the oath rise and come forward to swear."

There was silence within, rendered awful by the horrid cries of Death at the door. Not an ecclesiastic upon the right moved. There were three hundred members of the Convention; only twenty had seceded.

Meantime Larochejaquelein remained at Clisson with his friend and kinsman, the noble Lescure, afterwards one of the great leaders in the war of La Vendée. Meanwhile we shall glance at the origin of this struggle and the causes for the deep loyalty of the Vendean people.

The lords and commons of these western provinces of France had always lived in perfect harmony. Hence the latter, never feeling themselves oppressed, took no part in the widespread and revolting measures of the revolutionists. They loved and respected the king, and had no abuses of which to complain amongst the nobles. Moreover, being in complete submission to the laws of the Church, they shunned all intercourse with Illuminati or Carbonari, and despised or feared alike the doctrines of the socialist or nihilist. When the revolutionary movement began to be felt in France these people remained tranquilly in their homes unallured by visions of false liberty, and willing in all sincerity to render to Cæsar that which is Cæsar's.

Yet, when the first rumblings of the storm began to be heard in La Vendée, the peasants in their cabins around their fires of peat began to whisper the legend which had come down to them from their fathers. It was said that once the blessed Grignon de Montfort, founder of the missionaries of St. Laurent-sur-Sèvre, came to preach a mission in Bressuire. When the mission was over and the priest about to depart, he stood a moment in deep thought before a large stone cross. Suddenly he cried out:

"Brethren, for the punishment of sinners God will one day send into all this region a horrible war. Blood shall be shed; men shall be slain; the whole country shall be ravaged. These things shall come to pass when my cross is covered with moss."

The holy missionary departed; the hymns that had been sung at the mission service died away upon the Vendean air; but deep down in the hearts of the people dwelt this prophecy. Years passed on silently and swiftly; old men alone remembered the preacher's words, and in many a fireside chat related it, with the garrulousness of age, to their children and their children's children. All the while the soft green moss was stealing up the stony sides of the cross, covering it quietly, noiselessly, and surely, as time covers the surface of the earth with new-made graves. People passing the cross began to mutter with ominous shake of the head that the moss was creeping up. In 1793, when the storm had fairly burst over the land, the cross stood completely covered as in a garment of velvet green.*

Undismayed by the failure of their first rising at Bressuire, for they had risen, roused by the danger of their king to take part in the deadly struggle that was raging throughout France, the peasantry began to look abroad for leaders. Bonchamps, Charette, Stofflet, and d'Elbée

---

* History of the War in La Vendée. Life of Blessed Grignon de Montfort.

appeared upon the scene. But in the centre of the Bocage territory were numbers of royalists willing and even anxious to strike a blow in the good cause, if they only had a leader.

Larochejaquelein had meanwhile come out of his retirement at Clisson and joined the forces of Bonchamps and d'Elbée. Perceiving the need of a general rising in that portion of the country between Tiffanges and Chatillon, of which we have already spoken, he hastened to his own castle of St. Aubin to place himself at the head of the retainers and tenantry of his house. Badly armed, miserably undisciplined, poorly provisioned, they were wanting in everything but courage, trust in God, and a firm belief in the justice of their cause.

Of these forces Larochejaquelein now took command and marched at once to Aubiers, where the republicans had entrenched themselves. Before setting out the young leader made a soul-stirring address to his soldiers, concluding with the immortal words:

"My friends, if my father were here, you would have confidence in him. I am only a boy, but by my courage I will show myself worthy to command you. If I advance, follow me; if I flinch, cut me down; if I fall, avenge me!" *

Loud and prolonged was the applause which greeted the boy orator; for at this time our hero was scarcely twenty years of age. Full of enthusiasm, his soldiers called upon him to lead them to Aubiers, where a party of republicans were quartered.

An engagement took place there on the 13th of April. The enemy's forces were under the command of the celebrated Quetineau. Larochejaquelein placed detachments at various points of attack, where they lay con-

---

* Feller. Biographie Universelle.

cealed by hedges or shrubbery. He intrenched himself with the main body of his army in a garden, whence they made an assault upon Quetineau. The republican soldiers at once fell into disorder, were defeated and obliged to retreat.

Waving his sword above his head, Larochejaquelein rushed into the very thickest of the foe, shouting, "See, the Blues are flying. Charge!"

Charge they did, and were left masters of the field, the enemy having deserted their artillery, arms, and ammunition. Taking possession of these, the Vendeans hastened to Chatillon and Tiffanges, where they shared them with new volunteers who ranged themselves under Larochejaquelein's standard. Thus was begun in triumph that career which was destined to be so brief and glorious.

Lescure having left Clisson about this time in company with his friend Marigny to levy troops, if possible, for the royal cause, met a band of mounted royalists, crying as they rode, "Vive le roi!" To his great surprise and delight he discovered their leader to be his young kinsman Larochejaquelein. Warmly they congratulated each other on being at last in the service of the king; but their greetings were necessarily short, and, exchanging a cordial God-speed, each hastened upon his way.

The Vendean army now marched on to Thouars, a rock-built town upon the banks of the Thouet. It was among the most impregnable places in all that region, and was held by Quetineau with a considerable force. The royalist army advanced in four divisions, one being under the command of Larochejaquelein and his kinsman Lescure. They marched to Vrine, a village near Thouars. On a bridge of the same name a short but furious encounter took place. The ammunition failing, Larochejaquelein rode off to obtain supplies. In his absence Lescure, hoping to take the bridge, rushed down the slope, but found himself alone. Vainly he implored his soldiers to follow him; terror-stricken they remained as it were rooted to the spot. Suddenly a shout was heard, and Larochejaquelein was seen advancing at full gallop. With a simultaneous movement the whole force immediately rushed down the declivity and carried the bridge.

The army was now drawn up in several divisions before the walls of Thouars. Larochejaquelein began the escalade, calling upon his men to follow him. There were no scaling-ladders at hand, yet some effort had to be made to reach the walls. Mounting on the shoulders of a brave peasant, Tixier de Courlai, Larochejaquelein gained the summit and with his own hands began to tear away the stones. A breach was thus effected, and the besiegers gained an entrance at the same moment that another division of the Vendean troops had battered down the Pont-Neuf gate. The republicans at once laid down their arms and cried for quarter. To the lasting praise of the Vendeans, justly irritated as they were by a long course of cruelty and by provocation of every kind, they acted with remarkable moderation, showing mercy to all the prisoners. Truth to tell, they were more occupied in giving thanks to God than in taking vengeance on their foes. At Thouars they obtained reinforcements either of volunteers from among the republican troops or of royalists who had been within the town. They also came into possession of a quantity of artillery and ammunition, which they so much needed.

Having now gained some victories of minor importance, they hastened on to Chatillon, where twenty thousand insurgents had assembled. It was on the 23d of May. The royalists assisted at Mass in a body, after which the Penitential Psalms were sung and the soldiers knelt to receive a last benediction. Lescure, full of martial ardor, rushed forward alone to cheer on his division. He was greeted with a volley from the enemy's ranks which riddled his clothing and tore away his spurs. Undaunted he cried out, "See, the Blues do not know how to shoot!" The whole force now charged upon the enemy. In the very midst of the attack they knelt for a moment in prayer before a cross that stood in their way. Some of the officers objected, but Lescure interposed: "Let them pray," he said, "they will fight none the worse for it."

The result of the combat remained for some time doubtful. The republicans bravely held their ground and disputed every inch of the field. But Larochejaquelein with a few hundred men mounted on cart-horses turned the fortunes of the day by an irresistible charge. On they rushed, meeting and repulsing the enemy's cavalry. The onslaught was terrible; and the republicans, entirely defeated, laid down their arms and retreated in utter disorder. The royalists forthwith made themselves masters of Fontenay without the slightest opposition.

It was just after this victory that the royalists resolved to appoint a supreme council of administration, of which the Abbé Bernier, Father Jugault, a Benedictine, and the Abbé Brin were the most distinguished members. Especially famous was the Abbé Bernier, better known as the Curé of St. Laud's. He was unquestionably one of the great leaders in the Vendean rising. The council after much deliberation sent a proclamation from the Catholic armies to the Convention in which they declared "La Vendée victorious; the Holy Cross of Jesus Christ and the royal standard everywhere triumphant over the bloody flag of anarchy;" and added that " La Vendée desired to keep forever the Holy Catholic, apostolic and Roman faith, and to have a king who would be a father within and a protector without."

A comparison was drawn between the conduct of the Vendean and that of the republican army in their progress through Brittany and the Bocage. However, this appeal was totally disregarded by the Convention. New generals were sent into La Vendée to carry on the war, and amongst them were the celebrated Santerre, and Westermann, who was known as the " Butcher of the Vendeans."

The fortunes of the Vendeans were still, however, in the ascendant. They gained three important victories at Doué, Vihiers, and Montreuil. Concentrating their forces, they now marched on towards Saumur. Whilst Lescure was engaged at Fouchard Bridge, Cathelineau feigned an attack upon the castle, and Larochejaquelein led on his troops to surprise the enemy at Varin meadows. Leaving a small force to guard the Bridge of St. Just, which lay exactly in front of the enemy's camp, the young leader made an assault upon the rear. Throwing his cap over the ramparts, he cried:

"Soldiers, who will get me my cap?"

So saying, he leaped over himself, followed tumultuously by his men, while almost simultaneously the royalists entered the town from the opposite side. A portion of the republican troops made a stanch resistance and attempted to hold the castle. Darkness came down upon the combat; but the Vendean leaders determined that at dawn the enemy should be driven from their stronghold. When day broke it was discovered that the republicans had fled during the night from Saumur under cover of the darkness. Then did the harmonious clang of the bells delight the hearts of the soldiers; drums beat, clarions sounded shrill and high above the deafening shouts of "*Vive la religion catholique!*" "*Vive le roi!*"

One of the churches of the city had been made into a storehouse by the republicans, and the spoils of battle were now placed therein. On the morning after the victory Larochejaquelein was found standing as in deep reflection, with eyes cast down. A friend, approaching, asked him of what he was thinking.

"I am lost in astonishment," replied the young leader, "when I think of our success; it is clearly the hand of God."

To Larochejaquelein was now consigned the somewhat arduous post of keeping Saumur, which he did with equal courage and skill. It was on this occasion that the celebrated republican General Quetineau was taken prisoner. When he was afterwards released and sent to Paris, he died upon the scaffold, thus expiating his devotion to a bad cause. Nor was his execution the only instance of ingratitude upon the part of the Convention.

Meanwhile the Vendean army was making some important movements. Charette succeeded in taking Machecoul; he had hitherto acted independently, but now formed a conjunction with the other royalist leaders; the bulk of their forces after this laid siege to Nantes, where they were defeated. There they lost Cathelineau, one of the most able as well as popular leaders. While the Vendeans were encamped, Westermann, the republican leader, was passing with fire and sword through the Bocage territory, burning, devastating, slaying. He reduced to ashes the ancient château of Durbelières, the birth-place of Larochejaquelein.

The Vendeans were now divided into four divisions; Lescure was appointed to the command of one, and at once chose his young kinsman as his lieutenant-general. At Erigny Larochejaquelein made a gallant fight, aided by Bonchamps. He was struck by a ball, which carried away his thumb, but obstinately refused to leave the field, and ultimately won the day. A futile attempt was made by Lescure, Stofflet, and Larochejaquelein to cover Chatillon. The republicans were, however, in an immense majority, and the attempt was a failure in spite of the most determined bravery upon the part of the royalists. A bloody and desperate engagement took place, shortly before, between the Mayence men, under Kleber, and the Vendeans, under Bonchamps, d'Elbée, and Lescure, in conjunction with Charette and his gallant force. At sunset the republicans were driven in disorder from the field.

A plan of attack was now made to surprise the Blues on their march to Chollet. Lescure, who went out with a small force to reconnoitre, met the enemy in the avenue of Château la Tremblage, and at once gave battle. Fortune seemed to favor the royalists; they fought with their customary valor, and in spite of the odds the day might have been won; but a ball entered the eye of their leader; the soldiers became disheartened, and finally fell back. Lescure was carried to Beaupréau.

A movement was made on the 17th of October to surprise the republicans, now encamped before Beaupréau. Bonchamps and d'Elbée attacked the right wing, Larochejaquelein and Stofflet the centre; their vigorous charge completely broke the line. In vain did Kleber call upon the reserve force; it is said they retreated without having fired a shot, so great was their terror of the "Brigands of La Vendée." Larochejaquelein and Stofflet, pursuing their advantage, seized upon a park of artillery and turned it against the foe. Already were the Blues upon the eve of flight, when Haxo, one of their leaders, by an adroit movement, attacked the royalists in the flank. All thought of order or discipline was now abandoned; hand to hand, foot to foot, man to man, the opposing armies met. A panic spread among the peasants; in vain their despairing leaders called upon them, for the honor of God, by their love of country, by the memory of their martyred brethren, to remain and, if need be, die with them. Larochejaquelein, d'Elbée, and Bonchamps, filled with superhuman courage, refused to abandon the field. A few hundred rallied round them, and with this handful of faithful souls they charged again. The opposing forces far outnumbered them; they were surrounded on all sides; escape was impossible, and a glorious death was the only object of their hope. Night fell calmly and solemnly upon the tumult and disorder of the scene; upon the resolute faces of the men who had resolved to die as martyrs.

Vainly did their blows fall thick and fast upon the enemy; vainly did they shout defiance into the very teeth of their opponents. Bonchamps lay wounded on the spot where, a moment before, d'Elbée had fallen. Larochejaquelein continued to cheer his comrades with words of hope, whispering of the after-life, which at that solemn hour seemed so near. When the last glimmer of light had faded from the landscape, and the last gleam of hope from the hearts of the Vendeans, one alone remained full of undaunted valor, and that was Henri de Larochejaquelein. Nothing could subdue his dauntless spirit, so strong, so full of life and hope and valor. A reinforcement arrived in time to save him and carry the wounded leaders to Beaupréau, where already Lescure lay stricken unto death.

Utterly disheartened, the peasants proceeded in disorder to St. Florent, hoping to effect the passage of the Loire. Their hearts were full of deadly hatred against the foe that had devastated their lands and left their once happy homes in ruins. They were still smarting, too, under a sense of failure and defeat; and learning that four or five thousand republican prisoners were confined in an old church in the town, they would have massacred them but for the interposition of their leaders. A stormy meeting was held in the council-chamber; many of the leaders were in favor of condemning all the prisoners to instant execution, and thus acceding to the soldiers' demands. Lescure, who had been brought thither on a litter, raised his voice, feeble now with suffering, and cried, "Horrible! horrible!" But he was not heard, and already without in the streets the peasants, disregarding every authority, were pointing the cannon towards the church. Terror prevailed amongst the helpless republicans, not one of whom would, however, have hesitated under like circumstances to massacre his foe. But Bonchamps from his bed of death summoned the officers.

He addressed himself to Autichamps, saying:

"My friend, the last order I shall ever give you is that of saving the republicans. Tell me, I implore you, that it shall be done."

Autichamps promised, and rushed from the apartment. He silenced the tumultuous soldiery by an effort, and he told them what Bonchamps, whose face was already gray with the shadows of death, had commanded. With one accord the peasants cried:

"Quarter, quarter! Bonchamps commands it."

Before the quiet of another evening had fallen upon the town Bonchamps was at rest. Shortly before his death he received the Viaticum with extraordinary fervor. He had meted out mercy, and to him was mercy shown when, laying down his command, he appeared before the last tribunal. Over his grave at St. Florent stands his statue, and lower down upon the monument the record of that last heroic act of clemency:

"GRÂCE AUX PRISONNIERS! BONCHAMPS L'ORDONNE"* a fitting tribute to the noble and gentle qualities of the man.

Larochejaquelein now made every effort to oppose the passage of the Loire, which he knew would inevitably prove disastrous to the army in its present condition. But entreaty and remonstrance were alike unavailing; enfeebled by fatigue, half crazed with terror at the rumors which reached them of the cruelty of their foes, they rushed madly over that fatal river. Lescure, who had all along opposed the evacuation of La Vendée, permitted himself to be borne across, that he might spend the last moments of his life amongst the people whose cause he had so nobly espoused and gallantly supported. Larochejaquelein, at the suggestion of Lescure, was chosen commander-in-chief. With tears in his eyes he refused the honor, begging of them to elect one whose years and experience might the more readily inspire confidence. But Lescure persisted in declaring that he alone could restore the fallen fortunes of La Vendée, and the young soldier reluctantly accepted the arduous post of peril and of hardship.

There was little doubt of his ability to fill this important position. In age, it is true, he was the youngest of all the leaders of the rebellion; in judgment and experience he must necessarily have been inferior to many of his seniors; although it is unquestionable that he frequently exhibited the knowledge and military skill of a great general. In personal courage he was unsurpassed; his valor was reckless, indomitable, and almost superhuman. Yet, once the battle over, none gentler, more humane or generous than he. If he took a prisoner, he at once offered him the chance of single combat; while

---

* "Mercy for the prisoners. It is Bonchamps' order."

to the wounded, the dying, the helpless, the oppressed, he was a kind and resolute protector. In the council-chamber he was modest and even timid; yet on the rare occasions when he proffered advice, it was always good. When he was called upon for his opinion, he invariably replied: "Decide; I will execute." His motives were pure and lofty; no hope of gain or advancement ever quickened the beatings of his noble heart; his highest ambition was that, in the event of success, the king would give him command of a regiment of hussars. By the peasants he was fairly idolized; he was a leader after their own hearts; no royalist chief was ever so beloved as he. Every man would have drawn his sword and spilled his heart's best blood for "Master Henry," as they called him.

Such was the character and such were the qualifications of the man who was now summoned to the chief command of the Vendean army at the most critical moment of the campaign, when the sturdy hearts of the peasants were beginning to fail them, their arms to grow feeble, and their eyes to lose the olden fire.

However, the royalists now pressed forward to Laval, defeating a republican force at Château-Gonthier on their way thither. A division of the Blues was in position near the city of Laval, and upon it the royalists charged. The enemy retreated, hotly pursued by Larochejaquelein, who, in his impetuous ardor, did not perceive that he was alone. He was met in a narrow path by a republican, who at once attacked him with the utmost violence. Larochejaquelein was unarmed and partially disabled, one arm being quite helpless from a wound. Evading the blow, the hero rode up at full speed to the republican, threw him to the ground, and cried, whilst he prepared to defend himself against new assailants:

"Away, and tell your republicans that the royalist general, without weapons and with one arm disabled, threw you to the ground and then gave you your life." After which, putting spurs to his horse, he regained the camp.

All this time Westermann was upon the track of the royalists. They surprised him about three leagues from Laval, and a severe skirmish took place. The battle of Laval, which occurred before the heights of Entrames, was one of the most important of the campaign. Previous to the engagement, Lescure, who was dying, as it were, by inches, caused himself to be carried to a window, whence he addressed the soldiers in a few impressive words, which, coming as they did from a beloved leader now upon the very verge of the grave, were not without their effect. Larochejaquelein also harangued them, dwelling upon all that could inflame their patriotism or their thirst for glory. He pointed out on the one hand fame and the consciousness of well-doing as their reward, and on the other martyrdom.

The royal forces occupied the heights; the republicans, under Kleber and Westermann, advanced in formidable array. The engagement took place just below the heights, and lasted with determined bravery on both sides for some hours. The Mayence men proved most disastrous to the Vendeans. However, victory finally decided for the royalists, upon the bridge of Château-Gonthier, despite the gallant efforts of the republican General Bloss. The enemy was driven into the river, save a miserable remnant of their army, which took shelter within the walls of Château-Gonthier.

"What, my friends," cried Larochejaquelein, "are the conquerors to sleep outside and the vanquished within the walls? We have not finished yet."

In a few hours they had driven the enemy from the

town. Towards midnight, however, the Blues made a last effort to retrieve their losses, and were finally put to flight. Historians declare that by the skilful arrangement of his troops, his adroit manœuvres, no less than his wonderful intrepidity, Larochejaquelein on this occasion displayed the qualities of a great general.

He now divided his army into three great columns. Proceeding onwards, he gained fresh victories, and having carried Fougères and Ernée, began to contemplate an attack upon Dol. Whilst at Ernée, Larochejaquelein lost his kinsman and devoted friend. Lescure died a most saintly death, which is touchingly described by his widow in her memoirs of the time; to her he declared that besides leaving her unprotected, his sole regret in dying was that he could not place his king upon the throne. When the grief-stricken widow first met Larochejaquelein after her husband's death, she exclaimed:

"You have lost your best friend. After me, you were dearest to him of all in the world."

"Could my life restore him to you," replied Larochejaquelein, "take it."

The body of the departed chief was buried quietly. The traces of the hair-shirt which he had always worn were not needed to convince those who had been his associates of the holiness and austerity of his life.

On the evening of the 14th November, the royalists assailed Granville. The troops were, however, disheartened, and no efforts on the part of their leaders could rouse them to enthusiasm. Still, a small force of republicans sent to repulse the besiegers were defeated, and the royalists, approaching nearer, began a destructive fire upon the garrison. The republican commander, Lecarpentier, ordered the suburbs to be fired, but even this did not repel the dauntless Vendeans.

They seized upon some military stores, and would at once have commenced a breach, but for the want of proper artillery.

An escalade was suggested; but no scaling-ladders were at hand. After a moment of indecision, they thrust their bayonets into crevices of the wall, and mounted by that means. Larochejaquelein and Forestier, their leaders, had already reached the top, when some voices in the rear of the royal ranks raised the cry of treason. "We are betrayed; let us fly." The Vendeans who had followed their leaders to the ramparts rushed tumultuously back; the wildest disorder prevailed; the hope of the republicans revived, and in a short time victory was theirs.

In the gray dawn of the following morning, Larochejaquelein and Stofflet, in accordance with a pre-concerted plan, attacked the town by water. The attempt was a failure, the republicans having provided against it. Moreover, the royalists now met with a disappointment. Arms and ammunition from England had been promised them; they had refused to accept any other aid from a country which had ever been the enemy of France. No sign of the English fleet, however, appeared; and, more than ever disheartened, they were compelled to retreat from Granville.

A skirmish took place at Pontorson, upon which the Vendeans had fallen back. It proved disastrous to the republicans, the Vendeans gaining the day, with considerable loss to the enemy. Here, we are told, friend and foe alike demanded the aids of religion, and the priests hastened hither and thither, administering indiscriminately to republican and royalist.

The Vendeans were now destitute of everything, shoes, clothing, and, worst of all, food. Scores of gallant soldiers died of starvation, and those who survived endured the most terrible hardships. In this condition they were compelled to meet a numerous and well-provisioned army, under Kleber and Westermann. This engagement, which proved to be one of the most important of the campaign, took place at Dol. The republicans, burning to avenge their late defeats, and thirsting for the blood of the Vendean heroes, precipitated an engagement, which, but for the prudence and foresight of Larochejaquelein, who drew up his troops in order of battle, would have been fatal to the Catholic army.

The battle commenced soon after midnight. The night was intensely dark; the field was lit only by torches, and the flash of artillery and musketry was more appalling in the gloom. Noise and confusion prevailed throughout; it would seem that chaos had again come upon the earth. The courage of the royalists was at its lowest ebb; but their indomitable chief, still full of impetuous valor, sought to communicate to them a spark of his own ardor. With that wing of the army which was under his command, he succeeded in driving the vanguard of the foe back to Pontorson. Meanwhile Stofflet and Talmont were making a brave resistance; they succeeded, by a vigorous onslaught, in repulsing the republicans; but so terrific was the return charge of the enemy that the royalists were driven back, and even Stofflet compelled to leave the field. Larochejaquelein, appearing at the moment, and taking in at a glance the critical situation, rushed into their very midst, shouting the inspiring war-cry and calling upon the terrified peasants to rally. Deaf to every voice but that of fear, the royalists sought only for some means of escape. In their mad terror, women, children, the wounded, and the dying were left behind. At this juncture a venerable priest, the curé of Ste. Marie-de-Rhé, sprang upon a high mound of earth, and holding aloft a large crucifix, called upon the soldiers to take courage therefrom. He spoke to them sternly and authoritatively.

"Will you," he cried, "be guilty of the infamy of abandoning your wives and children to the knives of the Blues? Return and fight; it is the only way of saving them. Will you abandon your general in the midst of his foes? Come, my children, I will march at your head with the crucifix! Kneel down, you who are willing to follow me, and I will give you absolution; if you die, you will go to heaven; whilst those who betray God and leave their families to perish will go to perdition."

By a spontaneous impulse, two thousand men knelt to receive the remission of their sins; then, placing themselves under the standard of Larochejaquelein, they rushed once more to combat.

"Nous allons en paradis!" "Vive le roi!" * rang out in one enthusiastic shout which seemed to pierce the night-shadowed heavens.

When they reached their hero's side, he was standing alone, with his arms crossed upon his breast, facing a battery. When he saw that not a man remained by his side, and that resistance was useless, he stood thus, braving death, too proud to turn his back upon the foe. Never yet in all the fierce ordeals of many battles had he done so, nor would he now commence. News came to him that Talmont was endeavoring to keep another portion of the field with only eight hundred men. Hastening to his assistance, he succeeded in rallying upon the way a mere handful of men, but they managed to hold their position till the Curé of Ste. Marie came up with his two thousand followers. Almost simultaneously Stofflet returned, and the hard-fought field was won by

---

* "We are going to heaven!" "Long live the king!"

the royal forces. The Curé headed them on their entrance to the town, chanting the "Vexilla Regis," and holding aloft that crucifix the sight of which had so often inspired the men in the battle's fiercest rage.

This victory was but the beginning of a series of conquests by which the royalists were strengthened and encouraged. Larochejaquelein now suggested that they should return to Granville, and there await the English supplies, but the peasants loudly declared that they would return to La Vendée. Their leader, submitting, reluctantly proceeded towards Angers.

A noble act of mercy, said to have been first suggested by the Curé of Ste. Marie, was now performed. A hundred and fifty wounded republicans, who had been taken prisoners, were sent to their camp at Rennes with the message that "thus did the royal and Catholic army take vengeance on its foes." On the morning of the 4th December, the attack upon Angers took place. A heavy fire of artillery was continued during the day, but without much result. On the following day cannonading was again opened by the Vendeans upon St. Michael's Gate. After some hours' severe fighting a breach was made. Here, as everywhere else, the soldiers displayed indecision and discouragement; the chiefs gave them a noble example by rushing onwards themselves into the breach. Not a man followed, and all save Larochejaquelein, Piron, and Forestier perished. The remnant of the army retreated to Baugé.

When they had advanced within a short distance of La Flêche they found the bridge cut down and the opposite shore defended by a strong republican force. Larochejaquelein, leaving Piron to defend their first position, chose four hundred of the cavalry, each of whom took a foot-soldier upon his crupper. They rode some distance up the Loire, where they managed to ford the river, their leader going first. They met and surprised the garrison, took the town, regained the bridge, and saved the army by a vigorous charge. Larochejaquelein was hailed with acclamation as a great soldier and general, and upon his brow were bound fresh laurels.

The Vendeans were, however, in terrible straits; no provisions were to be had, and famine was daily and hourly enfeebling the remnants of that once vigorous army. Despair was in every heart and all too plainly written upon every face. Larochejaquelein alone, still undismayed, made an assault upon the town of Mans, which he succeeded in taking, and there a small supply of provisions was obtained. He made an effort to reach Ancenis, where he hoped to cross the Loire. He was terribly harassed upon the passage by the republicans. At Foultourte, a village through which they passed, the Blues, under Marceaux, a celebrated republican leader, supported by Kleber and Westermann, determined to stop the progress of the Vendeans towards Ancenis and cut off the remnant of their army.

Though fully aware of their slight chance of success, Larochejaquelein, with his usual energy and presence of mind, made every preparation for a determined resistance. He rallied his troops, especially the cavalry; and by prayers and entreaties prevailed upon the fugitives to return and share the fate of their comrades. Taking three thousand picked men, he placed them in ambush behind some fir-trees, whence they succeeded in repulsing Westermann and Müller.

This effort seemed to have exhausted their remaining strength, and the peasants began to waver. Larochejaquelein rushed forward, making a desperate charge upon the enemy's centre, but he was not supported. Returning, he called upon the haggard, hollow-eyed men who remained to follow him, besought them in tones of passionate entreaty, or commanded them resolutely and sternly; but alike in vain: they suffered him to rush on to the attack almost alone. Again the heroic chief returned, and made a third and last effort to rouse them; but again without avail. Loyalty, courage, honor, all seemed alike to have deserted the half-starving men. Hope was dead within their hearts, and again they met with a most disastrous defeat. Having retreated within the walls, they gave themselves up to utter despair. Westermann attacked them at midnight, and their indomitable leader again exhorted them at least to sell their lives dearly. But, alas! they only replied that a few hours longer or shorter mattered not, when they must die. For the first time positive despair and a sort of frenzy seemed to take possession of Larochejaquelein. Riding through the streets, he forced a few thousand men to take up arms, but the total want of discipline amongst them neutralized the efforts of their leaders. The battle was both fierce and bloody, but the final blow was dealt to the royalist cause in La Vendée. When the Vendeans began their retreat, Larochejaquelein with other leaders, amongst whom were the afterwards famous Jean Chouan and George Cadoudal, defended the town to the last, and covered the confused flight of their comrades.

An incident is here related of Stofflet which proves that the old chivalric spirit still remained amongst many of the royalist leaders. Having collected the tattered remnants of his flag, he was about leaving the town when in a narrow street he met an officer named de Scepaux, who with two comrades had mounted a gun in order to assist in covering the retreat of their companions. Stofflet stopped, ordered de Scepaux to mount his horse, take the flag, and leave him to serve the gun.

"No, my general," replied de Scepaux, "save the flag

yourself; it is in good hands. I remain here while a grain of powder or a ball is left."

"The Blues shall have me," replied Stofflet, "before they have our flag. If they send it to the Convention, they shall also send my head."

As Stofflet passed out of the town a poor woman who lay bleeding by the roadside recognized him, and begged him to save her child. "Give it here," he cried, and placing it in front of his horse, with the flag, rode out of the town. Years afterwards the child was restored to its mother, whose life had been preserved.

The royalists hastened on to Ancenis, hoping to cross the Loire. Larochejaquelein and Stofflet with eighteen men made the passage of the river in two frail fishing-smacks, their progress being watched with intense eagerness by the entire army. On landing they were attacked by a small force of republicans, and compelled to conceal themselves in the heart of the country.

Meanwhile a hostile vessel sailed down the river and sank some rafts on which the Vendeans had hoped to cross. Consternation spread through their ranks; a detachment of the enemy under Westermann coming up, an engagement was inevitable. The poor broken-spirited peasants, roused by the distant view of their fondly loved La Vendée, made one last effort and drove the republicans back. But the main body of their troops arriving, the peasants either fled in dismay or gave themselves up to their foes. Only a mere handful succeeded in crossing the river. Thus were they separated from their leader at the very crisis of their fate.

Larochejaquelein, having penetrated into the heart of the country, came, after many wanderings, to a farmhouse in Chatillon, where he took shelter. His adventures at this time remind us rather of those attributed to heroes of romance than of sober reality. Still fearful of discovery, he was driven to seek an asylum amid the ruins of his ancestral château of Durbelières. Here he remained for a considerable time; under cover of the darkness he stole out by night to seek provisions; and in this solitude lived over again the fierce, exciting, and most glorious struggle in which he had been engaged, devising new plans for a final effort in favor of God and king and country. For, inspired by the crumbling walls and ancient towers, by the storied tombs of his brave forefathers, he, their worthy descendant, full of indomitable valor, told himself that all was not lost, and that La Vendée should take the field again as the sworn champion of the good cause.

But even in this ruined haunt of the owl and bat he was not safe. News of his whereabouts having been conveyed to the republican camp hard by, a detachment was sent to make him prisoner. He concealed himself by lying on the entablature of that portion of the façade still remaining. After a hasty search the enemy withdrew, and Larochejaquelein escaped to Poitou, where he joined Charette.

This great leader, who, it seems, was jealous of Larochejaquelein's extraordinary influence over the peasantry of that region, received him with marked coldness. However, he said, "I am about departing for Mortagne; if you wish to follow me, I will see that you are provided with a horse."

"I follow you?" said Larochejaquelein haughtily. "I beg you to understand, Monsieur, that I am accustomed to lead, not to follow; and that I am in command here."

About eight hundred royalists consequently left Charette and ranged themselves under the banner of Larochejaquelein, whom they regarded as their hereditary chief. It is a matter of some surprise that the young hero should at such a crisis have shown himself so unusually mindful of his own interests. Hitherto his maxim had been that there must be no question of self when his country's welfare was at stake ; and upon this maxim he had invariably acted.

However, the country never had more need of gallant hearts than then. The republican army, under General Cordelier, with what was called the "infernal columns," was devastating La Vendée on every side. Larochejaquelein gained, soon after his arrival in Poitou, a series of victories over Cordelier. With such forces as he could collect he intrenched himself in the forest of Vezin. Their numbers were very few, but about that time they took among other prisoners an adjutant-general of the republican army, upon whom they found an order by which he was commanded to promise the peasants a safe-conduct, and having thus entrapped, to fall upon and slay them. So terrified were they that they flocked to join Larochejaquelein in great numbers.

Being therefore reinforced and in command of a large army, he attacked General Cordelier at several points, each time defeating him with considerable loss to the republican force. The troops who held the town of Chollet made a sortie with intent to burn the town of Noisailles. As they were applying their blazing torches to the walls, Larochejaquelein rode up at the head of a detachment and completely routed them. It was a decisive victory, but the last which Larochejaquelein was ever to gain for the cause he loved. Pursuing the fugitives, he discovered two grenadiers hidden behind a hedge. Approaching them, he cried:

"Surrender, and you shall have quarter!"

The grenadiers reluctantly acquiesced, and were about to give up their arms. But at the moment one of the Vendean officers, riding up, called his leader by name, imploring him to hold no further parley with the prisoners. Larochejaquelein disregarded the advice, and went nearer to question the republicans. As he stooped to seize his musket, one of the grenadiers, taking aim, fired, and the hero fell backwards in his saddle—dead.

So perished on the 4th of June, 1793, one of the brightest stars in that immortal galaxy of heroes, which La Vendée and its celebrated struggle produced. Great they were; but nowhere among them do we find one greater, more noble, more knightly than Henri de Larochejaquelein, the idolized boy-leader of La Vendée. He was buried quietly, without pomp or ceremony, so that perchance his death might escape the notice of the republicans, for well they knew the import of such a loss to the cause for which he had given his heart's blood. His soldiers bore him to a short distance from the place of his death, and there made him a grave where in summer-time the grass grew very green and a waving tree played at cross-bars with the sunshine. They laid him down softly and closed his bright eyes, those eyes which had flashed so proudly in the battle's fierce array; they smoothed back the hair from his forehead with almost woman's gentleness; they hung again around his neck the rosary, which was the distinctive mark of the Catholic and royal army, together with the scapular worn upon the breast, which they now placed over his quiet heart. They laid by as a relic the knot of white ribbon, the colors of the cause, which he had ever kept pure and unsullied. With bitter, burning tears they looked their last upon the young and ardent face that had been so loved throughout La Vendée; upon the figure of their boy-hero, who in spite of all obstacles, with an army miserably provisioned and undisciplined, had won them sixteen battles within ten months.

So the soldier of La Vendée was at rest, in the obscure grave wherein his body remained till 1815. It was then exhumed and conveyed to the parish church of Chollet, whence it was again removed. It was finally interred with the bones of his ancestors near the old feudal castle of St. Aubin, where, as a child, he had dreamed boyish dreams of fame and glory; where he had gazed with awe and wonder at the mail-clad figures of his forefathers, little guessing that he should take his place among them one day, adorned with a prouder title of nobility—the white streamer of La Vendée.

The ancient manor was, as we have seen, destroyed by republican incendiaries; the portraits of his race, in all likelihood, have perished with it. But not alone in feudal hall or ancestral castle was the portrait of Henri de Larochejaquelein preserved. Even to the smallest details of his personal appearance, it remains deep down in the hearts of the people, his memory enshrined with all that is most precious in their eyes, as a *preux chevalier* worthy to have lived in the grand old heroic times.

The peasant at his peat fire, the noble in his hall, nay, even the very republican, who, we are told, sincerely mourned his death, alike recall with enthusiastic admiration the name and deeds of this noblest of a noble race, Henri, Marquis de Larochejaquelein, whose short career came to a close while he was still in his twenty-second year.

Thus, O gallant boy, did thy young life flash out upon the midnight darkness of the revolutionary sky, and fade before the light of a new day had dawned for France. Many a fervent prayer was breathed over thy honored dust; many an eye has grown moist over the story of thy gallant deeds and untimely death; and many a young heart has caught from thine a kindred inspiration.

But thou hast slept soundly in thine early grave, leaving to fame a pure, noble, and unsullied record. What though evil times may come again for France; thy task is done, and thou art once more united to thy gallant comrades, whose names, like thine own, have gone down to posterity, synonymous with what is grandest and bravest and holiest; pure among the pure, valiant among the valiant, loyal among the loyal, to God, to king, to country, their names stand out upon the roll of fame—the heroes of La Vendée.

Henri de Larochejaquelein.

FROM THE FRENCH OF ADRIEN DÉZAMY.

I saw, as a child, in the depths of La Vendée,
    Just between Tiffanges and Tortoû,
A peasant old and lame, with deeply wrinkled face,
    Who was called the Sangenitou.
A last relic was he of that famous "Grand Guerre,"
    A Chouan and a hardy scout;
Oft I heard him relate to a rustic, gaping crowd
    His adventures thereabout.

"My children," said he, "as I ne'er knew how to read,
    I know not the reason why,
The Blues, first having killed the good king our sire,
    Burnt out such poor devils as I.
Then my heart grew full of vengeance and bitter hate;
    I felt I could never yield,
Seized a scythe, joined the men of Larochejaquelein,
    And rushed into the field.

They tracked us like wolves whom they sought to entrap
    For months, from morning till night;
We insurgents of le Bocage in our retreat
    Sustained a despairing fight.
Before the avalanche, forever at our head,
    Where danger was plainest to see,
With scapular on breast and the white royal scarf,
    Sword in hand, Monsieur Henri.

A simple chief was he, with no pride in the world,
  Reckless when peril was nigh;
I seem to see him now, his noble curling head
  When waving his hat on high.
He rushed to the front: " Forward, lads, for God and King,"
  Rang his words like trumpet-call;
" If I lead, follow me; if I flinch, cut me down;
  And avenge me, if I fall !"

Well, just then we had no balls, nor powder, nor bread,
  But at this inspiring cry
Our army in sabots like a mountain torrent rushed
  On the Blues and their outposts nigh.
I fell from the height of the talus above,
  My right leg was shattered before.
I have limped since that time, boys, 'tis now sixty years,
  Very soon I shall limp no more.

Thus he oft whiled away for us the long, dark nights;
  Round the wood fire, screened from cold,
That warrior of the past, with failing voice and slow,
  Evoked for us days of old.
Breathless and mute, we hung upon his words,
  While, with feeling rare to see,
He ended with a sob the mournful history
  Of his brave Monsieur Henri.

SIMON DE MONTFORT.

Champion of the Cross and Defender of the Faith.

Souls of the slain in holy war,
    Look from your sainted rest;
Tell us ye rose in glory's car,
    To mingle with the blest;
Tell us how short the death-pang's power,
How bright the joys of your immortal bower.

  Strike the loud harp, ye minstrel train!
    Pour forth your loftiest lays.
  Each heart shall echo to the strain
    Breath'd in the warrior's praise.
          Crusader's War Song.—HEMANS.

Simon de Montfort.

CHAMPION OF THE CROSS AND DEFENDER OF THE FAITH.

FROM the remote age which gave him birth comes down to us the grand historic name of Simon de Montfort, to which has been added by common consent the titles of Defender of the Faith and Macchabeus. Anti-Catholic writers of all times have been unsparing in their denunciations of him, and too often covered his name with unmerited obloquy. It is our task to glance at him in the light of a great Christian warrior, inspired with a lively zeal for the cause of religion and the welfare of his country.

Simon de Montfort, fourth Count of the name, was born in the latter half of the twelfth century, of a noble and distinguished family, who were seigneurs of a little town about ten leagues from Paris. They claimed descent from the illustrious house of Hainault. Of Simon's early life not many details come down to us, but we know that he was fortunate in his marriage with Alice de Montmorency. This lady was a worthy helpmate for so heroic a knight. She was full of the lofty spirit of her race, and no doubt had her share in the inspiration which marked her husband's proud career.

While De Montfort was still young an intense enthusiasm prevailed throughout Europe. From north to south, from east to west, innumerable warriors girded themselves for a mighty struggle. They received upon their shoulder the red cross of the Crusader, and forsook their homes and kindred; forsook the sunny shores of France, the homes of Saxon comfort or of Norman luxury, and set sail over the great waters to classic Greece or martial Cyprus, thence to Palestine. Montfort was young, ardent, chivalrous. Home was sweet and friends were dear, but mightier voices called him. Pope Innocent III. had proclaimed a fourth Crusade, and under the leadership of Boniface, Marquis of Montferrat, sailed Montfort. With this attempt, which only succeeded in establishing a short-lived Latin empire at Constantinople, our sketch has little to do.

Of Montfort we learn that he left his companions at Zara, and proceeded himself to Palestine. The day of his glory was yet, however, to come, and we shall now briefly glance at the train of events which made him at once the deliverer of his country and the protector of his co-religionists. During the absence of the western lords in Palestine a dangerous body of heretics had arisen, who were not only hostile to the Church, but subversive of all social order. They became known as Albigenses—most writers agree, from the province of Albi or Albigensis. Their doctrines were most repulsive and unnatural, and they were besides daring and unscrupulous rebels, dangerous to the peace and safety of the state.*

These heretics ravaged the lands, burned monasteries, assassinated priests, pillaged churches, and profaned holy things. For political reasons, a powerful leader of

---

* Notes to Alban Butler's Lives of the Saints, vol. viii.; Legendes des Croisades, by Collin de Plancy; Feller's Biographie Universelle, vol. vi.; Vaissette's Histoire Generale de Languedoc; Alzog's Hist. of the Universal Church, vol. ii.; Darras's General Hist. of the Church, vol. iii.

the day, Raymond, Count of Toulouse, espoused their cause, lending them every support in his power, and hoping by this means to increase his own estates. Innocent III., having, as his predecessors had, loudly denounced the heresy, sent into France his Legate, the saintly Peter of Castelnau, with various monks of the Order of Citeaux, to exercise their apostolate among these heretics. The Bishop of Osma, Diego, and some of the secular clergy, joined these devoted missionaries. Barefoot they went from city to city through the province of Languedoc, calling upon sinners to do penance for their sins and return to the way of God. Peter of Castelnau was often heard to say: "The cause of Christ cannot flourish in this country until one of the missionaries has shed his blood for the faith. May I be the first victim of the persecution!" Too surely was his prayer heard. On the 3d of January, 1208, the Legate was assassinated, as it was supposed by two of Raymond's officers. He died, crying out, "O Lord, forgive him as I do!"

This was the signal for a general rising against the Albigenses, who had already provoked the nation beyond the limits of endurance. "Military expeditions," says an eminent German writer, "sent against the Albigenses were laudable in their object and useful in their results. The spirit of their heresy was the overthrow of the essential principles which constitute society. A general cry of indignation went up from all the land. Like modern socialists, they put the torch to whatever the people had learned to love and respect. All the sovereigns of the day were unanimous in calling for their suppression. Frederic II., the bitterest enemy of the Pope, in framing laws for the government of Sicily decreed the most fearful punishments against these sectaries. When plundered monasteries, ruined churches, pillaged and wasted cities attested by their smoking ruins the fury of the fanatical sectaries, a general cry of indignation went up from all the land; and could we expect that the Christian society of the twelfth century should have stood a passive witness of these sacrilegious votaries? The outcry against these deeds of violence was not confined to the Pope and the Bishops. All the sovereigns of the day were unanimous in calling for their suppression."*

At this juncture God raised up to his people one who was to be a leader in Israel. St. Dominic was already the champion of the good cause by prayer and preaching, but Simon de Montfort was destined by the power of the sword to strike a definite blow at this monstrous evil. Innocent III. excommunicated Raymond, and called upon the knights, barons, and nobles of France to unite in a crusade for the peace and safety of their country and for the honor of God. Forty thousand men answered to the appeal, and at their head was Simon, whom a chronicler describes as "an equally fearless soldier and skilful captain, one of the finest types of the chivalry of the day." "A more intrepid warrior and faithful Christian could not have been chosen," continues the same author; "to the fearless daring of Cœur de Lion he joined the fervent piety of a religious."

Eagerly the proudest chivalry of France advanced to receive the sacred ensign of the cross, worn this time upon the breast, in contradistinction to those who fought in the Oriental wars, wearing it upon their shoulder. Amongst those who engaged in the enterprise was

---

* We have quoted thus at length from the Abbé Darras in his General Hist. of the Church, vol. iii. p. 423, because it seems of importance to establish the fact, in which all impartial historians concur, that these heretics were a social pest as well as a religious evil.

Louis, son of Philip Augustus, who was the then reigning king of France, and husband of Blanche of Castile, consequently the father of St. Louis. On this great day of enthusiastic demonstration the tall and martial figure of Montfort was everywhere conspicuous. The devoted multitude were fired with a holy zeal and ardent patriotism. Louis and Arnaud, the Abbot of Citeaux, who was the Papal Legate, united with Montfort in the leadership of the expedition. "I cannot fall," cried Montfort, setting out to battle, "for the whole Church is praying for me!" A campaign of three years was an uninterrupted series of attacks upon the various strongholds of the Albigenses, in most of which the standard of the cross was victorious. Béziers was the first place of importance taken by the Catholic army, but this victory was soon followed by that of Carcassonne. The surrender of this latter place was a fatal blow to the power of the heretics, and brought innumerable recruits to swell the ranks of the crusaders. Montfort had already distinguished himself by a valor remarkable even in those days of heroic enterprise. He was soon raised to the sole command of the army, and invested with the domains of the excommunicated Vicomte de Béziers.

Lavaus was a great stronghold of the enemy. Their infamous doctrines were rife among the townspeople. Melancholy spectacle! that Lavaus which had been so Catholic a city, where the solemn bells had been heard at evening recalling Christ's Incarnation; where on Sabbath mornings they had proclaimed the hour of Mass and filled with sweet sounds the air of Catholic France. There, in winter nights, old tales were told of the heroic men now mouldering into dust upon the sands of Palestine, the descendants of whom were swelling the Christian host which now beleaguered the walls of the once faithful town. There had been peace among the townspeople in days of old, the sunshine of God's peace, sweetening all their daily lives as they followed the faith of their fathers and worshipped at the same altars. But in their present repulsive creed, the green and beautiful earth and all the wonders of the universe were the creation of the rebel spirit Lucifer. They renounced all family ties and forbade the sacred bond of marriage. Hence the gloom of their unholy doctrines shadowed their streets and dwellings as with a pall.

On the plains outside the city was encamped the Christian army with Montfort at its head. Dawn broke cold and white upon the tents of the besiegers, and over the beleaguered town evening cast its myriad lights upon them; night came darkly, and the crusaders slept in the shadow of the walls which separated them from their foes. All was still save the footsteps of the sentinels, who kept their watch mute and vigilant as the stars above them.

Days passed into weeks, and weeks into months, before the day of victory came to gladden the hearts of the weary crusaders and strike terror into their foes. Montfort was at their head. His noble charger led the van; his warlike figure towered above his brother-knights. All day long the battle raged with undiminished fury. There was clashing of arms and clank of knightly steel, the neighing of war-horses, the shouts of the combatants, and the groans of the dying. High above all, mighty as the rushing of mountain torrents, was the sound of the hymns which the crusaders chanted to the God of Battles. Undaunted and indefatigable, Montfort was ever in the thickest of the fight. His very presence filled the soldiers with enthusiasm. Waving his sword above his head he cheered his followers on, or wielding his ponderous battle-axe he carried death to the ranks of the foemen. His clarion tones were heard ever and anon calling upon the Christian knighthood of France to follow him to the death for God, for France, and for their holy Church.

The charge was made, ardent and impetuous, fiery and irresistible; the walls were scaled, a breach effected. The God of Battles had given them the day. The city gates were thrown wide; the Christian army streamed through the portals.

Would that we might close our eyes upon the scene of carnage which ensued! The crusaders, infuriated by the long resistance offered them, put to the sword the hapless wretches who had been the city's defenders. It is but little extenuation of their cruelty that their enemies were stained with horrid crimes, or that they had massacred the consecrated ones of God and spread death and desolation through many fair provinces of France. The conquerors were Christians, knights and gentlemen; their gentle breeding and the noble cause they served would have been best honored by an exercise of mercy. But while we condemn them in all sincerity, and deplore that this stain should rest upon the character of Montfort, who in all other respects was the flower of Christian chivalry, let us remember that this stern and merciless justice which he meted out was the outcome of his century. A learned writer * remarks upon this subject: "A moment's reflection on the character and tendency of their teaching will go far to supply the motives of their severe treatment. The consequences of their spiritual tenets reached out until they embraced all the relations of political, commercial, and social life, and were subversive of them all." He goes on to say, in the same connection:

"When the sanguinary cruelties committed in the cru-

---

* Alzog, Hist. of the Universal Church, vol. ii,

sade came to the knowledge of Pope Innocent, he was borne down with grief. It was a source of sorrow to him that such deeds of violence should have been indulged in by those professing themselves the champions of the faith, and it was no alleviation of his feelings to know that the partisans of error had been equally guilty of them." *

We must, however, consider that the patience of the people of France had been sorely tried by the incessant misdemeanors of these fanatics, and that Simon de Montfort personally had an inherent horror of vice, which made their excesses peculiarly abhorrent to him. His predominant characteristic was justice. A justice severe and inexorable, indeed, but equally so to himself. He was never known to deviate in the smallest degree from his word nor from what he held to be the straight path of duty. In fine, let us remember that we can scarcely put ourselves in the identical circumstances in which he found himself, nor invest ourselves with the spirit of that age.

As we have glanced at this severity, which is seized upon by enemies of truth as the essential attribute of this illustrious warrior, let us pause a moment to consider those qualities in which he commands our highest admiration. Brave and intrepid to an unusual degree, even in an age of valor and great exploits, he united with this courage an imperturbable coolness which never deserted him even in the heat of battle. No emotion howsoever deep and powerful ever sufficed to throw him off his guard. This it was that made him unsurpassed as a leader. He was endowed, too, with a remarkably clear perception, and was in the council-chamber as wise and prudent as on the battle-field warlike and martial. He was affable and courteous in man-

---

* Alzog, vol. ii. p. 667; Hurter, Innocent III., vol. ii. p. 692.

ner, winning by his soldierly frankness of bearing the hearts of all who approached him.* So that old chroniclers tell us he had no other enemies than those of Holy Church, and though much respected by all who came in contact with him, was also much beloved. He was remarkably religious, never failing to hear Mass every day and to receive Holy Communion once a week. His zeal is said by historians to have been truly apostolic; and of his faith the following illustration is given: "He was told that our Saviour, under the Consecrated Host, had appeared visibly in the hands of the priest. Full of generous faith, he exclaimed, 'Let those go to see it who doubt it; as for myself, I believe firmly the truth of the Eucharistic Mystery as our Mother Church teaches it. Hence I hope to receive in heaven a crown more brilliant than those of the angels, for they, being face to face with God, have not the power to doubt.'" † Well might he be called "the gallant champion of the Cross and the invincible defender of the Catholic faith."

Meantime the fortunes of war turned steadily in favor of the crusaders, though Raymond of Toulouse had called to his assistance his brother-in-law, Peter of Arragon. Montfort, attacked in Castelnaudary by the heretics, made a sortie at the head of a handful of men, and gained a complete victory. He walked barefoot to the church in thanksgiving therefor. He was again besieged in Muret, a small town upon the Garonne, by a force of one hundred thousand, under the leadership of Counts Raymond, de Foix, and Comminges, supported by Peter of Arragon. To human eyes the fate of De Montfort and his valiant band was sealed. Within the walls de-

---

* See Joinville, edition of 1761; F. X. de Feller's Biographie Universelle, vol. vi.; Butler's Lives of the Saints, vol. viii.; Lacordaire's Vie de St. Dominique.

† Müller, Devotion of the Rosary.

spair was on every face save that of the gallant leader. Nobly he rallied his little garrison about him, and besought them by all they held dear to fight as men had never fought before. A sortie was planned and executed with the small force at his command.

On the morning of that eventful day he laid his sword upon the altar. When the hour of battle came he took it thence with these words: "From Thee, O Lord, do I this day receive my arms, since I must wield them in Thy holy cause." *

Can we wonder that a complete and glorious victory rewarded faith so sublime? Never in the annals of any wars was a battle gained under less auspicious circumstances. "His skilful dispositions, as well as his irresistible courage, disconcerted the confederates from the first." Peter of Arragon was killed. Montfort gave public thanks for the victory, and we are told disposed of the dead king's armor for the benefit of the poor.†

By the decision of the Fourth General Council of Lateran the possessions of the excommunicated Count of Toulouse were given to Simon de Montfort. He was obliged, however, to receive the investiture from the king of France and pay him feudal tribute. The domains were to revert to the son of Raymond, who was a good Catholic.

Under their intrepid leader the crusaders now swept all before them, and obtained possession of l'Agenais, the territory of Comminges, and all the Toulousian provinces.

The siege of Toulouse, which, we are told, "the intrepid Montfort, despising all obstacles and every peril, now undertook," was an occasion of much trial

---

* Darras, Hist. of the Church, vol. iii. p. 336.
† Gazeau, History of the Middle Ages.

and endurance for the Christian leader, and finally ended his glorious but all too brief career as defender of the Cross. After a siege of nine months he found himself totally without resource, his army discouraged and exhausted. He had, moreover, to accept with ready resignation the reproaches of those who should most have sustained him. But Montfort's indomitable heart rose superior to all misfortunes.* On the 25th of June, 1218, he went according to custom to early Mass. Just as Mass was beginning the sound of mail-clad feet was heard coming up the nave. A messenger advanced to where Montfort was kneeling.

"My lord count," said he, "the enemy has made a sally, and the Christian cause is in fearful peril. Our army wavers. Come, my lord, without delay, or the day is lost."

"Nevertheless," said Montfort tranquilly, "I will not leave the church until I adore my God."

Calmly he knelt, amid the dim religious quiet of the church, pondering upon that Mystery of the altar which he had spent years in defending. He prayed ardently, indeed, for the wavering Christian cause, and begged that the enemy might not prevail against it. The moment of Consecration came. Montfort, the greatest soldier of his age, prostrated himself with fervent, childlike faith. Adoring the Sacred Host, he exclaimed, "*Nunc Dimittis*"—" Now, O Lord, let Thy servant depart in peace." He had adored the living God for the last time upon earth. Immediately after the Elevation he rushed from the church, crying, "Now onward to death for Him who suffered death for us!" †

---

* Histoire de l'Église, par M. l'Abbé de Bérault-Bercastel, vol. xii. pp. 470–472, where can be found further particulars of the siege of Toulouse.

† Ibid.

He placed himself at the head of his knightly phalanx. He fought with an ardor which even he had never surpassed. That mighty sword, which, historians relate, carried terror by its every movement to the hearts of his foes, flashed in the thickest of the fight. The struggle was desperate, but Montfort succeeded in driving the enemy back within their ramparts. At the very moment when victory seemed theirs the illustrious leader fell mortally wounded amid a shower of arrows and stones. He beat his breast, recommending his soul to God and the Blessed Virgin, and so doing expired. Truly his was a death worthy a crusader, for he fell sword in hand, facing the enemy, and offering his soul to God.

A month later his son, Amauri, was obliged to raise the siege, but the power of the Albigenses in France was at an end. Montfort had overthrown this formidable enemy of his race and religion, and in the reign of St. Louis the last remnants of them disappeared. As a final testimony against these sectaries, for the downfall of whom the illustrious hero gave his life, we may quote the words of Raymond of Toulouse himself, when he appeared before the General Chapter of Citeaux, "complaining with tears that the Albigenses, for whom he had so long fought, wasted his territory and ruined his vassals." Bowed down by age and grief, he made the following energetic protest:

"My gray hairs," he said, "are outraged. Men are dragged along by the torrent of corruption. My decrees are despised; the laws of the Church are trampled upon; there is nothing left but to appeal to arms. I shall call upon the king of France to meet the heretics, and give the last drop of my own blood in this cause, too happy if I can but help to crush so dangerous a sect."*

---

* Darras, vol. iii.

The Abbé Darras adds: "The Church in organizing a crusade against these formidable enemies protected European unity, crushed the socialism of that day, secured general tranquillity and the existence of modern society."

So it was, indeed, in a glorious cause that Simon, Count de Montfort shed his blood and gave his noble life. To our thinking he is the grandest figure of his century, the model of an accomplished knight, and a fine example to Christians. If this sketch has lent its mite towards placing him in the true light before Catholics, our task is fully done and the slight labor it has cost us is amply repaid. Simon de Montfort belongs to that class of Christian heroes of all places and of all times, who are misunderstood even by their coreligionists. The key to the enigma is very simple. Such men have been maligned and misrepresented by authors hostile to the principles for which they strove, and it is the writings of these authors that are unfortunately most frequently brought before the eyes of the Catholic reading public. The larger portion of English literature deals out praise to heroes of a different kind. If the tribute we would fain offer to the memory of the illustrious Montfort falls far short of our subject and of our own desire, we can ask the indulgence of the reader. Simon de Montfort lives and must live forever. Well might he say, in the words of Horace:

> " I will tarry no longer
> On this earth; but victorious o'er envy, two-formed,
> I abandon the cities of men.
> I shall not pass away through the portals of death;
> I shall not be hemmed round by the waters of Styx.
> Not for me raise the death-dirge, my urn shall be empty;
> Hush the vain ceremonial of groans that degrade me,
> And waste not the honors ye pay to the dead
> On a tomb in whose silence I shall not repose."

CHRIST IN HIS CHURCH:

A CATHOLIC CHURCH HISTORY,

Translated and adapted from the German of Rev. L. C. BUSINGER,

By REV. RICHARD BRENNAN, LL.D.,

Together with an Historical Sketch of

THE CHURCH IN AMERICA,

By JOHN GILMARY SHEA, LL.D.

Crown 8vo., 426 pages.   Very Fully Illustrated.   Cloth, $2.00.

SPECIMEN ILLUSTRATION.

Mass in the Catacombs.

This, the first concise Catholic History of the Church ever published in English, has received the approbation of

HIS EMINENCE THE CARDINAL, Archbishop of New York,

THE MOST REVEREND ARCHBISHOP OF BALTIMORE,

The Right Rev. Bishops of

Buffalo,	Grass Valley,	Monterey and Los Angeles,
Covington,	Green Bay,	Natchez,
Erie,	London, Ont.,	St. Paul.

The Right Rev. Vicar Apostolic of Northern Minnesota.

BENZIGER BROTHERS, NEW YORK, CINCINNATI, AND ST. LOUIS.

"With supreme fortitude and constancy they have chosen to endure all sufferings rather than forsake, even in the least point, the faith of their fathers and their ancient fidelity to this Apostolic See. It is, moreover, their singular glory, enduring even to this day, that the noblest examples of all other virtues have never been wanting among them."—POPE LEO XIII. TO THE IRISH BISHOPS, JAN. 1881.

IRISH FAITH IN AMERICA;

RECOLLECTIONS OF A MISSIONARY.

TRANSLATED FROM THE FRENCH, BY MISS ELLA McMAHON.

Elegantly bound in Extra Cloth, with a Shamrock-crowned Cross on the side, in gold and ink. 16mo. 75 CENTS.

TESTIMONIALS OF THE CATHOLIC PRESS.

"A most loving tribute to the Catholic Irish race. It is not too much to say that every Catholic American of Irish blood should purchase the volume. It makes one love the Catholic Irish character. The work is full of interest; of wholesome and edifying instruction and incident. . . . Particularly we recommend this volume in these unsettling times that all may recognize the happy truth that the grandest characteristic of the Irish race is their thorough Catholicity."—Cleveland *Catholic Universe.*

"The ardor and fervency of the Irish in America for their Catholicity is eloquently told by the reverend writer."—Boston *Pilot.*

"A book written by a French priest who has learned to know and to love Ireland's sons and daughters. The work in question admirably combines pathos, humor, and genuine Christian truth and piety."—*Catholic Columbian.*

"This is a well-done translation. . . . Splendid tribute is paid to the excellencies of the Irish character by a Frenchman who had abundant opportunity for the study of it, and who, whilst he praises, does not lack the courage which marks the true friend—courage to admonish of a fault."—*The Catholic Fireside.*

"When a stranger, born and bred on foreign soil, speaking 'out of the abundance of his heart,' finds naught but praise for our people, we hardly know how to thank him for his generous honesty. We heartily commend the book to our readers, assured that while moved by its pathos, enlivened by its genuine humor, 'racy of the soil,' they will feel proud of this tribute to their faith and patriotism."—*The Irish American.*

"A sprightly and interesting volume, replete with Irish repartee and wit, in which we are called upon to contemplate an entire people as the Apostle of the Most High. Every race has a mission to fulfill and the Irish nation seems especially to be the Missionary people. An eloquent tribute is paid to this nation of laborers, by whose efforts Religion is preserved and extended. Every Catholic will derive benefit from a perusal of the book."—*Hibernian Record.*

"A book that contains many interesting illustrations of the devotion of the Irish race to the holy Catholic Church. It is replete with interesting anecdotes, and is a book that should be read in every Irish Catholic family."—New York *Sunday Union.*

"We have seen many books neither so well brought out nor containing such useful and interesting matter sold for over three times the price. The author had varied opportunities of noting down facts connected with the fidelity of the Irish in America, and he seems to have lost no opportunity in noting the leading characteristics of those amongst whom he labored long and zealously. It is full of information well and simply told."—Lawrence, Mass., *Catholic Herald.*

"We hope every reader of the Monitor will secure a copy of it, in order to learn how well the Irish race have preserved and propagated the faith in this land. The work was originally written in French, by a missionary priest who lived in this country for many years, and has been translated by Misss ELLA McMAHON very faithfully."—San Francisco *Monitor.*

"A most interesting book. . . . . It is not only a deserved tribute to our Irish Catholic people, but will prove appreciative and instructive to all Catholics in this country."—Louisville *Central Catholic Advocate.*

"Were the book written by an Irishman, we might think it the happy conceit for which that nation is famed, but as the author is French, we cannot fail to be gratified and thankful for his good opinion of us."—Richmond, Va., *Catholic Visitor.*

BENZIGER BROTHERS, NEW YORK, CINCINNATI, AND ST. LOUIS.

www.ingramcontent.com/pod-product-compliance
Lightning Source LLC
Chambersburg PA
CBHW032135230426
43672CB00011B/2345